First published in 2015 by Motorbooks, an imprint of Quarto Publishing Group USA Inc.,
400 First Avenue North, Suite 400, Minneapolis, MN 55401 USA

Motorbooks titles are also available at discounts in bulk quantity for industrial or sales-promotional
use. For details write to Special Sales Manager at Quarto Publishing Group USA Inc., 400 First Avenue
North, Suite 400, Minneapolis, MN 55401 USA.

To find out more about our books, visit us online at www.motorbooks.com.

ISBN: 978-0-7603-4727-0

   Library of Congress Cataloging-in-Publication Data

Falloon, Ian.
   The complete book of BMW motorcycles : every model since 1923 / Ian Falloon.
      pages cm
   Includes index.
   ISBN 978-0-7603-4727-0 (hc w/jacket)
   1. BMW motorcycle--History. I. Title.
   TL448.B18F35224 2015
   629.227'5--dc23
                                   2015004890

Acquisitions Editor: Darwin Holmstrom
Project Manager: Jordan Wiklund
Art Director: Cindy Samargia Laun
Cover Design: Simon Larkin
Book Design and Layout: Simon Larkin

On the front cover: The S1000RR. *BMW Group Press*
On the back cover: (Left) BMW's first motorcycle was the R32, and it introduced many design
   features that would characterize BMW motorcycles for the next 90 years. *BMW Group Press*
   (Right) Significantly updated for 2015, the F800R now had new styling, an upside-down fork
   and radial front brakes. *BMW Group Press*
On the frontis: Josef Stelzer was one of BMW's most successful riders in the 1920s. Here he is with
   the R39 that won the 1925 250cc German road-racing championship. *BMW Group Archives*

Printed in China

10 9 8 7 6 5 4 3 2 1

THE **COMPLETE** BOOK OF
BMW
MOTORCYCLES

EVERY MODEL SINCE 1923

IAN FALLOON

motorbooks

CONTENTS

ACKNOWLEDGMENTS

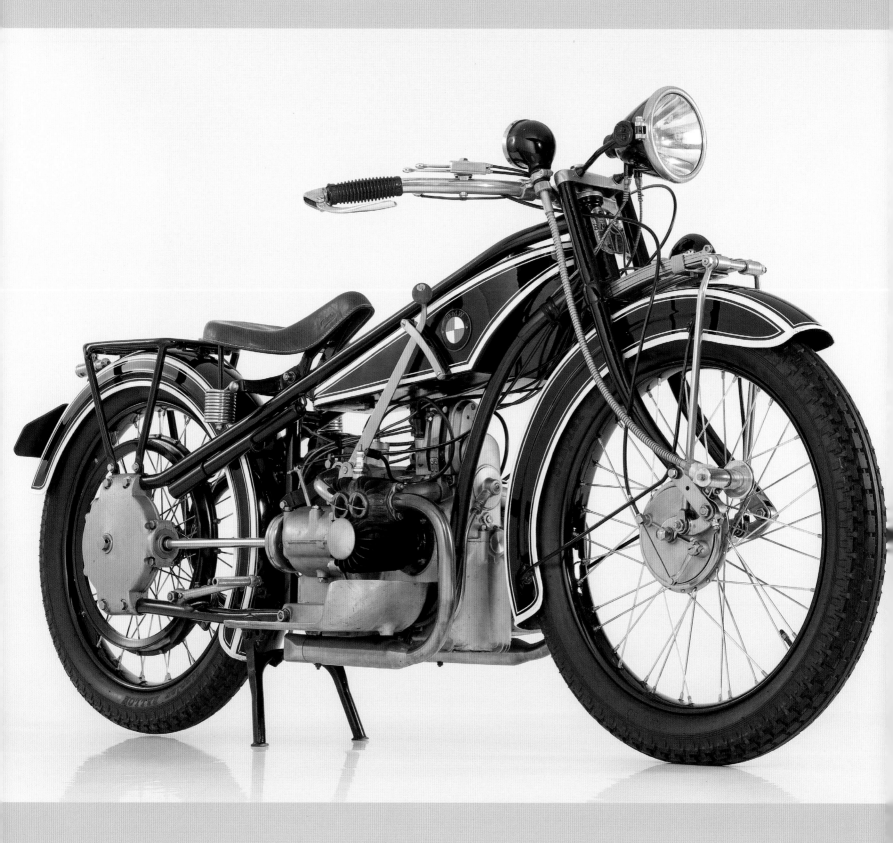

With five BMW motorcycle titles already under my belt, this comprehensive history presented a new challenge: to include as many previously unpublished pictures as possible. Fortunately Fred Jakobs and Ruth Standfuss of BMW Group Archives came to my aid, responding to all my requests for photos, and without their support, this project would not have been possible. Others who contributed photographic material were Lothar Mildebrath, Udo Gietl, Mac Kirkpatrick, Don Kotchoff, and Damien Cook. The legendary racing RS54s and derivatives are only covered sketchily here, and for more information on these fantastic machines I suggest the study of Lothar Mildebrath's definitive book on this subject—*Münchener Meistermacher Maschinen BMW RS 54 and Family* (German-English) (ISBN 978-3-00-042687-2; rs.bmw-veteranenclub.de).

At Motorbooks, my Acquisitions Editor Darwin Holmstrom and Project Manager Jordan Wiklund were continually helpful, while on the home front the support of my family—Miriam, Ben, and Tim—was unabated. As always, they put up with the all-consuming motorcycle discourse without complaint.

← **BMW's first motorcycle was the R32, and it introduced many design features that would characterize BMW motorcycles for the next 90 years.** *BMW Group Press*

↓ **Celebrating 90 years of the boxer twin—the magnificent R nineT.** *BMW Group Press*

INTRODUCTION
BEGINNINGS:
FROM AIRCRAFT TO MOTORCYCLES

BMW's beginnings go back to 1913 when, in Schleibheim Street in Munich, Karl Rapp established a factory to manufacture aircraft engines. Although his engines were unreliable, the outbreak of war provided Rapp a reprieve, and in 1916 the Rapp Motor Works received a lucrative war contract. But because of Rapp's dubious reputation, the Austrian War Ministry insisted on appointing a supervisor, Franz Josef Popp, a 30-year-old Austrian lieutenant and qualified engineer, to oversee production. Popp soon saw the only solution for survival was to remove Rapp's name from the company, and in July 1917, the Rapp Motor Works became the Bavarian Motor Works. Then on October 5, Popp registered the distinctive rotating propeller trademark. Slightly earlier, in 1916, engineer and pilot Gustav Otto established a neighboring Bayerische Flugzeug-Werke (Bavarian Aircraft Works), and although BMW and BFW coexisted as separate entities until 1922, they would eventually merge.

Engineer Max Friz joined Rapp Motor Works in January 1917, Popp engaging him to redesign Rapp's problematic six-cylinder engine. The result was an engine that no longer vibrated and produced 160 horsepower at 3,000 meters. Friz convinced the authorities in Berlin the advantages of his new engine, the IIIa, and by the end of 1917, it was successfully tested in the air. The IIIa was so superior to other designs that by the middle of 1918 the Prussian military ordered 2,000 engines. Although Ernst Udet achieved 30 victories with his BMW IIIa-powered Fokker D VII fighter plane, and new BMW II and IV engines were about to enter production, it was too late.

← Max Friz, the father of the BMW motorcycle, was also involved in the design of the successful 1914 Mercedes-Benz Grand Prix car. Following the release of the R32, Friz became a director of BMW AG, and from 1925 until 1937 he was their chief designer. He was general manager of the Munich plant from 1935 until 1937, and then at Eisenach until 1944. Friz retired in 1945 and died in 1966. *BMW Group Archives*

↙ BMW's first aero engine was Max Friz's IIIa. This was highly successful over its short life, primarily due to the superiority of Friz's high altitude carburetor. But as it arrived toward the end of World War I, it was too late to make much of an impression. *BMW Group Archives*

The end of the war arrived on November 11, and although production ceased three weeks later, Popp managed to reopen the factory in February 1919, enabling further development of the BMW IV engine. This was a development of the IIIa, Franz Zeno Diemer using it to reach an altitude of 9,760 meters. Although a world record, as Germany was a defeated power, the FAI international authority didn't ratify it. Only 11 days after Diemer's repeat flight on June 17, the Treaty of Versailles was signed and Germany was forbidden involvement in the manufacture of aircraft and engines until midway through 1920. Popp was now in a dilemma as to what BMW was to manufacture, salvation coming from experienced foreman Martin Stolle. Stolle was a committed motorcyclist, winning third prize on a 1913 model English Douglas in a Vienna-to-Munich race in 1914. Impressed with the Douglas flat-twin's reliability, he persuaded Popp to sanction the development of a similar motorcycle engine.

Early in 1920, Stolle acquired a 1914–1915 Model B 500cc Douglas and stripped it down on Friz's workbench. Every part was measured and reluctantly drawn up by Friz, an innovator loath to copying. Stolle then persuaded the Victoria Works in Nuremberg to fit the engine in their frame, creating the Victoria KR1. Ostensibly the M2 B15 (2 for two cylinders and B for boxer) was a copy of the 494cc Douglas, sharing the side-valve layout and 68x68mm bore and stroke. Friz incorporated enclosed valves and force-fed gear lubrication, and with a single carburetor it produced a modest 6.5 horsepower at 3,000 rpm. Positioned in the frame longitudinally like the Douglas, with either belt or chain final drive, the M2 B15 soon found its way into other motorcycles besides the Victoria.

Also unable to produce aircraft, Bayerische Flugzeug-Werke was in a similar predicament to BMW, and an opportunity arose to produce a simple motorized bicycle, the 143cc two-stroke Flink. This proved quite successful during 1920, and in 1921 BFW decided to compete with the Victoria, creating the Helios, also with the BMW M2 B15 engine. But by the end of 1921, BFW was close to bankruptcy, and BMW was forced into producing railway brakes. Popp saw a future in motorcycle production, and in May 1922 BFW merged with BMW, moving into BFW's premises. As Victoria no longer required the M2 B15 engine, Popp asked Friz to design a completely new motorcycle, and in 1923 BMW graduated from an engine producer to motorcycle manufacturer.

← Franz Zeno Diemer, prior to his second altitude record attempt on June 17, 1919. Earlier he set a new altitude record of 9,760 meters, but this wasn't officially recognized. *BMW Group Archives*

↓ Martin Stolle with the Victoria KR1 powered by the BMW M2 B15 engine. In March 1921, Stolle rode a Victoria KR1 in the 370-kilometer Bavarian Motorcycle Derby. Although Stolle created this engine, he left BMW in 1922 after BMW refused to pay 100 marks in trip expenses. Stolle later built an overhead-valve engine that powered the most successful sporting motorcycle in Germany at the time, the Victoria KR2. This was also superior to the new BMW R32 at Solitude in June 1923, where none of the three special overhead-valve BMWs finished. *BMW Group Archives*

THE 1920S
ESTABLISHING THE DNA:
EARLY BOXERS AND SINGLES

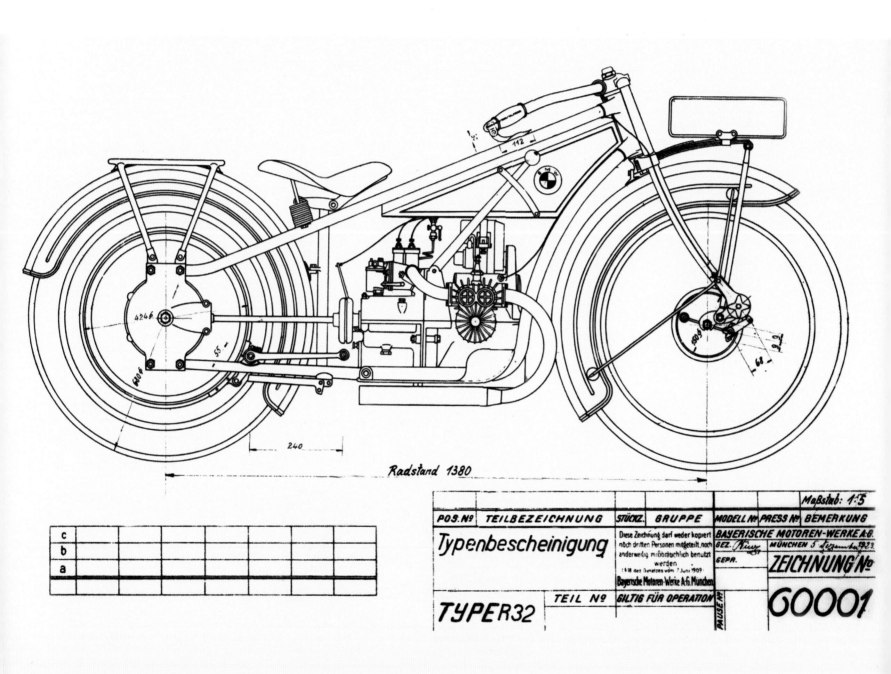

Radstand 1380

240

112

4240

55

60

9.2

c										
b										
a										

					Maßstab: 1:5
POS. N°	TEILBEZEICHNUNG	STÜCKZ.	GRUPPE	MODELL N° PRESS N° BEMERKUNG		
Typenbescheinigung		Diese Zeichnung darf weder kopiert noch dritten Personen mitgeteilt, noch anderweitig mißbräuchlich benutzt werden (§18 des Gesetzes vom 7.Juni 1909) Bayerische Motoren-Werke A-G. München		BAYERISCHE MOTOREN-WERKE A.G. GEZ. München 5 Dezember 1923 GEPR.		ZEICHNUNG N°
TYPE R32	TEIL N°	GILTIG FÜR OPERATION				60001

R32

As BMW already had the M2 B15 500cc horizontally opposed twin-cylinder engine, Friz used this as a basis for his new design. The rear cylinder tended to overheat on the Victoria and Helios, so Friz decided to mount the engine transversely, adding a shaft drive. The rigid frame meant the driveshaft didn't require a universal joint, a rubber disc was a sufficient shock absorber, and Friz had the drawings completed by December 1922. Although the 1919 English Sopwith ABC motorcycle also featured a transverse twin-cylinder engine (without shaft drive), Friz claimed he was unaware of the ABC at the time. ABC's designer Granville Bradshaw later accused BMW of copying the ABC, but there were too many detail differences for this to be substantiated.

The R32 side-valve engine produced only slightly more horsepower than the M2 B15, but its design and execution were groundbreaking. Concentrating on reliability and ease of maintenance, the engine, including the valve timing system, was fully encased. Due to the shaft final drive and inline crankshaft, no chains required adjustment. So compared to other 500s, the R32 was revolutionary. A hand lever operated the three-speed grease-filled gearbox, and the ignition was by a magneto generator with a rather complicated set of handlebar controls.

← The R32 drawings were completed in only four months. The front brake appeared in 1925. *BMW Group Archives*

↙ BMW's first engine was the M2 B15, and Friz used this as a basis for the R32. *BMW Group Archives*

↓ Advertising for the first BMW motorcycle. As was usual in the 1920s, the R32 had a rigid frame and the rear brake was a block type. As early versions didn't have a front brake, and the R32 was capable of close to 60 miles per hour, it was fortunate the roads weren't congested in Germany in 1932. BMW continually refined the R32 over its short life, establishing a program of development that would characterize BMW motorcycles. *BMW Group Press*

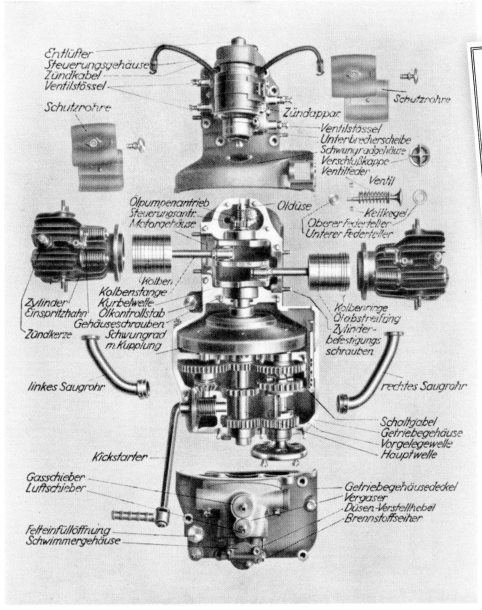

DAS NEUE

B.M.W.=RAD

DER

BAYER. MOTOREN=WERKE

A.=G.

MÜNCHEN

↑ **Test rider Rudi Reich with an R32. This test model has an unpainted fuel tank.** *BMW Group Press*

↓ **Instrumentation was minimal on the R32, but the detailing was superb.** *BMW Group Press*

Friz installed this engine in a closed twin-loop tubular-steel frame, with the gas tank underneath the upper frame tubes. The frame was brazed and sleeved, but the workers lacked experience in brazing, and fractures on the solder joints were a problem until the introduction of pressed-steel frames in 1929. The front suspension consisted of a short swinging fork with a cantilever-plate spring beneath the steering stem. Initially the only brake was a rear wheel–block type operated by the rider's heel, but by 1925, a front 150mm drum brake was introduced. The R32 (R for *Rad* meaning wheel, but the 32 remains a mystery) not only offered a top speed around 55 miles per hour, but the low center of gravity promised safe and manageable handling for a touring motorcycle on the poor quality roads of the day. In May 1923, Friz himself tested the R32, finishing the "Fahrt durch Bayerns Berge" trial through the Bavarian mountains without incurring any penalties. The R32 was launched at Berlin in September 1923, one month before the Paris Car Show, where it was a star attraction, establishing a boxer-twin shaft-drive format that would characterize many BMW motorcycles for the next 90 years. The initial response was mixed. Skeptics feared the engine could be easily damaged in a fall, others felt it was underpowered, but no one could deny the compact engine and transmission unit was a brilliant design and beautifully executed.

The release of the R32 coincided with the stability of the German mark, but at 2,200 marks (or 2,600 marks with light, horn, pillion seat, and speedometer), it still represented a significant investment. Yet the motorcycle market was flourishing in Germany. Cars were for the wealthy few, and with the demand for motorcycles strong, BMW managed to sell 1,500 R32s by the end of 1924.

1923-1926 **R32**

Engine designation	**M2 B33 or M33a**
Type	**Four-stroke, twin-cylinder, flat-twin**
Bore x stroke	**68x68mm**
Displacement	**494cc**
Power	**8.5 horsepower at 3,200rpm**
Compression ratio	**5.0:1**
Valves	**Side-valve**
Carburetion	**1xBMW Special 22mm**
Gears	**3-speed**
Ignition	**Bosch magneto**
Frame	**Twin-loop tubular-steel**
Front suspension	**Twin cantilever spring**
Rear suspension	**Rigid**
Wheels	**26x2.5**
Tires	**26x3 front and rear**
Brakes	**150mm front drum (second series) block rear**
Wheelbase	**1380mm (54.3 inches)**
Dry weight	**122kg (269 lbs.)**
Engine numbers	**31000 to 34100**
Frame numbers	**1001 to 4100**
Numbers produced	**3,090**

↓ The R32's flat-twin, shaft-drive layout established a design format that continues today. It also encapsulated BMW's philosophy of innovative engineering and high build quality. *BMW Group Archives*

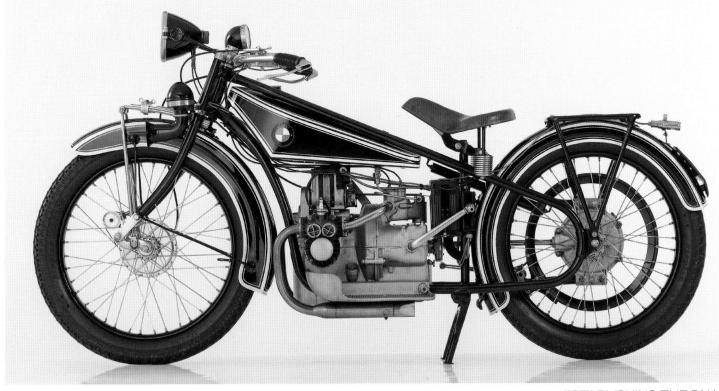

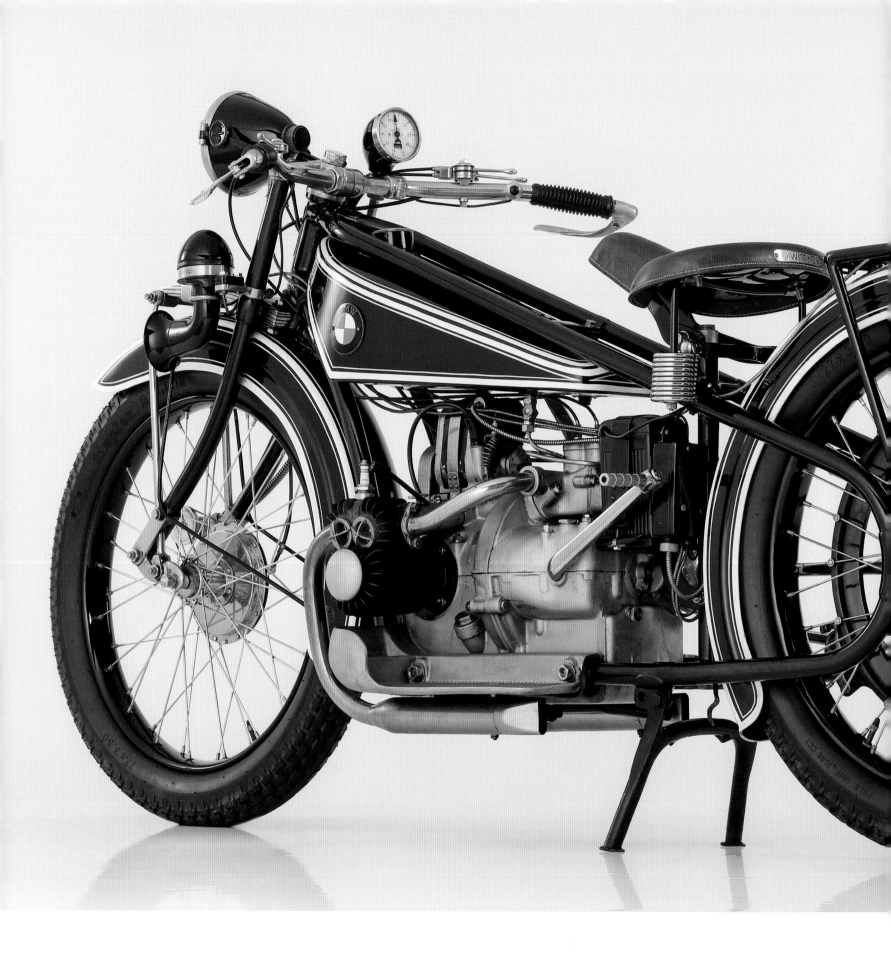

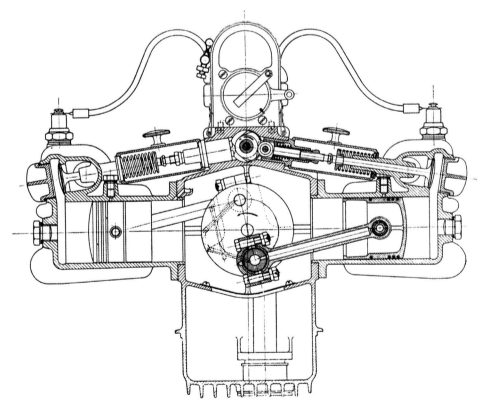

↑ The R32 had rudimentary cantilever-plate spring front suspension and a brazed tubular-steel frame. With its fully enclosed engine and drivetrain, it was oil tight and much more modern than other motorcycles in 1923. The rear-drive unit connected directly to the frame, increasing overall rigidity. Characterized by many beautiful details, the R32 was an outstanding example of high-quality engineering. *BMW Group Press*

⇑ A hand lever operated the R32's three-speed grease-filled gearbox. The side-valve engine was based on the M2 15B, which was strongly derived from the British Douglas. Innovations extended to the monobloc engine, the two bronze screw caps allowing access to the valves for removal. The air intake was through the flywheel chamber rather than the carburetor. *BMW Group Archives*

↑ As the R32 side-valve engine layout was quite simple, it was very reliable and helped establish BMW's reputation for exceptional reliability. Innovative features included the use of alloy pistons. *BMW Group Press*

R37

BMW knew racing success was required to establish the company's name, and while the side-valve R32 was a solid touring motorcycle, it was soon evident it wasn't competitive against the overhead-valve Victoria KR2. In June 1923 the R32s were humiliated at Solitude, near Stuttgart, so for the next year BMW returned with an overhead-valve version, the R37. Designed by 26-year-old Rudolf Schleicher who had joined BMW in 1922, the R37 was similar to the R32, except for a light aluminum cylinder head with fully enclosed and lubricated overhead valves set at an included angle of 90 degrees. This was quite a radical development as valves at that time were usually exposed to dust and water and often required manual lubrication of the rocker shafts. To achieve improved cooling, Schleicher incorporated (and patented) circumferential cooling fins with cooling passages around the valves. This engine, the M2 B36, was installed in a chassis that was similar to the R32's.

↑ **Franz Bieber won the 1924 Eifelbergrennen race on the R37 and went on to take the German championship.** *BMW Group Archives*

→ **Rudolf Schleicher with his very successful overhead-valve R37.** *BMW Group Archives*

← Franz Bieber, Rudolf Schleicher, and Rudi Reich with the new R37 at the Solitude hillclimb in 1924. The new R37 produced a claimed 22 horsepower and won three categories, with Reich setting the fastest time of the day and beating Josef Maier on Martin Stolle's Viktoria. *BMW Group Archives*

↓ While the R37 was extremely successful in German competition, winning 100 events during 1925, the R32 also remained popular. Here are three R32s with an R37 during 1925. *BMW Group Archives*

⇟ Rudi Reich on an R37 at Solitude in 1925. *BMW Group Archives*

After providing BMW's first motorsport victory in February 1924 at the Mittenwalder Steig hillclimb, Rudolf Schleicher headed a team of three at Solitude. Joined by Franz Bieber and Rudi Reich, Schleicher and the other riders on the new R37s won three categories, with Reich setting the fastest time of the day. This success continued as Bieber claimed the German 500cc championship. The R37 then went into limited production during 1925, albeit at a price of 2,900 marks, making it the most expensive German motorcycle, but also one of the fastest with its 72-mile-per-hour top speed. It produced a claimed 22 horsepower.

It wasn't until 1926 that the R37 managed to capture attention outside Germany. Schleicher and his friend Fritz Roth ventured to England on production R37s as private entrants in the Six-Day Race. Not realizing that off-road tires were necessary, and unable to source any, they fronted with conventional tires and low pressures. Almost laughed out of the race when they arrived, Schleicher crossed the finish line with a gold medal. The British press sat up and took notice, and Professor A. M. Low wrote in the *Auto-Cycle Union* magazine, "After the toughest days in the field, we could not find a single oil leak, the machine was beautifully quiet, and seemed to possess great reserves of power. From a design point of view it is miles ahead of any British machine."

1925-1926 R37 *(DIFFERING FROM THE R32)*

Engine designation	**M2 B36 or M36a**
Power	**16 horsepower at 4,000 rpm**
Compression ratio	**6.2:1**
Valves	**Overhead-valve**
Carburetion	**1xBMW Special three-slide 26mm**
Front brake	**150mm front drum**
Dry weight	**134 kg (295 lbs.)**
Engine numbers	**35001–35175**
Frame numbers	**100–275**
Numbers produced	**152**

↑ **Josef Stelzer was one of BMW's most successful riders in the 1920s. Here he is with the R39 that won the 1925 250cc German road-racing championship.** *BMW Group Archives*

R39

As the R32 twin was sold as a premium motorcycle, production levels were necessarily low and the profitability in difficult times dubious. BMW's management team wanted to expand aircraft engine and car production, but team members insisted the motorcycle operation be profitable, requiring a lower-priced model to supplement the R32, opening the door to a broader range of buyers. Development of a single-cylinder model began in April 1924, and the R39 made its first appearance at the Berlin Show at the end of the year. Although it was ready to go, tire supply problems saw production of the R39 delayed until September 1925. While it was intended as a budget model, the specification was surprisingly high. Like the boxer twins, the 250cc engine (designation M40a) was mounted longitudinally in the frame, but with a vertical cylinder and shaft drive. The alloy overhead-valve cylinder head came from the sporting R37, and a three-speed gearbox bolted directly to the crankcase, driven through a single-plate dry clutch mounted to the flywheel.

   The R39 frame was a twin tube design like the R32, but the rear brake was an external shoe acting on a drum on the driveshaft, rather than the earlier wedge-shaped brake block. But the high specification came at a cost, 1,870 marks, close to that of the R32. While the performance for a 250 was outstanding (the top speed of more than 60 miles per hour was more than the R32), sales dwindled following reports of problems with cylinder bore wear and excessive oil consumption. Josef Stelzer rode an R39 to victory in the 1925 250cc German road racing championships, but this wasn't enough to save it. Production ended in 1926, but the R39 was offered well into 1927.

1925-1927 R39

Engine designation	**M40**
Type	**Four-stroke, vertical single-cylinder**
Bore x stroke	**68x68mm**
Displacement	**247cc**
Power	**6.5 horsepower at 4,500 rpm**
Compression ratio	**6.0:1**
Valves	**Overhead-valve**
Carburetion	**1xBMW Special 20mm**
Gears	**3-speed**
Ignition	**Bosch magneto**
Frame	**Twin-loop tubular-steel**
Front suspension	**Four-plate spring**
Rear suspension	**Rigid**
Wheels	**27x3.5**
Tires	**27x3 front and rear**
Brakes	**150mm front drum, external shoe rear**
Dry weight	**110 kg (242 lbs.)**
Engine numbers	**36000–36900**
Frame numbers	**8000–8900**
Numbers produced	**855**

↓ The R39 of 1925 was BMW's first single. Although it was quite successful as a racer, it didn't sell well.
BMW Group Archives

R42

The R32 established BMW as a manufacturer of quality motorcycles, but after two years it required replacement. A redesigned touring twin appeared alongside the R32 at the end of 1925 and superseded it during 1926. Although still a side-valve 500, the R42 incorporated a number of updates, including a wedge-shaped combustion chamber, new cylinders with the cooling fins set across the barrel, and the beautifully sculptured detachable alloy cylinder heads. Schleicher found some new slotted pistons in the United States, these running cooler and quieter, while the new two-valve carburetor was easier to keep in tune. Although significantly more powerful, the R42's top speed of 59 miles per hour wasn't much more than the R32's.

Accompanying the engine development was a new frame, with straight downtubes, and the engine was located further toward the rear for superior weight distribution. This improved the rather top-heavy feeling of the R32, resulting in more secure handling. The R39 single's heel-operated driveshaft brake also was featured on the R42, and a sidecar mount was provided on the rear driveshaft housing. By 1926, BMW was expanding, and with a reduction in price of the R42 to 1,510 marks, it became one of BMW's most successful motorcycles of the 1920s.

↓ Offering improved performance, the side-valve R42 replaced the R32 during 1926. This would be one of BMW's most successful models during the 1920s. *BMW Group Archives*

1926-1928 **R42** *(DIFFERING FROM THE R32)*

Engine designation	**M43**
Power	**12 horsepower at 3,400 rpm**
Compression ratio	**4.9:1**
Carburetion	**1xBMW Special two-valve 22mm**
Front suspension	**Five-plate spring**
Wheels	**19x3 or 21x2.5**
Tires	**26x3.5 or 27x2.75**
Brakes	**150mm front drum, external shoe rear**
Wheelbase	**1,410mm (55.5 inches)**
Dry weight	**126 kg (278 lbs.)**
Engine numbers	**40001–46999**
Frame numbers	**10001–16999**
Numbers produced	**6,502**

↑ Although the R47 wasn't a specific racing model like the R37 it replaced, BMW offered sports and Werks Rennmaschine versions. Here are two R47s (#50 in the center and #54 on the left) at the start of the 1926 Schleiz Three-Point Race. *BMW Group Archives*

R47

One year later an overhead-valve version of the R42, the R47, replaced the R37. Not as pure a racing machine as its predecessor, the R47 featured the touring R42 chassis, complete with sidecar option. Engine updates included cast-iron barrels with the valve covers retained by a single fastener. Instead of the R37's three-slide carburetor, the R47 shared its BMW Special carburetor with the R42. The top speed was a little less than the R37, at 68 miles per hour, but because the price was reduced significantly, to 1,850 marks, the R47 was much more popular. A 22-horsepower R47 special sports variant was also available, and the R47 also was offered as a 28-horsepower Werkes-Rennmaschine, or Works Racer.

← The R47 Special Sport was one of the highest performing 500s of the late 1920s. *BMW Group Press*

↓ Karl Gall on an R47 in the 1927 Tauern race. Gall would become one of BMW's leading riders during the 1930s. *BMW Group Press*

1927-1928 **R47** *(DIFFERING FROM THE R42)*

Engine designation	**M51**
Power	**18 horsepower at 4,000 rpm**
Compression ratio	**5.8:1**
Valves	**Overhead-valve**
Carburetion	**1xBMW Special two-valve 22mm**
Wheels	**CC1**
Tires	**27x3.5 (low pressure) or 26x3 (high pressure)**
Dry weight	**130 kg (287 lbs.)**
Engine numbers	**34201–35999**
Frame numbers	**4201–5999**
Numbers produced	**1,720**

R52, R57, R62, AND R63

By 1928, BMW was established as a premier manufacturer of touring motorcycles and four new models were released using a new chassis. Two 750cc versions, one overhead-valve and one side-valve engine, joined the two 500cc models, but these were new designs with a pressed-up crankshaft instead of the earlier one-piece type. The 750s also included a redesigned lubrication system. The side-valve engines now featured a longer 78mm stroke, while the overhead-valve engines retained the earlier 68mm stroke. Although they looked visually similar to the previous version, the side-valve cylinder heads incorporated a new mounting system. The 750cc R63 was the highest performing BMW motorcycle yet. While the claimed top speed was 75 miles per hour, this was conservative, and the R63 was one of the fastest machines available in 1928. It also came at the premium price of 2,100 marks, and as with the R47, a 36-horsepower sporting version was available. BMW also produced a 40-horsepower 749cc racing machine during this period.

All four new models came with a magneto-generator electrical system, with Bosch lights optional until 1929 when they became standard. The stronger three-speed gearbox was oil lubricated (instead of grease), with a new hand change mechanism. Underneath the gearbox was a useful toolbox, with a hinged door. Also for the first time the kick-start was side-mounted, kicking out to the side, and would be a BMW feature for many years to come. The clutch was also originally a single plate but was changed in 1929 to a twin plate. Except for a larger front brake and a six-leaf spring for the front fork, the new chassis was similar to that of the R42 and R47. A triangular gas tank mounted between the engine and the top frame tubes distinguished all these models. Also they weighed more than previous models. The majority produced were side-valve versions, and with annual production now around 5,000 motorcycles, BMW had come a long way in the six years since the release of the R32. At the end of 1929, the company introduced a new motorcycle lineup, but not before Ernst Henne provided BMW with its first motorcycle speed record on a supercharged R63.

↑ For 1928, the R52 replaced the R42. Still a 500cc side-valve, this was basically a smaller version of the new 750cc R62, sharing the same long stroke.
BMW Group Archives

1928-1929 R52 *(DIFFERING FROM THE R42)*

Engine designation	**M57**
Bore x stroke	**63x78mm**
Displacement	**486cc**
Compression ratio	**5.0:1**
Carburetion	**1xBMW special two-valve 22mm**
Gears	**3-speed**
Ignition	**Bosch magneto**
Frame designation	**F56**
Front suspension	**Six-plate spring**
Wheels	**Deep bed 19x3**
Tires	**26x3.5 (low pressure), 26x3.25 (high pressure) front & rear**
Brakes	**200mm front drum, external shoe rear**
Wheelbase	**1,400mm (55.1 inches)**
Dry weight	**152 kg (335 lbs.)**
Engine numbers	**47001–51383**
Frame numbers	**20000–30600**
Numbers produced	**4,377**

↑ BMW test riders with the R52 and R57. *BMW Group Press*

← "Running in" new R52s on the BMW test track in 1928. *BMW Group Press*

↓ The R57/63 was the performance model of the late 1920s and even into the 1930s. This is Oswald Müller at the 100-kilomer race in Santiago, Chile, in 1931. *BMW Group Archives*

1928-1930 **R57** *(DIFFERING FROM THE R52)*

Engine designation	**M56**
Bore x stroke	**68x68mm**
Displacement	**494cc**
Power	**18 horsepower at 4,000 rpm**
Compression ratio	**5.8:1**
Valves	**Overhead-valve**
Carburetion	**1xBMW Special two-valve 24mm**
Wheels	**Deep bed 19x3 or 21x3.5**
Tires	**26x3.5 or 27x2.75 front and rear**
Dry weight	**150 kg (331 lbs.)**
Engine numbers	**70001–71012**
Frame numbers	**20000–30600**
Numbers produced	**1,005**

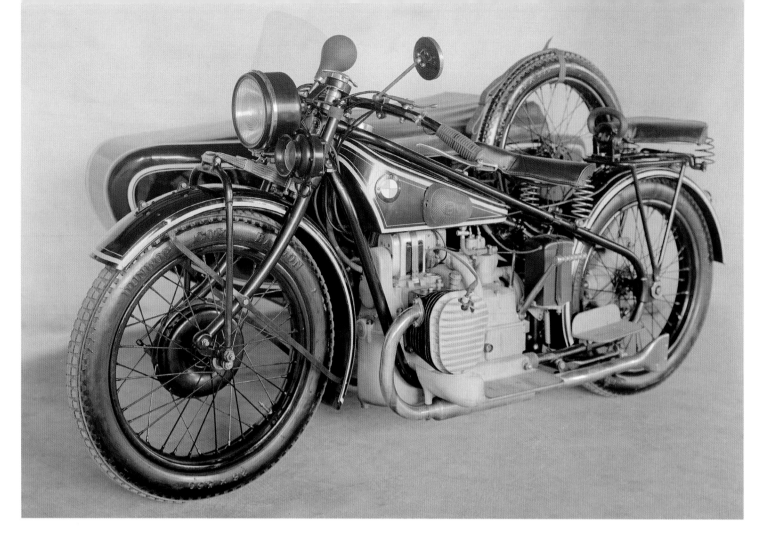

↑ BMW's first production 750 was the 1928 side-valve R62. This was particularly suited to sidecar use.
BMW Group Archives

↓ The overhead-valve R63 was one of the fastest motorcycles available in Germany after 1928, and both WR750 racing versions, were extremely successful. Here is Fritz Wiese, 1930 German over 500cc motorcycle champion, on an R63 before the start of the Schleiz Three-Point Race.
BMW Group Archives

1928-1929 **R62** *(DIFFERING FROM THE R52)*

Engine designation	M56
Bore x stroke	78x78mm
Displacement	745cc
Power	18 horsepower at 3,400 rpm
Compression ratio	5.5:1
Dry weight	155 kg (342 lbs.)
Engine numbers	60001–65000
Frame numbers	20000–30600
Numbers produced	4,355

1928-1929 **R63** *(DIFFERING FROM THE R57)*

Engine designation	M60
Bore x stroke	83x68mm
Displacement	735cc
Power	24 horsepower at 4,000 rpm
Compression ratio	6.2:1
Dry weight	152 kg (335 lbs.)
Engine numbers	75001–76000
Frame numbers	20000–30600
Numbers produced	794

← Prior to attempting world speed records, Ernst Henne was a very successful road racer, winning the 1926 German 500cc championship on an R37. *BMW Group Press*

↓ Ernst Henne on the supercharged 750 would become BMW's most successful world record exponent, breaking 76 records between 1929 and 1937. Early attempts were with an unfaired machine, and Henne wore a streamlined helmet and tailpiece. *BMW Group Archives*

As the BMW still lacked the handling finesse of the British competition, supercharging was featured on racing versions beginning in 1928. Rudolf Schleicher initially instigated supercharging during 1927, and Max Friz continued development after Schleicher left BMW. Friz installed a French Cozette centrifugal supercharger and later a Zoller rotary-vane type, horizontally above the engine and gearbox where an oil-bathed chain from the crankshaft drove it. This was extremely effective, providing the racing R57 with around 55 horsepower and the R63 with 75 horsepower, and during 1929, the racing BMWs were virtually unbeatable in German competition.

Hans Soenius won three consecutive German championships, from 1927 to 1929, and another of BMW's outstanding riders was Ernst Henne. Henne won the German 500cc road racing championship in 1926 and the 750cc championship in 1927. In 1928 Henne won the Targa Florio in Sicily and in 1929 was convinced he could take the world speed record away from the British riders Oliver Baldwin (Zenith JAP) and Bert le Vack (Brough Superior). Henne persuaded Friz to prepare a short-stroke supercharged 750. On September 19, 1929, on the narrow tree-lined Ingolstädt road near Munich, Henne raised the absolute motorcycle world one-mile speed record to 134.67

miles per hour. The BMW was unfaired, but Henne wore a streamlined helmet and tail attached to his riding suit.

Henne's success initiated competition between BMW, Brough Superior, and Gilera for the world speed record that would last throughout the next decade. It also culminated an extremely profitable decade for BMW. Not only were nearly 20,000 motorcycles produced during the 1920s, but also aircraft engine manufacture was well underway again. Production of the type VI V-12 began during 1926 and 7,000 units were sold by the

mid-1930s, and in 1928, BMW signed a license agreement with the American company Pratt & Whitney to produce radial aircraft engines.

Another significant development during 1928 was the purchase of the Eisenach car plant near Frankfurt, along with the license to build a copy of the British Austin Seven, called the Dixi. BMW then became a car manufacturer, with cars manufactured at Eisenach throughout the 1930s, while motorcycle and aircraft engine production remained at Munich. But despite this new emphasis, motorcycle production remained pivotal.

1930–1945
FOLLOW THE LEADER:
INNOVATION AND SPEED RECORDS

By the end of the 1920s, motorcycle technology was developing rapidly, new models appeared at a surprising rate, and after only a year, the four-model range released in 1928 was discontinued. Although selling well, problems with frame fractures and collapsing front forks (particularly when adapted for a sidecar) prompted the release of two new 750s for 1929, the R11 and R16. Distinguished by the cheaper, pressed-steel frame, these became known as the star-framed models, the word *star* probably a corruption of the German *stark*, meaning strong. Other German manufacturers soon followed BMW's lead, establishing a new German school of motorcycles, but as the pressed-steel frame was almost universally abhorred, this was a dubious connotation. The single-cylinder BMW motorcycle also made a comeback, and while never as popular as the twins, it was continually developed during the 1930s.

← At the 1929 London Motorcycle Exhibition, BMW released the R11 (left rear) and R16 (center) alongside the existing range. In the front on the left is an overhead-valve R57 or R63, with a side-valve R52 or R62 front right. *BMW Group Archives*

1930–1934 FLAT-TWINS

R11 and R16 Series 1

The R11's side-valve engine carried over from the R62, while the R16 featured the overhead-valve R63 engine. Apart from larger carburetors, these were unchanged, but the riveted pressed-steel frame set the new machines apart. Although undeniably stronger, the pressed-steel frame was also heavier, but in the eyes of many, it was ugly, scarring Friz's creation.

The chassis of the R11 and R16 consisted of two loops in a single pressing, joined by crossmembers. These strengthening sheets were also riveted at the front and into the fork blades. The only welding was at the front where the two halves joined together over the steering head. The trailing link front forks were also pressed steel, with nine-leaf spring front suspension, and the fuel tank was almost hidden by the heavy gusseting around the steering head. The result was a machine that conveyed a solidity and robustness that appealed to commercial and military interests but was hardly a sporting mount. The weight was around 20 pounds more than the R62 and R63, and while the R16 was capable of 75 miles per hour, the R11 struggled to better 60 miles per hour.

After production was delayed during 1929 due to some front fork problems, by 1930 the pressed-steel models replaced the tubular steel-framed versions. Only the sporting overhead-valve 500cc R57 remained through 1930, while the side-valve R52 disappeared altogether. The R11 and R16 were then developed through five series until 1934. Considering its heft, the R16 was a surprisingly effective racing motorcycle, and in 1933 BMW achieved its most significant sporting success to date. Sepp Stelzer, Ernst Henne, and Joseph Mauermayer won the 15th International Six-Day Trophy in Wales. Of the 143 entries, only three were BMWs, and they won two gold medals and one silver medal, also taking the trophy home to Germany. The ISDT was held at Garmisch Partenkirchen in Germany in 1934, again the R16 riders going home with gold. This was also a test run for the new telescopic front fork that would appear on production models during 1935.

Ernst Henne ushered in the new decade with his world speed record, but this was short-lived and he soon lost it to Joe Wright on the JAP-powered OEC Temple. Henne soon set about regaining it, and on September 30, 1930, he raised the record to 137.66 miles per hour. Economically, this was a difficult time and records were significant, both for BMW's importance as a world marque, and for national pride. Motorcycle sales were directly related to Henne's achievements. After losing the record again to Wright, who raised it to an astonishing 150.72 miles per hour in November 1931, at Cork in Ireland, Henne attempted to regain it in during 1932. After Henne had several failed attempts on the Neunkirchner Allee, a long straight road south of Vienna, motorcycle sales slumped.

Production slipped from 6,681 in 1931 to 4,652 in 1932.

Salvation for Henne and BMW came with the return of Rudolf Schleicher. During 1930, Henne persuaded Popp to entice Schleicher's return, and with Sepp Hopf, Schleicher designed a new multiplate supercharger. On November 3, 1932, in Tata, Hungary, in front of a full military lineup and the governor of Hungary, Admiral Horthy, Henne beat Wright's record, achieving 151.86 miles per hour. Two years later, in October 1934 in Gyon, Hungary, Henne went slightly faster at 152.9 miles per hour, and in 1935, he gave the supercharged overhead-valve 750 its final record. On the new Frankfurt-Darmstadt autobahn, he went 159.09 miles per hour. Things were looking up, and it coincided with Schleicher's return.

← Although Henne spent most of the year battling with Joe Wright for the world speed record, in May 1930 he found time to indulge in ice records at Ostersund in Sweden. For the frozen Storsee lake, his supercharged 500cc twin was fitted with studded tires, and in 7-degree F temperatures, after crashing and sliding 1,600 feet along the ice, Henne managed 123.2 miles per hour. *BMW Group Archives*

↑ Henne at speed on the Neunkirchner Allee near Vienna in April 1931, and although he managed 147.98 miles per hour, it wasn't enough to take the record. This would have to wait until later the following year. *BMW Group Archives*

↙ The two main protagonists responsible for BMW's success during the early 1930s. Rudolf Schleicher on the left, here congratulating Ernst Henne after his April 1931 attempt. *BMW Group Archives*

↑ Henne also set several sidecar world records. In April 1932 he raised his 1931 record of 118.48 miles per hour to 128.98 miles per hour. This would last until Wilhelm Noll beat it in 1955. *BMW Group Archives*

↓ Ernst Henne with the streamlined helmet and tail prior to a world record attempt near Vienna in April 1931. Fellow BMW racer Franz Bieber is in the center. *BMW Group Press*

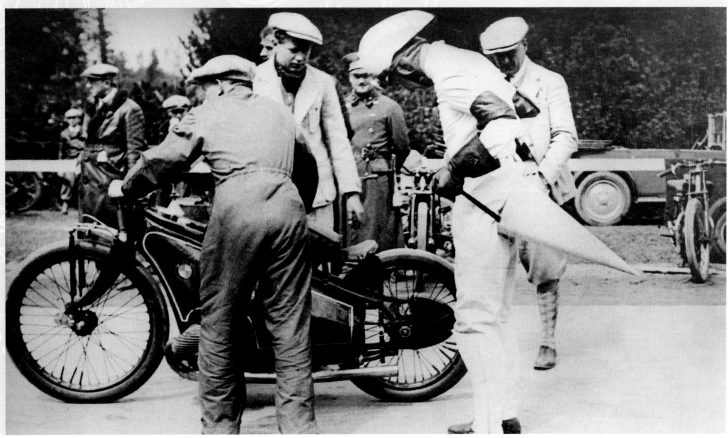

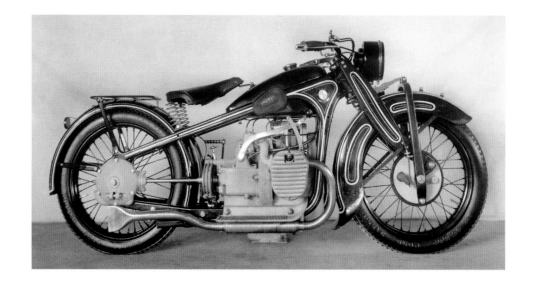

→ A heavy and ugly pressed-steel frame distinguished the R11, but it soon earned a reputation for ruggedness and was extremely popular. *BMW Group Archives*

1929-1930 **R11** SERIES 1

Engine designation	**M56**
Type	**Four-stroke, twin-cylinder, flat-twin**
Bore x stroke	**78x78mm**
Displacement	**745cc**
Power	**18 horsepower at 3,400 rpm**
Compression ratio	**5.5:1**
Valves	**Side-valve**
Carburetion	**1xBMW 24mm**
Gears	**3-speed**
Ignition	**Bosch magneto**
Frame designation	**F66**
Frame	**Twin-loop pressed-steel**
Front suspension	**Nine-plate spring**
Rear suspension	**Rigid**
Wheels	**26x3.5**
Tires	**26x3.5 (low pressure), 26x3.25 (high pressure) front & rear**
Brakes	**200mm front drum, 37mm rear shaft brake**
Wheelbase	**1,380mm (54.3 inches)**
Dry weight	**162 kg (357 lbs.)**
Engine numbers	**60001–73984 (Series 1–5)**
Frame numbers	**P101–P9893 (Series 1–5)**
Numbers produced	**7,500 (Series 1–5)**

↑ The R16 shared the short-stroke 750cc overhead-valve engine with the previous sporting R63. *BMW Group Archives*

1929-1930 **R16** SERIES 1 *(DIFFERING FROM THE R11 SERIES 1)*

Engine designation	**M60**
Bore x stroke	**83x68mm**
Displacement	**736cc**
Power	**25 horsepower at 4,000 rpm**
Compression ratio	**6.5:1**
Valves	**Overhead-valve**
Carburetion	**1 x BMW Special 26mm**
Dry weight	**165 kg (364 lbs.)**
Engine numbers	**75001–76956 (Series 1–5)**
Frame numbers	**P101–P9893 (Series 1–5)**
Numbers produced	**1,106 (Series 1–5)**

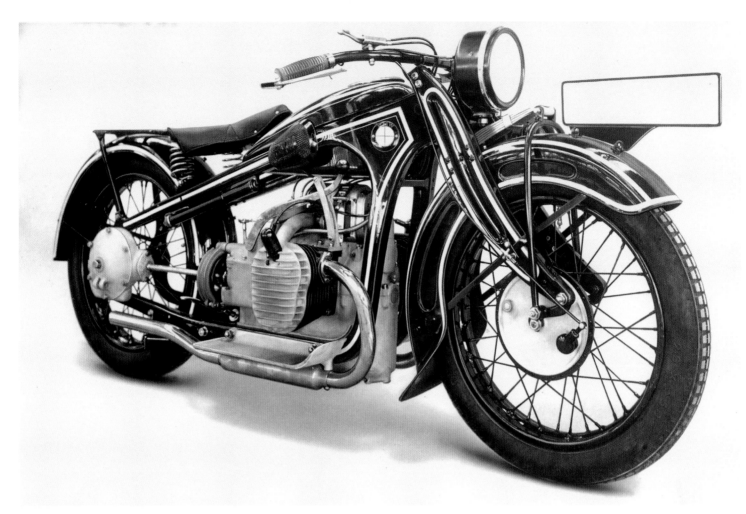

R11 and R16 Series 2

During 1930, the Series 2 R11 and R16 appeared. A stronger thrust bearing was added to the twin-plate clutch, along with an additional bearing in the rear drive, while the rear driveshaft brake shoes were increased. During this series, the Bosch headlamp changed from the older drum style to a more modern cup shape.

↑ Little changed from the Series 1, the R11 Series 2 appeared during 1930. This example still has the earlier drum headlamp. *BMW Group Archives*

↙ A lineup of new overhead-valve R16 Series 2s. These have the newer cup-style headlamp. *BMW Group Archives*

1930-1931 **R11 AND R16** SERIES 2 (DIFFERING FROM THE SERIES 1)	
Engine designation	**M56 S2 (R11), M60 S2 (R16)**
Frame designation	**F66 S2**
Brakes	**55mm rear shaft brake**

↑ **Section view of the 1932 R11 Series 3.**
BMW Group Archives

R11 and R16 Series 3

New carburetors appeared on the R11 and R16 Series 3 engines for 1932. The R11 carburetor was now a SUM from Berlin, with preheated secondary air drawn through a tube on the exhaust manifold. On the R16, the compression ratio was increased with twin 1-inch Amal carburetors (made under license by Fischer in Frankfurt) bolted directly on the intake manifolds of each cylinder head. This was enough to see a dramatic power increase, with a top speed of 78 miles per hour.

1931-1932 **R11 AND R16** SERIES 3 *(DIFFERING FROM THE SERIES 2)*	
Engine designation	**M56 S3 (R11), M60 S3 (R16)**
Power	**33 horsepower at 4,500 rpm (R16)**
Compression ratio	**7:1 (R16)**
Carburetion	**1 x Sum CK 3/500 F1 24mm (R11)** **2x Amal type 6/011 25mm (R16)**
Frame designation	**F66 S3**

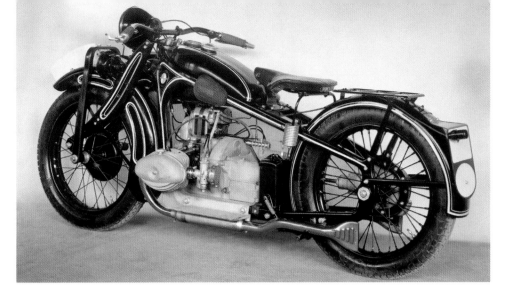

← The evolutionary R16 Series 4, now with optional battery ignition.
BMW Group Archives

↓ Setting the 1933 R11 Series 4 apart were the saddle extension springs.
BMW Group Archives

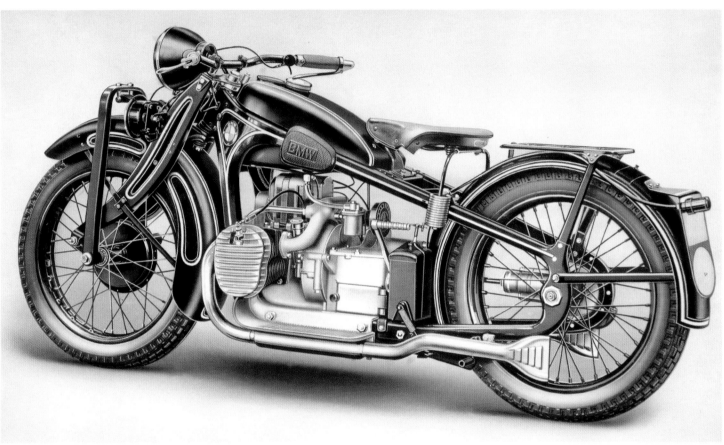

R11 and R16 Series 4

For the R11 and R16 Series 4 engines, new single-row caged roller big-end bearings replaced the earlier twin-row rollers. The gear change mechanism was moved to a gate underneath the knee rubber on the right, while the saddle now had extension springs. Battery ignition was also offered on the R16.

1933-1934 R11 AND R16 SERIES 4
(DIFFERING FROM THE SERIES 3)

Engine designation	**M56 S4 (R11), M60 S4 (R16)**
Frame designation	**F66 S4**

↑ With a pair of Amal carburetors, the R11 Series 5 was now capable of 70 miles per hour. *BMW Group Archives*

→ Setting the R16 Series 5 apart were the fishtail mufflers, and inside the engine a timing chain replaced the gears. *BMW Group Archives*

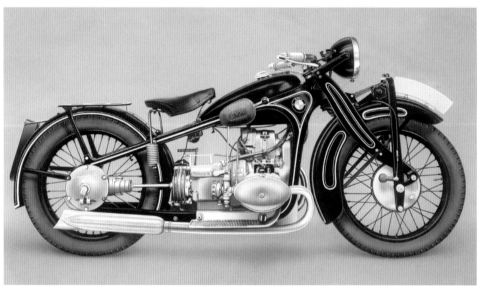

R11 and R16 Series 5

For the final series, the R11 and R16 received a roller timing chain, replacing the gears driving the camshaft from the front of the crankshaft. The R11 and R16 Series 5 featured battery and coil ignition, a first for a BMW motorcycle. The R11 and R16 now had a revised and more efficient fishtail silencer, the R11 with twin Amal carburetors, the power increase allowing a top speed of 70 miles per hour. A specific single carburetor army R11/5 RW was also produced, and a few R11/6s with a three-shaft four-speed gearbox, as a precursor to the R12.

1934 R11 AND R16 SERIES 5
(DIFFERING FROM THE SERIES 4)

Engine designation	M56 S3 (R11), M60 S3 (R16)
Power	20 horsepower at 4,000 rpm (R11)
Compression ratio	6.5:1 (R16 toward the end)
Carburetion	Amal 6/406 SP and 6/407 SP 25mm (R11)
Ignition	Battery (R11 and R16)
Frame designation	F66 S5

SINGLE CYLINDERS 1931–1937

R2 Series 1

The R39's failure deterred BMW from producing another single until 1931, but with changing economic circumstances and registration requirements in Germany, BMW now required an entry-level model. After April 1, 1928, the registration rules were amended so that motorcycles under 200cc could be used without road tax and ridden without a license. This resulted in DKW mass producing small two-stroke motorcycles, and while BMW wasn't initially interested in competing in this market, the company was forced into it following the deteriorating economic climate after the Wall Street crash of October 1929.

Unlike with the R39, BMW managed to find the right formula with the R2. It was no easy feat trying to combine traditional BMW four-stroke quality but at a price people could afford. Also retaining the shaft drive, the R2 engine was mounted longitudinally in the frame, with a three-speed gearbox bolted behind. The only anomaly was the exposed overhead valves, these oil-spraying components seemingly incongruous with the clean shaft final drive. The crankcase was a one-piece tunnel design, later to be featured on all air-cooled BMWs. Ignition was by battery and coil and the power enough to propel the rather heavy R2 to around 59 miles per hour, with excellent fuel economy.

The pressed-steel frame and cantilever fork were similar to the R11 and R16, but the engine was offset to the right to allow for a direct driveline in top gear from the crankshaft to minimize power loss. An internally expanding rear drum brake instead of the earlier driveshaft brake was an improvement. The R2 was designed with practicality and ease of ownership in mind, even including a front stand to assist wheel removal. Although it sold for 975 marks, three times the cheapest DKW, the R2 was immediately successful.

↑ BMW's smallest model of the twentieth century, the R2. The capacity allowed it to slip under the 200cc German tax limit. This Series 1 version has exposed valves. *BMW Group Archives*

↓ Cutaway of the R2 Series 1. *BMW Group Archives*

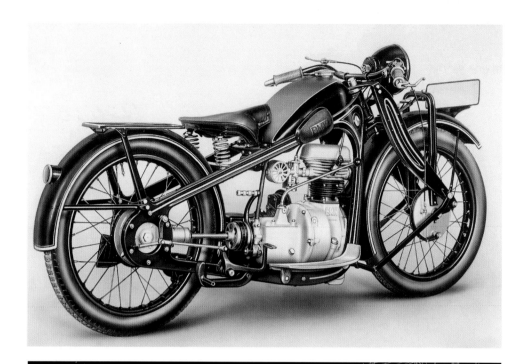

→ The R2 Series 2 received enclosed
valves and a new gear lever.
BMW Group Archives

1931 **R2** SERIES 1

Engine designation	**M67**
Type	**Four-stroke, vertical single-cylinder**
Bore x stroke	**63x64mm**
Displacement	**198cc**
Power	**6 horsepower at 3,500 rpm**
Compression ratio	**6.7:1**
Valves	**Overhead-valve**
Carburetion	**1 x Sum 19mm**
Gears	**3-speed**
Ignition	**Battery**
Frame designation	**F67**
Frame	**Pressed-steel duplex**
Front suspension	**Nine-plate cantilever spring**
Rear suspension	**Rigid**
Wheels	**25x3**
Tires	**25x3 front and rear**
Brakes	**180mm drum front and rear**
Wheelbase	**1,320mm (52 inches)**
Dry weight	**130 kg (287 lbs.)**
Engine numbers	**101–15402; P80001–P97700 (Series 1–5)**
Frame numbers	**P15000–P19260 (Series 1–5)**
Numbers produced	**4,161 (Series 1)**

1932–1933 **R2** SERIES 2A AND 2/33
(DIFFERING FROM THE SERIES 1)

Engine designation	**M67 S II and M67 S II 33**
Carburetion	**1 x Sum type K5/250, some with Amal (Series 2/33)**
Frame designation	**F67 S II and F67 S II 33**
Frame	**Pressed-steel duplex**
Front suspension	**Front damper (S2/33 from June 1933)**
Numbers produced	**1,850 (2a); 2,000 approx. (Series 2/33)**

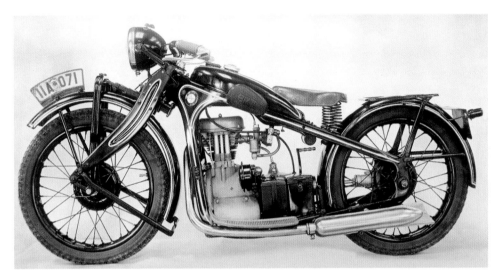

↑ A Theo Schoth dealer meeting in Berlin, 1934. From right to left: a R4, R11, R2, R47, and another R11. *BMW Group Archives*

← The 200cc R2 was one of the most popular BMW motorcycles of the early and mid-1930s, lasting to this Series 5 version of 1936. *BMW Group Archives*

R2 Series 2a and 2/33

For 1932, the R2 engine received an enclosed valve gear, a new SUM carburetor, and a new gearlever. Another series 2 was introduced during 1933 with 80 examples having an Amal carburetor. However, the main updates were to the chassis that from June 1933 on incorporated a friction damper with scissors on the front fork.

R2 Series 3, 4, and 5

All 1934 R2 engines received the Fischer-made Amal push-in carburetor and a new camshaft, slightly increasing the power. The 6-volt 30-watt generator on the left side of the engine was now encased under an aluminum cover, and the wheelbase was reduced slightly. For the 1935 R2 Series 4, the gas tank was smaller and longer, a rubber saddle also replaced the leatherette type, and a new type of Bosch headlamp was fitted. The final R2 was the 1936 Series 5, with a new Amal carburetor, a revised driveshaft, and a wider rear wheel mudguard and number plate. With more than 15,000 produced, the R2 was the right bike at the right time, and one of BMW's motorcycle production mainstays between 1931 and 1936.

1934–1936 R2 SERIES 3, 4, AND 5
(DIFFERING FROM THE SERIES 2A AND 2/33)

Engine designation	M67 S III, S IV, S V
Power	8 horsepower at 4,500 rpm
Carburetion	1 x Amal 18.2mm, Amal type 74/412S (Series 5)
Frame designation	F67 S III, S IV, S V
Wheelbase	1,303mm (51.3 inches)
Numbers produced	2,077 (Series 3), 2,700 (Series 4), 2,500 (Series 5)

→ With deep fenders and unusual right-side kick-starts, most of the 15,295 R4s produced between 1932 and 1937 ended up in military or police use. This is the Series 1. *BMW Group Archives*

R4 Series 1

Following the demise of the 500cc R52 and R57 in 1930, there was a gap in the lineup between the 200cc R2 and 750cc R11 and R16. Rather than build another expensive twin, BMW opted for expediency, creating the 400cc R4 single for 1932. The engine had enclosed valves and was based on the R2's powerplant. Producing enough power to propel the R4 to 62 miles per hour, it was designed primarily for military and police duties. As a military prerequisite, the R4 had a right-side kick-start, one of the few BMW motorcycles so equipped.

Although the chassis was fundamentally the same as the R2, the pressed-steel forks featured additional strengthening steel strips, the deep front fender was similar to the R11, and the tires had a slightly larger section. From July 1932, the front fork incorporated a friction damper, and the R4 gained a reputation for indestructability.

1932 R4 SERIES 1

Engine designation	**M69 S1**
Type	**Four-stroke, vertical single-cylinder**
Bore x stroke	**78x84mm**
Displacement	**398cc**
Power	**12 horsepower at 4,000 rpm**
Compression ratio	**5.7:1**
Valves	**Overhead-valve**
Carburetion	**1 x Sum CK 3/500 Fr 25mm**
Gears	**3-speed**
Ignition	**Battery**
Frame designation	**F69 S1**
Frame	**Pressed-steel duplex**
Front suspension	**Nine-plate cantilever spring with friction damper**
Rear suspension	**Rigid**
Wheels	**26x3.5**
Tires	**26x3.5 SS front and rear**
Brakes	**180mm drum front and rear**
Wheelbase	**1,300mm (51.2 inches)**
Dry weight	**137 kg (302 lbs.)**
Engine numbers	**80001–95280 (Series 1–5)**
Frame numbers	**P80001–P97700; P1001–P10437 (Series 1–5)**
Numbers produced	**1,101 (Series 1)**

R4 Series 2, 3, 4, and 5

For 1933, the R4 received a four-speed gearbox, the engine with a new gear lever and kick-start (no longer transversely, but longitudinally) and a copper-wool air filter. The Series 2 chassis incorporated some styling revisions, notably an extender spring saddle and new rubber-covered footrests in place of the alloy boards. The 1934 Series 3 received a new cylinder head, increasing the power slightly, and an enclosed left side generator with a second chain drive. The gearshift was now in a gate near the fuel tank (as on the 1933 R11), and chassis updates included a larger gas tank (3 gallons). On the 1935 Series 4, the toolbox was integrated into the crankcase, with the generator on top of the crankcase driven by a V belt from the crankshaft, and the battery was in a separate box near the gearbox. The chassis received a new headlamp, and the forks had twin friction dampers. For 1936–1937 R4 Series 5, the gear case was updated, with new gears, and the oil cap repositioned. The chassis was much as before, and this final series was produced in relatively large numbers for military use.

As the R4 wasn't able to compete with the more powerful overhead-valve 500s, it was seen an alternative to the more mundane side-valve models. The price of 1,150 marks may have deterred it from younger buyers, but it soon earned a reputation for ruggedness and reliability that made it the standard training and dispatch model for the military and police. The R4 was also used in trials events and offered for a while as an off-road sports model, albeit without any modifications from standard.

↑ For the 1935 R4 Series 4, the generator was positioned above the crankcase. *BMW Group Archives*

← An R4 Series 3 on a test at the Nürburgring 1934. *BMW Group Archives*

1933–1937 **R4** SERIES 2, 3, 4, 5
(DIFFERING FROM THE SERIES 1)

Engine designation	**M69 S2, S3, S4, S5**
Power	**14 horsepower at 4,000 rpm (From Series 3)**
Gears	**4-speed**
Frame designation	**F69 S2, S3, S4, S5**
Front suspension	**2 friction dampers (From Series 4)**
Numbers produced	**1,737 (Series 2), 3,671 (Series 3), 3,651 (Series 4), 5,033 (Series 5)**

1) Eine BMW R 4-400 ccm zur Testfahrt auf dem Nürburgring.

The R3

Joining the range of singles for 1936 was a small-bore version of the R4, the R3. But without the performance of the R4 or the tax and license advantages of the R2, this long-stroke single was dropped after only one year.

1936 **R3** (DIFFERING FROM THE R4)	
Engine designation	**203/1**
Bore x stroke	**68x84mm**
Displacement	**305cc**
Power	**11 horsepower at 4,200 rpm**
Compression ratio	**6.0:1**
Carburetion	**1 x Sum Register type CK3/500 25mm**
Gears	**4-speed**
Frame designation	**203/1**
Wheels	**19x2.5**
Tires	**26x3.5 balloon front and rear**
Wheelbase	**1,320mm (52 inches)**
Dry weight	**149 kg (328 lbs.)**
Engine numbers	**20001–20740**
Frame numbers	**P1001–P1740**
Numbers produced	**740**

↓ **The R12 and R17 were the first production motorcycles to feature a telescopic front fork, but the ride was poor and travel limited.**
BMW Group Archives

1935–1937 FLAT-TWINS

R12 and R17

During 1934, motorcycle production more than doubled, from 4,734 in 1933 to 9,689, encouraging the development of two new 750cc models. These were the side-valve R12 and overhead-valve R17, first displayed at the Berlin Motor Show in February 1935. The engines were based on the powerplants used in the earlier R11 and R16, but with a four-speed gearbox, and while retaining the pressed-steel frame, what set the new machines apart was Rudolf Schleicher's oil-damped telescopic front fork. These first appeared on Alfred Böning's radical R7 prototype of 1934 and was the first modern-style hydraulic fork fitted to a motorcycle. The R12 and R17 were a curious combination of the old and new, still retaining a rigid rear end when many British motorcycles featured rear suspension. Even Hitler was surprised as he passed the BMW stand at the 1935 Berlin Motor Show, asking Schleicher, "And when are we going to get rear suspension?" Schleicher later admitted he was filled with embarrassment and consternation by Hitler's question, but it would still be two years before rear suspension appeared. Schleicher already had Böning's Norton-based rear suspension design but was unhappy with it. He then had Alexander von Falkenhausen design a new system, with sliding tubes housing the driveshaft and springs at the frame ends.

The R12 and R17 four-speed engines featured stronger crankshafts, but retained the hand change through a gate on the right side. The R12 also came with a choice of a single Sum carburetor or twin Amals, the power identical to the two similar R11s. As the flagship of the range, the R17 only came with twin Amal carburetors, but revved out to 5,000 rpm and topped out at an impressive 87 miles per hour. The R17's weakness was the heavy pressed-steel chassis,

↑ Heavy and solid, the R12 was particularly suited to military use. The large, sweeping valanced fenders appeared for 1936.
BMW Group Archives

← Most R12s were single carburetor, with two preheater pipes running back to the manifold from the exhaust ports.
BMW Group Archives

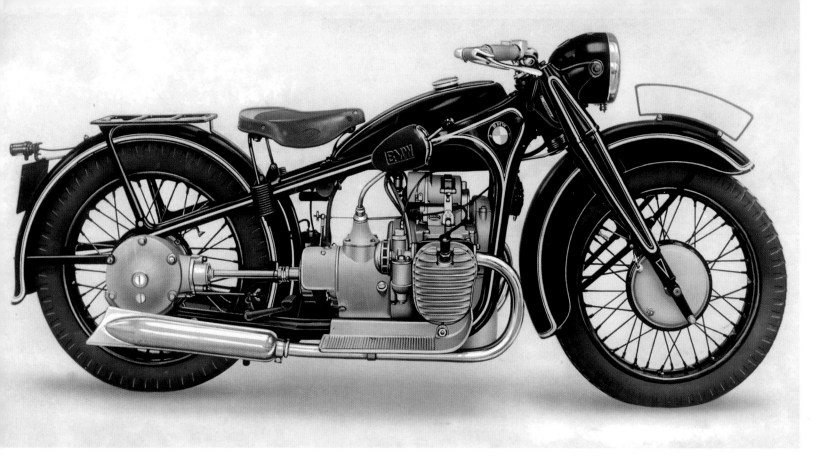

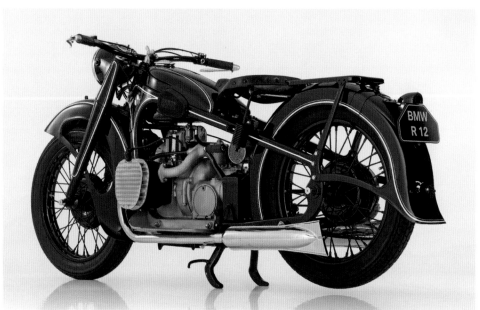

suitable for military and sidecar duties, and shared with the R12 workhorse. The rear brake was now a drum instead of the driveshaft type, enabling the front and rear 19-inch wheels to be interchangeable. And while they were revolutionary for 1935, the telescopic forks were decidedly underdeveloped with only meager one-way damping and 75mm of movement.

It was also difficult to disguise the heavy pressed-steel frame, and for 1936 the R12 and R17 received sweeping fenders, imitating the styling of contemporary luxury German cars. While the R12, at 1,630 marks, would become the most popular prewar BMW motorcycle, the princely sum of 2,040 marks made the R17 the most expensive German motorcycle available in its day and only for the fortunate few. If viewed as a comfortable touring machine for straight smooth roads rather than a sporting motorcycle, the R17 was successful. It epitomized the best German attributes—solidity and efficiency—but by 1936 the time was right for a completely new sporting machine. The R12 in the meantime would soldier on until 1942, predominantly as a single-carburetor military machine and only for the military after 1938. It would serve as the Wehrmacht's principal motorcycle in the early stages of World War II.

1935–1942 R12 *(SINGLE AND DUAL CARBURETOR)*

Engine designation	M56 S6 or 212
Type	Four-stroke, twin-cylinder, flat-twin
Bore x stroke	78x78mm
Displacement	745cc
Power	18 horsepower at 3,400 rpm, 20 horsepower at 4,000 rpm (Dual carb)
Compression ratio	5.2:1
Valves	Side-valve
Carburetion	1 x Sum CK 25mm, 2 x Amal 6/406/407 23.8mm (Dual carb)
Gears	4-speed
Ignition	Magneto or battery
Frame designation	F66
Frame	Twin-loop pressed-steel
Front suspension	Telescopic fork
Rear suspension	Rigid
Wheels	3x19
Tires	3.5x19 front and rear
Brakes	200mm drum front and rear
Wheelbase	1,380mm (54.3 inches)
Dry weight	185 kg (408 lbs.) approx.
Engine numbers	501–24149 and 25001–37161
Frame numbers	P501–P24149 and P25001–P37161
Numbers produced	36,008

↓ It may have had interchangeable wheels, a telescopic front fork, and be the fastest and most expensive motorcycle available in Germany, but the heavy R12 frame disadvantaged the R17 as a sporting motorcycle. *BMW Group Archives*

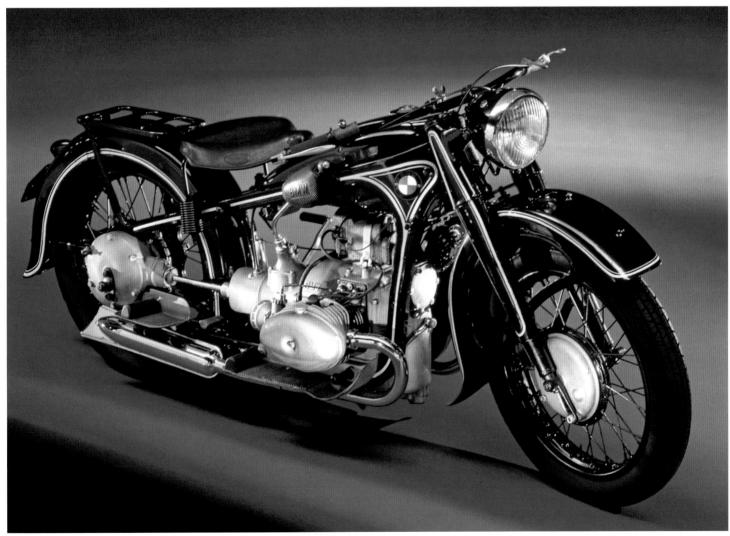

In January 1933, Hitler became chancellor of Germany and the Nazis were well aware of the morale boost associated with competition success. As part of their nationalistic propaganda program, they encouraged German manufacturers to embark in racing, and one result was a new 500cc supercharged BMW twin that would eventually inspire a range of production models.

Instead of developing the existing overhead-valve design, the 500 Kompressor was a purpose-built Grand Prix racer. Back in 1928, drawings were made for an overhead camshaft engine, and considerable time was spent investigating bevel gear-driven overhead camshaft systems until 1932. Four versions were built, two 500cc (M250/1, M255/1) and two 600cc (M260/1, M265/1), with or without a supercharger. The bore and stroke of the 500 was 66x72 mm, with 72.2x72mm for the 600, with the valves operated by bevel gear-driven twin overhead camshafts in the cylinder head. Each pair of camshafts was geared directly to each other and opened the valves through short rockers. The Zoller multicell vane-type supercharger was now

spline-driven from the front of the crankshaft, with a single 27mm Fischer-Amal side-mounted carburetor on the right. Because the supercharger ran at engine speed, it provided boost of around 15 psi, the power delivery was very smooth, and the Kompressor would pull cleanly from as low as 2,500 rpm. Many of the castings were lightweight Elektron magnesium, including the crankcases and gearbox housing, and for the first time for BMW, the four-speed gearbox had a positive foot gearshift.

Instead of the heavy R11 and R16 pressed-steel frame, the Kompressor featured Schleicher's electrically arc-welded tubular-steel frame and incorporated his own design of oil-filled 28mm telescopic front fork. This was the first time oil-damped telescopic forks appeared on a motorcycle, but the rigid rear end remained. The Kompressor debuted at the high-speed banked Avus circuit near Berlin in June 1935. It was ridden by Ludwig "Wiggerl" Kraus, but Ragnar Sunqvist on the Swedish Husqvarna V-twin won at an average speed of 105.6 miles per hour. There were no more outings that year except for the International Six-Day Trial, again held in Germany, where the German trophy team of Kraus, Stelzer, and Henne rode detuned Kompressors to victory.

⇑ The BMW team on 500 Kompressors at the 1935 ISDT. Henne, Stelzer, and Kraus/Müller succeeded in winning the trophy. *BMW Group Archives*

↑ For the 1937 season, the Kompressor received plunger rear suspension. This is Karl Gall's German championship–winning machine. *BMW Group Archives*

← The 500cc Type 255 Kompressor engine was one of the greatest racing motorcycle engines of the 1930s. The supercharger, mounted in front of the engine, fed a long, smooth intake running underneath the cylinders. Shaft-driven bevel gears operated the double-overhead camshafts in each cylinder head. *BMW Group Archives*

For the 1936 season, Otto Ley and Karl Gall received works Kompressors, Ley taking second in the Swiss Grand Prix behind Jimmy Guthrie on the Norton. Despite its superior power, the Kompressor was a handful and difficult to ride. Ley managed another second at Assen before the Kompressor achieved its first victory in Sweden in August. Ley and Gall finished first and second ahead of the Norton, FN, and DKW works teams. In the meantime, the world speed record was lost to Eric Fernihough on the Brough Superior, so Schleicher prepared a fully streamlined 500 Kompressor. In October 1936, on the Frankfurt-Darmstadt autobahn, Henne set a new record of 169.02 miles per hour. BMW now looked optimistically toward the 1937 season, along with Alexander von Falkenhausen's new rear suspension. Faced with reluctance to race with it by the riders, von Falkenhausen proved the superiority of his rear suspension by successfully riding the machine himself in the International Six-Day event at Füssen. The plunger rear suspension featured straight-guide sleeves in vertical tubes, and the driveshaft required a universal joint.

In the hands of Ley and Gall, the fully sprung Kompressor now proved a match for the British machines. Gall outpaced the Nortons

↗ Henne inside the fully faired Kompressor, prior to a run on the autobahn near Frankfurt in 1937.
BMW Group Press

→ Jock West and his German mechanic with the factory Kompressor on their way to the Isle of Man in 1937.
BMW Group Press

at the Dutch TT to take the victory, also winning the German Grand Prix at the Sachsenring after Guthrie was killed on the last lap. Ley won the Swedish TT and Jock West the Ulster, giving BMW four out of seven Grand Prix victories in 1937. Jock West also rode a solitary Kompressor at the Isle of Man, finishing a creditable sixth, and Gall won the German championship. The year ended with Henne responding to Fernihough and Piero Taruffi's new world speed records. With wind tunnel–tested streamlining, on November 28, 1937, Henne managed 173.68 miles per hour on the 90-horsepower 500. This record would last until 1951 as Fernihough was killed at Gyon in April 1938 trying to beat it.

The Isle of Man TT was the first event for 1938 and BMW fielded a three-man team. Developments saw the power up to 55 horsepower at 7,000 rpm, running on petrol-benzol and with larger full-width brakes. With the Nazi decree that a German should win on

a German machine, Georg (Schorsch) Meier replaced the aging Ley, alongside Gall, while West filled out the team. Gall crashed heavily during practice, and Meier was unable to remove the soft warmup spark plugs on the start line, so West was left as the only BMW in the race. West acquitted himself well, finishing fifth, while Harold Daniell won on the works Norton. Meier then went on to win the Belgian Grand Prix, the Dutch TT, and the German Grand Prix to take the European Championship. West again won the Ulster Grand Prix.

With war clouds looming, Norton withdrew from racing for 1939, BMW now battling Gilera for 500cc honors. Meier, Gall, and West again traveled to the Isle of Man in June, Gall crashing at Ballaugh Bridge during practice. Barely recovering from the skull fracture he received in the 1938 crash, he died four days later. Despite this setback, Meier won the Senior TT at 89.38 miles per hour, with West second,

↑ In October 1936, Ernst Henne attempted the world speed record near Frankfurt with this fully enclosed 500cc Kompressor, nicknamed "The Egg." He managed 168.92 miles per hour, setting a new record. *BMW Group Archives*

↑ For the November 1937 attempt, Henne's Komprssor had new wind tunnel– tested streamlining. *BMW Group Press*

→ Henne about to set his final world speed record, achieving 173.7 miles per hour, a record that would stand for 14 years. *BMW Group Archives*

more than two minutes behind. Meier followed his TT victory with wins at the Dutch TT and the Belgian Grand Prix. Here he lapped at 100.63 miles per hour, the first time a "ton" lap was achieved in a classic event. A crash in Sweden saw Meier out of the German Grand Prix due to injury, and the outbreak of war ended the season after Ulster. The final Kompressor was a formidable machine, if somewhat a beast to ride. When weighed after the TT, Meier's machine was found to be the lightest finisher at only 137 kilograms.

During the World War II, all the factory racing machines were transferred to Berg on Lake Starnberg for safekeeping, but Meier managed to retrieve the Isle of Man machine in 1943, hiding it away in a hay barn. When he wheeled it out for a demonstration race against the NSU at Solitude in 1947, hundreds of thousands turned out to watch. Meier then set up a motorcycle dealership in Munich, continuing to successfully race the Kompressor in German events and winning five German championships between 1947 and 1953.

↑ Englishman John "Jock" West came in second at the 1939 Isle of Man Senior TT. The jovial West was sales manager for the British BMW importer, and while unpaid as a racer, he became the face of BMW abroad in the late 1930s. With tension increasing between the two governments, as a British rider in a German team, West was often put in an uncomfortable position. *BMW Group Archives*

↑ Meier on his way to winning the 1939 Isle of Man TT. This was the first victory at the Isle of Man by a foreign rider on a foreign make and provided BMW great publicity, even if it was short-lived as war was declared three months later. After joining the Bavarian State Police in 1929, Georg, known as Schorsch, Meier soon attracted attention for his ability on a motorcycle, and the fact that he rode too fast on the Bavarian country roads. In 1935, Meier joined the German Army and was German Army Champion in 1935 and 1936. He began his racing career as Henne's substitute in the 1937 ISDT at Donington, England, winning a gold medal and earning a ride in the BMW road racing team. *BMW Group Archives*

↑ Sweeping fenders in the style of contemporary luxury German cars characterized the second series R17. *Ian Falloon*

1935–1937 **R17** *(DIFFERING FROM THE R12)*

Engine designation	**M60**
Bore x stroke	**83x68mm**
Displacement	**736cc**
Power	**33 horsepower at 5,000 rpm**
Compression ratio	**6.5:1**
Valves	**Overhead-valve**
Carburetion	**2 x Amal 76/424 1-inch**
Dry weight	**165 kg (364 lbs.) approx.**
Engine numbers	**77001–77436**
Frame numbers	**P501–P24738**
Numbers produced	**434**

1936–1937 FLAT-TWINS

R5

When the R5 was released at the Berlin Motor Show in February 1936, it heralded a new era of innovation for BMW. The R5 was arguably the most advanced motorcycle available at that time, not only looking much more modern than the R17, but it was significantly lighter and cost only 1,550 marks. Overnight BMW had made its R17 sporting flagship obsolete. These were sanguine times in Germany, and BMW benefited. Production climbed from 10,005 in 1935, to 11,922 in 1936, and to 12,549 in 1937.

Designed by Leonhard Ischinger, the R5 drew heavily on the 500 Kompressor and was the first 500cc overhead-valve production BMW since the demise of the R57. The engine was all new, with the crankcase a one-piece tunnel-type similar to that of the singles. The crankshaft was inserted from the front and, with two chain-driven camshafts instead of one, positioned over the crank to allow for shorter tappets and pushrods. The timing chain also drove the Bosch generator on top of the crankcase, with the ignition coil and distributor positioned inside the front cover. The included valve angle was reduced to 80 degrees, the rocker arms pivoting in needle roller bearings, with double hairpin valve springs to provide safety at higher rpm.

The four-speed gearbox was foot operated by a linkage on the left, although the right-hand lever was retained primarily as a quicker way to select neutral. As this positive stop gearshift design originated with Harold Willis' 1928 Velocette, it demonstrated BMW's openness to

↑ The R5 was one of the greatest motorcycles of the decade. Innovations included a positive stop gearshift and a steering damper for the telescopic front fork. Many aficionados consider the R5 the best looking of all BMWs. *BMW Group Archives*

↓ The R5 engine was all new and now featured a one-piece tunnel crankcase with twin camshafts. This 1937 version has a central air filter built into the gearbox casing. *BMW Group Archives*

incorporating new ideas, even foreign. Carburetion was by twin Amal carburetors, each with a small ear-type air filter, but these proved unsatisfactory. For 1937, a central wire-mesh air filter built into an extension of the gearbox casing replaced them. Although the power output was less than that of the R17, the R5 was a much more sporting motorcycle.

The main reason for the R5's superiority was the electrically arc-welded (a process termed Arcatron) tubular-steel duplex frame, similar in design to that of the 500 Kompressor. Schleicher used the same oval-section conical tubing, and not only did the frame impart a more modern appearance, but the weight was considerably reduced. Completing the improved chassis specification was an adjustable external steering damper for the telescopic fork, and it was primarily the rigid rear end that limited the ride quality. However, a softly sprung Pagusa rubber seat compensated for this, and the R5 provided exceptional sporting performance for the mid-1930s. The top speed was around 84 miles per hour and many enthusiasts rated the handling of the rigid-frame R5 superior to the later R51. The R5 was a milestone motorcycle for BMW, finally challenging the British in performance and handling. One of the standout machines of the decade, the R5 also provided the basis for BMW twins for the next 20 years.

↑ Not only did the R5 look more modern than the pressed-steel frame R17, it was lighter and functionally superior. Although still with a rigid rear end, the R5's handling was considered better than later versions with plunger rear suspension. *BMW Group Archives*

↑ Also new was a tubular-steel frame, an exotic combination of round and oval section tubing, selected according to the load expected and joined by electric and gas welding. The rear drum brake casting and small-diameter driveshaft were beautifully executed. *BMW Group Archives*

1936–1937 **R5**

Engine designation	**254**
Type	**Four-stroke, twin-cylinder, flat-twin**
Bore x stroke	**68x68mm**
Displacement	**494cc**
Power	**24 horsepower at 5,500 rpm**
Compression ratio	**6.7:1**
Valves	**Overhead-valve**
Carburetion	**2 x Amal 5/423 22.2mm**
Gears	**4-speed foot shift with auxiliary manual lever**
Ignition	**Battery**
Frame designation	**250**
Frame	**Twin-loop tubular-steel**
Front suspension	**Telescopic fork**
Rear suspension	**Rigid**
Wheels	**3x19**
Tires	**3.5x19 front and rear**
Brakes	**200mm drum front and rear**
Wheelbase	**1,400mm (55 inches)**
Dry weight	**165 kg (364 lbs.)**
Engine numbers	**8001–9504 and 500001–502786**
Frame numbers	**8001–9504 and 500001–503085**
Numbers produced	**2,652**

↑ Even after it was superseded by the R51, the R5 continued as a competitive racer, here during the 1938 German Alpine Rally. *BMW Group Press*

↓ A London stunt rider demonstrating the R5's stability. *BMW Group Press*

R6

Joining the R5 for 1937 was a side-valve 600, the R6. Side-valve engines were considered better suited for sidecars and BMW was optimistic for sales of the new R5 and R6 to the German military. Unfortunately, the company's optimism proved unfounded, as the German army authorities were more interested in the heavy and solid, but proven, pressed-steel frame 750cc R12. The R6 chassis was identical to the sporting R5's, but the engine was new. Instead of twin camshafts, as in the earlier engines, spur gears drove single central camshaft. With twin Amal carburetors, the power was unremarkable and the top speed barely reached 78 miles per hour. Although the long-stroke motor's torque made it suitable for sidecar use, this still didn't save the R6, and it only lasted one year.

1937 R6 (DIFFERING FROM THE R5)	
Engine designation	261
Bore x stroke	70x78mm
Displacement	596cc
Power	18 horsepower at 4,500 rpm
Compression ratio	6.0:1
Valves	Side-valve
Carburetion	2 x Amal M75/426/S 22.2mm
Dry weight	175 kg (386 lbs.)
Engine numbers	600001–601850
Frame numbers	500001–503085
Numbers produced	1,850

↓ Both the R5 and R6 shared the new tubular-steel chassis, but the 600cc side-valve R6 was aimed at sidecar users. It didn't prove popular and lasted only one year.
BMW Group Archives

1937–1940 SINGLES

R35

The final pressed-steel frame single was the R35, this replacing the R4 during 1937. Although the capacity was slightly less, the power was unchanged. The R35 received a front telescopic fork, but this was rather rudimentary in design and didn't incorporate the R5's hydraulic damping. During this time of BMW's technical innovation, the R35 was still very much an anachronism, but was very popular with the German military, which bought it in large numbers, just as it had the R4. Although production ended at Munich in 1940, production continued from 1947 at the Eisenach plant, now in East Germany, to use up parts stock. The EMW (Eisenacher Motorenwerke) R35 and R35-3 (with plunger rear suspension) remained in production through 1955. Of the 80,000 examples produced, only a handful ever made it to the West.

↑ The final BMW motorcycle with the pressed-steel frame was the single-cylinder R35. Now with a telescopic front fork and 19-inch wheels, the R35 replaced the R4 and unsuccessful R3, and it proved extremely popular, both with the general public and military. *BMW Group Archives*

1937–1940 R35 (DIFFERING FROM THE R4 SERIES 5)	
Engine designation	**M69 and 235**
Bore x stroke	**72x84mm**
Displacement	**342cc**
Power	**14 horsepower at 4,500 rpm**
Compression ratio	**6.0:1**
Carburetion	**1 x Sum CK 9/22mm**
Frame designation	**235**
Front suspension	**Telescopic fork**
Wheels	**3x19**
Tires	**3.50x19 front and rear**
Wheelbase	**1,400mm (55.1 inches)**
Dry weight	**155 kg (342 lbs.)**
Engine numbers	**300001–315387**
Frame numbers	**300001–315654**
Numbers produced	**15,386**

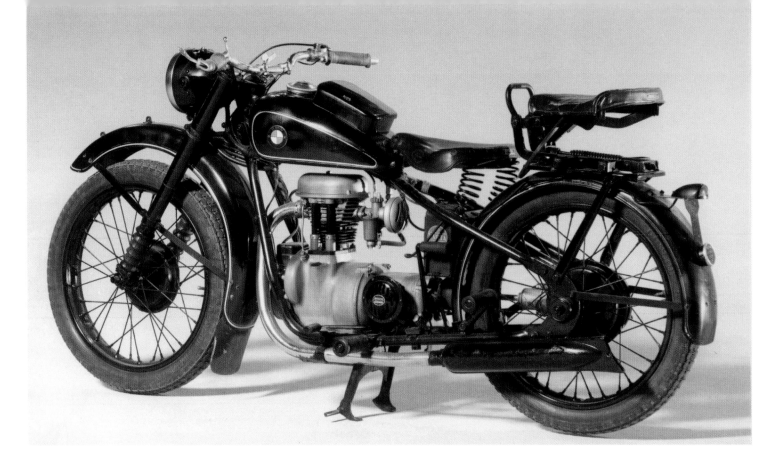

↑ A more modern R20 single replaced the extremely popular "people's bike" R2 for 1937. The frame was now tubular steel but with a rigid rear end, and this example has an optional pillion seat. *BMW Group Archives*

R20 and R23

Also introduced for 1937 was the R2 replacement, the R20. With its tubular-steel frame, this was more modern than the R35, and the overhead-valve engine was an all-new design, with different dimensions. As the crankshaft-driven generator was positioned in front of the timing cover, the engine's appearance was cleaner and tidier. The gearbox reverted to three speeds with a foot gearshift, and the R20 frame consisted of bolted-together butted-end tubes with an undamped R35-type telescopic front fork. After June 1938, new traffic regulations in Germany no longer exempted 200cc machines, and there was a new restricted license for motorcycles up to 250cc. BMW then responded by creating the 250cc R23 by boring the R20 engine. Apart from a toolbox now incorporated inside the fuel tank, the R23 was identical to the R20. Relatively large numbers of both the R20 and R23 were produced, but the outbreak of World War II saw their demise.

1937–1938 R20 *(DIFFERING FROM THE R2 SERIES 5)*

Engine designation	220/1
Bore x stroke	60x68mm
Displacement	192cc
Power	8 horsepower at 5,400 rpm
Compression ratio	6.0:1
Carburetion	1 x Amal push-in M 74/428 18.2mm
Frame designation	220/1
Frame	Bolted twin-loop
Front suspension	Telescopic fork
Wheels	2.5x19
Tires	3.00x19 front and rear
Wheelbase	1,330mm (52.4 inches)
Engine numbers	100001–105004
Frame numbers	100001–105029
Numbers produced	5,000

1938–1940 R23 *(DIFFERING FROM THE R20)*

Engine designation	**223/1**
Bore x stroke	**68x68mm**
Displacement	**247cc**
Carburetion	**1 x Amal push-in M74/435S 18.2mm**
Dry weight	**135 kg (298 lbs.)**
Engine numbers	**106001–104021**
Frame numbers	**106001–104203**
Numbers produced	**8,021**

↓ New regulations saw the 250cc R23 replace the 200cc R20 for 1938. *BMW Group Archives*

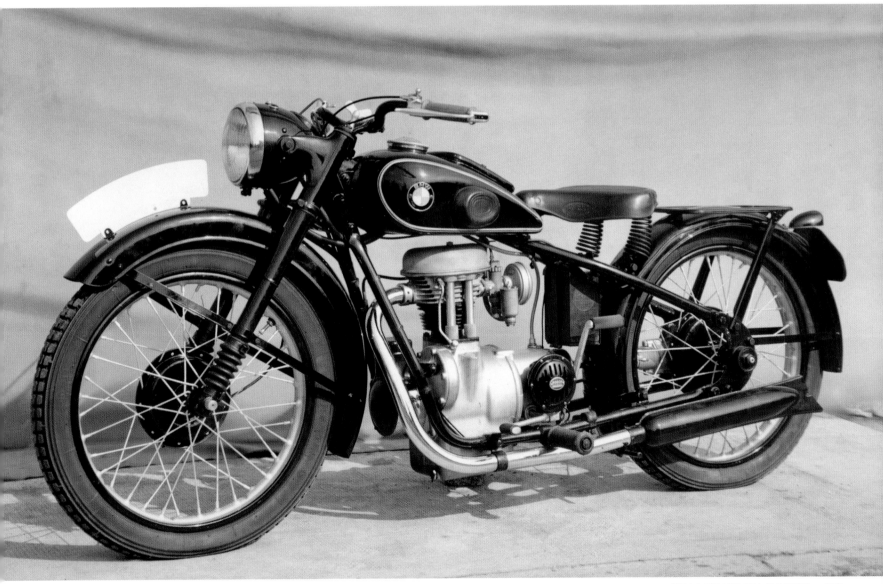

→ For the 1937 ISDT in Wales, BMW prepared new sprung-frame R51s for the German trophy team of Ludwig Kraus, Josef Stelzer, and Georg Meier. The German team narrowly lost to Britain. *BMW Group Press*

1938–1941 FLAT-TWINS

R51, R61, R66, and R71

As the works Kompressor racers successfully introduced Alex von Falkenhausen's plunger rear suspension during 1937, the release of a new range of fully sprung models at the Berlin Show in February 1938 wasn't unexpected. The R51 replaced the R5, and the R61 the R6, and two new models joined them: the R66 and R71. The R71 was a 750cc side-valve sidecar machine, ostensibly to replace the R12 that was by now only a single-carburetor version and purely for the military. The 600cc overhead-valve R66 assumed the position as the top-of-the-range sportster, with a price of 1,695 reichsmarks.

Apart from a slightly lower compression ratio for the R61, there were few changes to the engines for the R51 and R61. As chrome was in short supply, mostly earmarked for gun barrels, the mufflers were generally painted black. The plunger telescopic rear suspension set the new machines apart, all sharing the same chassis, accompanied by a weight increase.

Based on the R61, the R71's capacity increase to 745cc came through a larger bore. This was to be BMW's last side-valve model, and apart from the older-style cylinders heads, it otherwise looked identical to the 600cc R61. Undoubtedly the most exciting of the new models was the R66. Instead of basing the engine on the R5/R51 twin-camshaft type, with its long cam chain, the 600cc R66 engine included the R61 side-valve crankcases with one central gear-driven camshaft and a wider cylinder base to incorporate the pushrod tubes. The cylinder heads with hairpin valve springs were shared with the R51, but unique to the R66 were cylinders and heads tilted 5 degrees forward to provide more foot room. With larger Amal carburetors, the R66 was capable of 90 miles per hour, and even with a sidecar, it was good for 71 miles per hour. Production of the four models lasted well into the war years, finally ending in 1941 (although the R51 finished in 1940). BMW's racetrack success was also reflected in sales, production soaring in 1938 to 17,300 and in 1939 to 21,667.

1938–1940 R51 *(DIFFERING FROM THE R5)*	
Engine designation	254/1
Frame designation	250/1
Rear suspension	Plunger
Dry weight	182 kg (401 lbs.)
Engine numbers	503001–506172
Frame numbers	505001–515164
Numbers produced	3,775

← W. Ehrich on an R51 during the Six-Days Trial in Austria late in August 1939, only days before the outbreak of war. *BMW Group Archives*

↓ The R51 was a competent and versatile motorcycle; it is seen here with the Swedish rider Ake Laurin in the 1938 Jasna off-road event. *BMW Group Archives*

1938–1941 **R61** *(DIFFERING FROM THE R6)*

Engine designation	**261/1**
Compression ratio	**5.7:1**
Frame designation	**251/1**
Rear suspension	**Plunger**
Dry weight	**184 kg (406 lbs.)**
Engine numbers	**603001–606080 and 607001–607340**
Frame numbers	**505001–515164 and 607001–607340**
Numbers produced	**3,747**

↑ The 600cc R66 was BMW's top sporting motorcycle from 1938. Not only did this feature the sprung frame with plunger suspension, the engine was unique. Based on the side-valve engine with its single central camshaft, the overhead-valve R66 featured tilted-forward cylinders and heads.
BMW Group Archives

→ The side-valve R61 was ostensibly an R6 with plunger rear suspension.
BMW Group Archives

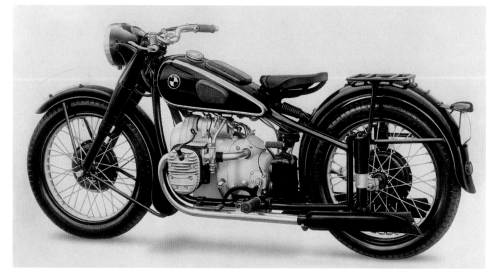

1938–1941 R66 *(DIFFERING FROM THE R5)*

Engine designation	**266/1**
Bore x stroke	**69.8x78mm**
Displacement	**595cc**
Power	**30 horsepower at 5,300 rpm**
Compression ratio	**6.8:1**
Carburetion	**2 x Amal 6/420S 23.8mm**
Frame designation	**251/1**
Rear suspension	**Plunger**
Dry weight	**187 kg (412 lbs.)**
Engine numbers	**660001–661629 and 662001–662039**
Frame numbers	**505001–515164 and 662001–662039**
Numbers produced	**1,669**

↑ Although not possessing the aesthetic balance of the rigid-frame R5, the R66 was arguably the finest of all prewar BMW motorcycles. *BMW Group Press*

← Although the 750cc side-valve R12 continued in production for military use only, in 1938 the tubular-frame R71 replaced it for general duties. Still popular for the military, the R71 was also built in relatively large numbers and inspired the postwar Soviet M-72 and Chinese Chang Jiang 750. This continued as a side-valve until the mid-1980s, when an overhead-valve version replaced it. *BMW Group Archives*

1938–1941 R71 (DIFFERING FROM THE R6)

Engine designation	271/1
Bore x stroke	78x78mm
Displacement	746cc
Power	22 horsepower at 4,600 rpm
Compression ratio	5.5:1
Carburetion	2 x Graetzin G24mm
Frame designation	251/1
Rear suspension	Plunger
Dry weight	187 kg (412 lbs.)
Engine numbers	700001–702200 and 703001–703511
Frame numbers	505001–515164 and 703001–703511
Numbers produced	3,458

While the double-overhead camshaft 500 Kompressor always remained a factory racer, in 1937 a small number, about 50, R5SS (Super Sport) production racers were made available for selected riders. Although not offered to the public, the R5SS was fundamentally a modified R5 without lights or mufflers, and outside, rather than inverted, handlebar levers. The power output was around 4 horsepower more than the R5, achieved through different valve timing, polished ports, and stronger valve springs, and carburetors with velocity stacks. The top speed was approximately 100 miles per hour. Prior to the release of the sprung-frame R51, BMW also built an R51SS during 1937, with limited

production continuing into 1938, and a higher performance R51RS for 1939. The R51SS featured a special gearbox with higher ratios, higher compression ratio of 8:1, and 6/432 Amal/Fischer 24mm carburetors. The power was 28 horsepower and the R51SS retained head and taillights. With a similar tank and seat to the works racers, the R51RS (Rennsport or Racing Sport) had 21- and 20-inch wheels and brakes with stiffening ribs. Although the engine was based on the pushrod R51, spur gears replaced the long camshaft timing chain and the cylinder barrels were the R66 type. With an output of 36 horsepower, the R51RS was capable of around 112 miles per hour. As only 17 of these machines were built, they are now extremely rare and desirable.

↑ As the Kompressor was for factory riders only, the R51RS was offered as a customer racer. *BMW Group Archives*

↓ After Karl Gall's death, BMW still wanted to win the team prize, coopting Tim Reid into the team on a R51RS for the 1939 Isle of Man Senior TT. Reid failed to finish. *BMW Group Press*

The Military R75

As the German army rolled relentlessly across Europe in 1940, its principal BMW motorcycle was still the rigid pressed-steel frame side-valve R12. Production of the R12 continued until 1942, but as early as the winter of 1937 and 1938, both Zündapp in Nuremberg and BMW were commissioned to design new 750cc military motorcycles. BMW decided to adapt the side-valve R71 engine with a split-bolted tubular-steel frame, to allow easy engine installation and removal, and a rigid rear end. Zündapp developed its KS750, and this model proved superior to the BMW offering: the R72. The R72's 800cc side-valve engine overheated at slow speeds, and BMW subsequently tested a fan-cooled version. Although BMW then considered licensed production of the Zündapp, during 1939 the company undertook development of a new design, the R75.

The most important design features of the R75 were its suitability for sidecar use and the ability to sustain a marching speed of 2 miles per hour without overheating. Thus it included sidecar wheel drive, a locking differential, and cross-country and reverse gears. The engine had overhead valves with the camshaft, Noris generator, and magneto all driven by aluminum gears. Unlike earlier twins with integrally cast rocker posts, underneath the two-piece rocker covers were separately bolted rocker posts. Twin Graetzin carburetors fed the engine, with the air cleaned by a single, moist felt air filter, along with an oil strainer and sump prefilter to ensure no dust entered the engine. This was initially positioned above the gearbox, but during June 1942 it was moved to the top of the fuel tank underneath a metal helmet-like cover. To overcome cooling problems in North Africa, Schleicher also developed a fan-cooled engine during 1942. The magneto provided automatic ignition advance, and the tuning emphasis was on low-end torque. As the fully equipped outfit could weigh half a ton, it was important the R75 could successfully negotiate difficult conditions such as mud and sand.

The four-speed transmission included a dog clutch and four lower ratios for off-road use, the power-dividing crown wheel differential at the rear equalizing any varying speeds of the two driven wheels. This allowed the R75 to perform as well as a four-wheeler and reduced tire wear. The rear wheels, on stub axles, used the same 4.50x16-inch tires as the VW Kübelwagen and featured hydraulic brakes. Up front the double-action hydraulic telescopic fork was a strengthened version of earlier BMW types and framed a lattice-girder type with a strong central box section that could be dismantled into individual parts for easy repair.

Another design criteria for the R75 (and Zündapp KS750) was load capacity. Experience with the R12 in field conditions led to the Wehrmacht requesting a load of 500 kilograms (1,100 pounds), corresponding to the weight of three soldiers and their equipment. However, the tire suppliers set the maximum load at 270 kilograms (600 pounds), well under Wehrmacht requirements. To avoid any bureaucratic problems, the R75 had two maximum total weights listed: an official figure of 670 kilograms (1,477 pounds) and a Wehrmacht figure of 840 kilograms (1,852 pounds). Most R75s were overloaded, and rear tire life was only around 2,000 to 4,000 miles. As tire supply was restricted, the delivery of bikes was also sporadic.

Development of the R75 concluded in February 1941, with the first motorcycle leaving the production line in July 1941. After the construction of 6,000 examples, more space was required in Munich for aircraft engine manufacture and production moved to Eisenach from July 1942 (against Popp's recommendation). The GBK (Bike Select Committee) also decided that the Zündapp KS750 was a better machine than the R75 and by August 1942 instructed BMW to cease R75 manufacture in favor of the KS750. The R75 was proving too expensive to produce and the front forks were often too weak for the war's heavy loads. The GBK requested the R75 be equipped the KS750 parallelogram fork, but because BMW still had 5,000 telescopic forks in stock, this didn't occur. BMW was also reluctant to embark on the production of a competitor's bike on the command of the Wehrmacht.

↑ The military R75 was a tribute to BMW's engineering expertise, but it was expensive to produce and the Wehrmacht considered it inferior to the Zündapp KS750. Exclusively designed for use with a sidecar, it had a sophisticated gearbox and reverse gear driving both the motorcycle and sidecar. The front brake was a large mechanical inboard drum, and unlike the similar Zündapp's, the front suspension was by a telescopic fork. The helmet-like cover on the gas tank covered the air filter.
BMW Group Archives

1941–1944 R75 SIDECAR

Engine designation	**275/2**
Type	**Four-stroke, twin-cylinder, flat-twin**
Bore x stroke	**78x78mm**
Displacement	**745cc**
Power	**26 horsepower at 4,000 rpm**
Compression ratio	**5.8:1**
Valves	**Overhead-valve**
Carburetion	**2 x Graetzin Sa 24mm**
Gears	**4-speed plus reverse, 3-speed plus reverse off-road**
Ignition	**Noris magneto**
Frame designation	**275/1**
Frame	**Bolted tubular-steel**
Front suspension	**Telescopic fork**
Rear suspension	**Rigid-plate and tube springs sidecar**
Wheels	**3Dx16**
Tires	**4.5x16 front, rear, and sidecar**
Brakes	**250mm drum front & rear, 250 hydraulic drum sidecar**
Wheelbase	**1,444mm (56.9 inches)**
Dry weight	**400 kg (882 lbs.) with sidecar**
Engine numbers	**750001–768000+**
Frame numbers	**750001–768000+**
Numbers produced	**17,635**

The R75 earned a reprieve and production continued at Eisenach. This stalled as German workers would lose their reserved occupation status and were likely to be called up for military service; they were loath to move from Munich. BMW requested foreign workers, and around 1,000 Russian prisoners of war were trained to manufacture R12s and R75s. As a result, R75 production numbers were considerably below expectations, with around 2,000 less than anticipated by the end of 1942.

Circumstances changed during 1943. A shortage of raw materials saw the aluminum castings sourced from outside with a resulting loss in quality. Combined with foreign workers who lacked training and motivation, production costs escalated as it now took an additional two hours to repair defects after the first test drive. At a cost of 2,000 reichsmarks each, the Wehrmacht placed their final order of 2,000 machines during 1943 and it was inevitable that R75 production would cease. Although astonishingly dependable, and able to operate in appalling conditions with little maintenance and inferior fuel, the R75 was complicated, expensive, and considered inferior to the KS750. The army now preferred the cheaper mass-produced four-wheeled VW Kübelwagen, and despite some export orders (to unspecified armies), the initial target was to cease R75 production in May 1944, releasing workers for aircraft manufacture. This was later amended to the end of December 1944 when it became clear the May goal couldn't be met.

By the end of March 1944, close to 18,000 machines had been delivered, but air raids in July began to interrupt production. After three raids, production ended on October 18, 1944, and when US troops occupied the factory in April 1945, 60 percent of the buildings were destroyed. Eisenach subsequently became part of East Germany, and a few R75s were produced out of spare parts during 1946 and delivered to Russia. Although Eisenach began developing an updated R75 military motorcycle during 1952, this never reached the production stage.

At around the same time as the air raids on Eisenach, the Allies began bombing BMW in Bavaria in earnest. There were now two plants, one in Allach in addition to Milbertshofen at Oberwiesenfeld. Allach was to the north west of Munich, close to the concentration camp at Dachau, and was largely spared Allied bombing, but the RAF bombed Milbertshofen as early as September 1940. The RAF bombed again in March 1943, but when the American Air Force Squadrons began their barraging on June 9, 1944, more damage was sustained. After eight air offensives, through September 22, 1944, more than half of the Milbertshofen works was destroyed. Although stripped and looted, the undamaged Allach works became a US Army supply and transport depot.

After differences of opinion with the Reich's Aviation Ministry, Popp resigned as BMW chairman in June 1942, but remained a member of the supervisory board of BMW AG until May 8, 1945. Popp was always wary of the Nazis, maintaining his loyalty to BMW rather than the Third Reich, something he reiterated in the denazification court of 1947. On April 11, 1945, Hitler issued his "scorched earth" policy that required the destruction of all military assets, including BMW, but Albert Speer thwarted this on the grounds that "we should not destroy what generations have built up before us." This still didn't save BMW as the company was on the Allies' blacklist, probably due to its development of the 003 jet engine. On October 1, 1945, the order came for the leveling of BMW factories 1 and 2, and it looked unlikely that the company would survive.

This was where Kurt Donath, Milbersthofen works manager since 1942, and non-Nazi party member appointed by the Allies in 1945, intervened. He managed to save the works and initiate the manufacture of saucepans, agricultural machinery, and bicycles. But a stroke of luck enabled BMW to rebuild as a motorcycle manufacturer. Currency reform and a relaxation of economic restraints during 1948 meant confiscated assets suddenly became "free," and it was discovered that the Reich owed BMW 63.5 million marks from Deutsche Bank checks dating back to April 28, 1945. Donath now had the cash to get the company rolling again, and just as BMW did after World War I, he decided to build motorcycles.

↑ Alexander von Falkenhausen, here on an R75 in 1942, headed the R75's engineering team. Although complex, the R750 proved exceptionally rugged, particularly in difficult environments. A standard MG34 (7.92mm) infantry weapon was also fitted in the sidecar to many examples, particularly those for the paratroop units.
BMW Group Archives

1946–1959
AFTER THE WAR:
NEW SINGLES AND EARLES FORK TWINS

When BMW decided to resume motorcycle production after the war, Allied requirements initially restricted the displacement to 60cc. BMW wasn't interested in such a small displacement motorcycle, but in 1947 it was permitted to build a small number of prewar R23s out of spare parts in warehouses. This led to the limit being raised to 250cc, but as all the production drawings were lost to the Soviets when they took over the Eisenach factory, BMW stripped down a prewar R23, minutely measuring each part. New drawings were complete by summer 1947, but a complete machine took another year to materialize. When the R24 was first shown in the Geneva Show in March 1948, most of the basic components were missing (but disguised by wooden mockups), but at the Export Fair in Hanover in May, it was only minus a gearbox, gearwheels, and crankshaft. There was an overwhelmingly positive response to the R24, with 2,500 advance orders, but material shortages delayed production until December 1948.

1949

R24

Although based on the R23, the R24 engine featured a number of new components and design features, notably a new cylinder head, strongly influenced by the design of the wartime R75. The valve angle was altered, the rocker arm bearing blocks were bolted-on pillars rather than cast bosses, and the pushrods were inserted through tunnels in the cylinder head. Like the R75, the valve covers were in two pieces, held by a clamp with a single bolt. The compression ratio was increased slightly, as was the power, and drive was by a four-speed gearbox, while at the front of the crankshaft was a Noris dynamo, with the battery ignition incorporating centrifugal advance. The chassis was similar to the R23, with a bolted rigid tubular-steel frame and telescopic front fork. Also inspired by the R75, the bolted cradle frame allowed easier maintenance, but this didn't appear on any other model.

With a chromed fishtail exhaust and trim embellishments on the fenders, the finish and appearance were of high quality. And although the R24 was also the most expensive German motorcycle, Schorsch Meier's exploits on the 500 Kompressor boosted sales and 9,400 R24s were sold in 1949. By now 800 workers were building 50 R24s a week, helped by the acquisition of new machine tools to replace those lost in reparation. R24 production continued until May 1950, when the R25 replaced it.

↑ The R24 engine followed the form of the R23's, but apart from the same bore and stroke, it was otherwise new. Positioned above and to the left of the five-section crankshaft, the chain-driven camshaft drove pushrods enclosed in separate tubes. Unlike in the R23, pillars rising above the cylinders supported the rockers. The carburetor was a Bing, and the power increased to 12 horsepower. *BMW Group Archives*

← BMW's first postwar motorcycle was the single-cylinder R24. This was quite similar to the prewar R23 but included a new engine and bolted-together frame. *BMW Group Archives*

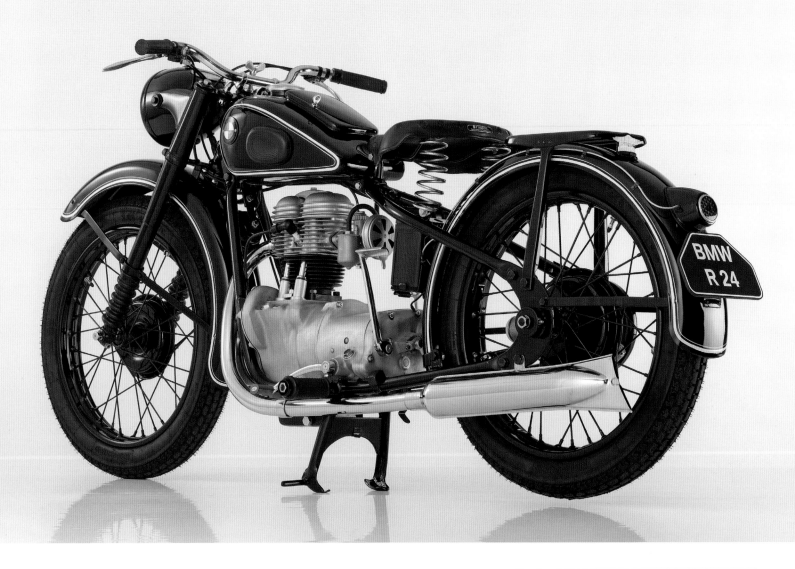

↑ Extremely popular with German authorities, the R24 retained the black wheel finish and distinctive fishtail muffler. *BMW Group Archives*

↓ The rigid rear end and shaft final drive was very similar to that of the R23. A useful addition on the R24 was the incorporation a spring and cush drive to spread the drive load. *BMW Group Archives*

1948–1950 R24

Engine designation	224/1
Bore x stroke	68x68mm
Displacement	247cc
Power	12 horsepower at 5,600 rpm
Compression ratio	6.75:1
Carburetion	1 x Bing AJ1/22/140b 22mm
Gears	4-speed
Frame designation	224/1
Frame	Closed steel-bolted twin-loop
Front suspension	Telescopic fork
Wheels	2.5x19 deep-bed
Tires	3x19 front and rear
Brakes	160mm drum front and rear
Dry weight	130 kg (287 lbs.)
Engine numbers	200001–212007
Frame numbers	200001–212007
Numbers produced	12,020

1950

R25

Despite being the most expensive motorcycle in its class, demand for the BMW 250cc single remained strong, and updates for the 1950 R25 centered on simplifying the design. The engine received a single-piece crankshaft, replacing the previous five-sectioned type. Other developments included a 2mm larger inlet valve and a larger Bing carburetor. However, a more significant improvement was the incorporation of a welded tubular-steel frame, making it suitable for sidecar attachment, and plunger rear suspension—a first for a BMW single. Also setting the R25 apart was a deeply valanced front fender, and the R25 proved even more successful than the R24.

1950–1951 **R25** *(DIFFERING FROM THE R24)*	
Engine designation	**224/2**
Compression ratio	**6.5:1**
Carburetion	**1 x Bing type 1/22/28 24mm**
Frame designation	**225/1**
Frame	**Closed-steel twin-loop**
Rear suspension	**Plunger**
Wheels	**2.5x19 deep-bed**
Tires	**3.25x19 front and rear**
Dry weight	**140 kg (309 lbs.)**
Engine numbers	**220001–243210**
Frame numbers	**220001–243210**
Numbers produced	**23,400**

↓ The R25 was the first BMW single with plunger rear suspension, while the front suspension remained the rudimentary prewar telescopic fork. This is an off-road sport version with a high-level exhaust system.
BMW Group Archives

CHAPTER 3

↑ BMW's first postwar twin, the R51/2.
Only the deeply flared front fender and
split valve covers distinguished it from
the prewar R51. *Ian Falloon*

R51/2

After the war, most demand was for low-cost transport, and although BMW was only building
250cc singles, their high specification ensured these weren't totally suitable for the budget
conscious. BMW was known for quality, and this was a mantel difficult to eschew, even in the
face of postwar austerity. But a new door opened for BMW when, during the summer of 1949,
the Allied force's restriction on motorcycle displacement was lifted for German motorcycle
manufacturers. As there was still little money for development, the 500 twin was initially
based on a prewar design, in this case the 1938 R51. BMW was fortunate that the R51 was an
advanced design for its day, and although its foundations went back to the even earlier R5,
BMW confidently displayed the R51/2 in Geneva in March 1950, and at the Chicago Trade Fair
in August. But production at this time still favored the R25 single two to one, and more than
three-quarters of the new twins were destined for the German market.

Apart from the split valve covers (similar to those of the R75), and a pair of inclined Bing
carburetors, the engine of the R51/2 was virtually identical to that of the prewar R51. New
cylinder heads included coil valve springs, but the chain-driven twin camshaft setup was the
same. Ignition was still by battery and coil, and the R51/2 retained the exposed generator
with distinctive finned clamp on top of the engine. Updates included a coil spring damper on
the gearbox mainshaft and a revised lubrication system with pressurized oil to the camshaft
bearings, but the air cleaner element was still inside the gearbox casing, exactly as it was prewar.

Except for two additional strengthening tubes, the electrically welded oval section tubular-
steel frame was the same as the final 1941 R51 of 1941, and the telescopic fork gained two-way
damping. The R51/2 certainly reestablished BMW as a prominent motorcycle manufacturer,
but as a prewar design, it was always only going to be a stopgap. After only a year, BMW
released the R51/3, with a new engine.

↑ The R51/2 front fork was improved over its prewar predecessor with two-way damping. *BMW Group Archives*

1950–1951 **R51/2** *(DIFFERING FROM THE R51)*

Engine designation	**254/3**
Power	**24 horsepower at 5,800 rpm**
Compression ratio	**6.4:1**
Carburetion	**Bing 1/22/39 and 1/22/40**
Frame designation	**251/2**
Dry weight	**185 kg (408 lbs.)**
Engine numbers	**516000–521005**
Frame numbers	**516000–521005**
Numbers produced	**5,000**

1951

R25/2, R51/3, and R67

As motorcycle production continued to climb, from 9,400 in 1949 to 25,101 in 1951, BMW began to establish distribution in other markets, notably Britain and the United States. While the quality was indisputable, the main impediment to sales was the price. In England an R51/3 cost double a comparable British twin, and in the United States the R51/3 was $1,126. In Germany the R51/3 may have been the only 500cc motorcycle readily available, but in export markets the British twins offered superior performance at a much lower price. This year BMW also decided to contest the ISDT for the first time since 1939 at the 1951 ISDT held in Varese, Italy. Special R51/3s with high-rise exhaust systems were prepared for Georg Meier and Walter Zeller, with a sidecar version for Ludwig Kraus, with Zeller achieving a silver medal.

R25/2

The R25/2 replaced the R25 during 1951, the engine reverting to earlier R24 specification with the smaller intake valve and carburetor, either a Bing or SAWE. Detail updates to the cycle parts included horizontal seat springs (instead of vertical), two-tone black wheel rims, and a less valanced front fender. The R25/2 was extremely successful, many sold with an optional Steib sidecar.

1951–1953 R25/2 (DIFFERING FROM THE R25)	
Engine designation	224/3
Compression ratio	6.5:1
Carburetion	1 x Bing type 1/22/44 or SAWE type K22F
Frame designation	225/2
Wheelbase	1,335mm (52.5 inches)
Dry weight	142 kg (313 lbs.)
Engine numbers	245000–283650
Frame numbers	245000–283650
Numbers produced	38,651

→ The R25/2 had horizontal seat springs but was quite similar to the R25. *BMW Group Archives*

R51/3

When unveiled at the Amsterdam Motor Show in February 1951, apart from slightly different pinstriping on the front fender, most observers believed the R51/3 was nearly identical to the R51/2. But although the power was unchanged, inside the redesigned engine cases was a completely new engine design, one that would power all BMW twins through 1969. While the crankshaft was still a built-up type, with two ball bearings at the front and a ball bearing at the rear, and the connecting rods still run on roller bearings, replacing the twin camshafts and long timing chain was a single camshaft above the crankshaft. Driven by helical gears, this allowed for a much narrower crankcase with a Noris magneto driven from the crankshaft and a contact breaker and automatic advance from the front of the camshaft. A third gear drove the oil pump, and as everything was encased in smooth new covers, the engine looked much more modern. The pistons also featured five (rather than four) rings. Along with new pistons, cylinders, and heads, the 34 and 32mm valves retaining an 80-degree included angle, the two-piece valve covers disappeared, making way for new distinctive rocker covers. The Knecht oil-soaked wire-mesh air filter was also now mounted in a special casing above the gearbox.

The engine may have looked more up to date, and except for the addition of a small top-mounted engine clamp, the chassis was initially almost identical to that of the R51/2. Thus three series of R51/3 followed, the 1951 version with a R51/2 prewar-style fully enclosed steel front fork and single-sided front brake. For 1952 the front fork received rubber gaiters, the air filter cover was redesigned and painted silver, and the front brake was a twin-leading shoe. The third series of 1954 had full-width duplex brakes front and rear, aluminum wheel rims, and raised mufflers to increase ground clearance.

↑ While the R51/3 looked very similar to the R51/2, the engine was completely new. This 1952 version has rubber gaiters on the front fork and a twin-leading shoe front brake. *BMW Group Press*

↓ New cylinder head covers and a slimmer crankcase distinguished the R51/3, and inside the engine was a single camshaft and gear-driven valvetrain. A new silver-painted air filter cover appeared for 1952, this including a lever to restrict air for cold starts. *BMW Group Press*

1951–1954 **R51/3** *(DIFFERING FROM THE R51/2)*

Engine designation	**254/3**
Compression ratio	**6.3:1**
Carburetion	**Bing 1/22/41–1/22/42 or 1/22/61–1/22/66 22mm**
Frame designation	**251/3 (1951), 251/4 (1952–1954)**
Brakes	**200mm front and rear (Duplex front 1952; Full hub front and rear 1954)**
Wheelbase	**1,400mm (55 inches)**
Dry weight	**190 kg (419 lbs.)**
Engine numbers	**522001–540950**
Frame numbers	**522001–540950**
Numbers produced	**18,420**

↑ The R51/3 headlight unit with integral speedometer and ignition switch. These were standard fare for BMW motorcycles until 1954.
BMW Group Press

↗ The R51/3's plunger rear suspension was similar to that of the R51/2, as was the half-hub rear brake.
BMW Group Press

→ Bridging the prewar and postwar eras with its redesigned engine in the earlier chassis, the R51/3 typified the early 1950s BMW motorcycle.
BMW Group Press

R67

Alongside the R51/3 for 1951 was the similar 600cc R67. Unlike the prewar sporting R66, the R67 was intended mainly as a sidecar machine and provided sedate performance. Both the chassis and engine included the updates incorporated with the 1951 model R51/3, but the R67 was short-lived and replaced for 1952.

1951 **R67** (DIFFERING FROM THE R51/3)	
Engine designation	**267/1**
Bore x stroke	**72x73mm**
Displacement	**594cc**
Power	**26 horsepower at 5,500 rpm**
Compression ratio	**5.6:1**
Carburetion	**Bing 1/24/15–1/24/16**
Dry weight	**192 kg (423 lbs.)**
Engine numbers	**610001–611449**
Frame numbers	**610001–611449**
Numbers produced	**1,470**

↓ Only lasting one year, the R67 was designed primarily for sidecar use. As on the first series R51/3, the front fork was the prewar-style fully enclosed steel type. *BMW Group Archives*

1952

R68 and R67/2

Changes to the existing models were minimal, the R51/3 receiving fork gaiters and a new front brake, with the R67/2 replacing the R67. The twins' air filters were also updated to a paper Eberspaecher type. By far the most popular model was still the single-cylinder R25/2, this continuing unchanged for 1952. But with Triumph and BSA about to release higher performance 650s, Munich needed a more powerful model, and this year saw the long-awaited introduction of the company's sporting flagship, the R68, and BMW's first 100-mile-per-hour production motorcycle. BMW also continued its ISDT involvement with an entry of six special R68s. Max Klankermeier and Kraus won gold medals on their sidecar machines, as did solo-mounted Georg and Hans Meier, and Walter Zeller.

↑ The 1952 range at the Nellemann dealership in Aarhus, Denmark, in late 1951 or early 1952. The new R68 is on the stand, an R25/2 is in the left foreground, and the R51/3 and R67/2 are on the right. *BMW Group Archives*

← The official BMW International Six-Days Trial team outside the factory prior to the event at Bad Aussee in Austria in September 1952. From the left are Georg Meier, Walter Zeller, Hans Roth, Hans Meier, Ludwig Kraus, and Max Klankermeier. *BMW Group Archives*

R68

Released at the Frankfurt motorcycle show at the end of 1951, the R68 was the first real sporting BMW motorcycle since the R66 and has rightly earned a place as one of the most desirable postwar production models. The uprated engine included unique barrels and heads, larger 38mm and 34mm valves, a fiercer camshaft, rockers pivoting on needle rollers under the new twin-rib valve covers, and a barrel-shaped roller bearing for the rear of the crankshaft. Other detail differences included finned exhaust clamps, and the initial show bike featured an upswept two-into-one exhaust system resembling that of the 1951 Varese International Six-Day Trial factory R51/3 racers of Meier, Zeller, and Kraus. This exhaust system didn't make it to the 1952 production R68 that wore standard fishtail exhausts, but the 2-1 remained an optional accessory.

Although the R68 chassis was fundamentally identical to the R67/2, several features set it apart. The front mudguard was narrower, with a steel brace, and an optional sprung pillion pad was available, although this was primarily to allow the rider to adopt a more prone riding position. R68s also included a manual spark control lever on the handlebar clutch control and a rear chrome grab handle. The claimed top speed was 100 miles per hour, and the brakes were the same 200mm duplex of the 1952 R51/3.

There were few changes for 1953. By late 1952 rubber gaiters appeared on the front fork, the mufflers were now the nonfinned torpedo type, and the two-piece canister air filter was painted silver. After July 1953 a sidecar mount was provided on the frame, and updates for 1954 included light alloy wheel rims, a full-width front brake, and a larger headlamp. Arguably obsolete, even by 1952 the short-travel plunger rear suspension was considered archaic; the expensive R68 continued a BMW tradition that made it available only to a fortunate few.

↑ The R68 front fork gained rubber gaiters for 1953 and was sometimes fitted with a high-rise exhaust system patterned on the ISDT bikes. *Ian Falloon*

→ All R68s had the swinging pillion saddle and chrome grab handle and narrow front fender. This 1953 version shares the R51/3's straight exhaust system. *BMW Group Archives*

↖ R68 engine assembly, on a conveyer belt in 1952. *BMW Group Archives*

← The earliest R68 retained the shrouded-steel front fork. *BMW Group Archives*

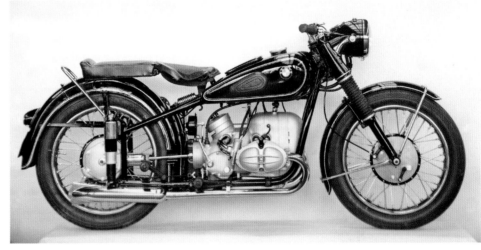

1952–1954 R68 *(DIFFERING FROM THE R67)*

Engine designation	**268/1**
Power	**35 horsepower at 7,000 rpm**
Compression ratio	**8:1**
Carburetion	**Bing 1/26/9–1/26/10**
Frame designation	**251/4**
Brakes	**200mm Duplex front, Simplex rear (Full hub 1954)**
Dry weight	**190 kg (419 lbs.)**
Engine numbers	**650001–651453**
Frame numbers	**650001–651453**
Numbers produced	**1,452**

R67/2

For 1952 the R67/2 received a marginal power increase, and as the chassis was identical to the R51/3, the R67/2 received the 1952 R51/3 updates, including fork gaiters and a new front brake. Primarily designed for sidecar use, with a Spezial model also available that had a sprung Steib sidecar with a hydraulic brake, the R67/2 continued until 1954, now with full-width brakes.

1952–1954 **R67/2** *(DIFFERING FROM THE R67)*	
Engine designation	**267/2**
Power	**28 horsepower at 5,600 rpm**
Compression ratio	**6.5:1**
Carburetion	**Bing 1/24/25–1/24/26**
Frame designation	**251/4**
Brakes	**200mm Duplex front (Full hub 1954)**
Engine numbers	**612001–616261**
Frame numbers	**612001–616261**
Numbers produced	**4,234**

↓ **Largely intended for official use, this R67/2 is fitted with a sidecar for ADAC (German automobile club) roadside assistance.** *BMW Group Archives*

1953

The twin-cylinder R68, R67/2, and R51/3 continued with minor updates, notably fork gaiters, torpedo mufflers, and a new Knecht air cleaner. The fork gaiters were designed to reduce wear from dirt that could enter underneath the metal covers and also included improved seals. The single-cylinder R25 series was still by far the most popular model, the R25/2 continuing much as before, but during 1953 a new R25/3 was introduced, initially primarily for military use. Eventually the R25/3 replaced the R25/2, becoming the most successful BMW motorcycle of the 1950s, and later that year the 100,000th BMW motorcycle rolled off the Munich production line.

R25/3

BMW introduced a number of new features with the R25/3, and although the power wasn't dramatically increased, a new air intake curving up from the larger 24mm carburetor through a long tube from the front of the tank contributed to more midrange torque. To improve heat dissipation, the cylinder head was painted black, while the right side auxiliary gear lever was deleted. Chassis updates extended to a new front fork, with hydraulic damping and more travel; 18-inch wheels with alloy rims and full-width brakes, and a reshaped gas tank with a toolkit incorporated in the left side instead of the top. The R25/3 looked lower and leaner than the R25/2, and the performance was surprising for a 250 single, with a top speed around 74 miles per hour.

↑ BMW's most popular model of the mid-1950s, the R25/3 introduced an unusual air intake system and 18-inch wheels. This is at Luanda airport, Angola, in 1956. *BMW Group Archives*

1953–1956 R67/2 *(DIFFERING FROM THE R25/2)*	
Engine designation	224/4
Power	13 horsepower at 5,800 rpm
Compression ratio	7:1
Carburetion	1 x Bing type 1/24/41 or SAWE type K24F
Frame designation	225/3
Wheels	3x18 deep-bed
Tires	3.25x18 front and rear
Wheelbase	1,365mm (53.7 inches)
Dry weight	150 kg (331 lbs.)
Engine numbers	284001–331705
Frame numbers	284001–331705
Numbers produced	47,700

As Germany was forbidden from international competition immediately after the end World War II, Georg Meier and Ludwig Kraus resurrected the prewar Type 255 Kompressor for the German championship. This proved inspirational, and between 1947 and 1949, the Kompressor was virtually unbeatable in Germany. The machine was ostensibly that of 1939, but with more up-to-date suspension, including a leading-axle telescopic fork and rear dampers with protective gaiters. Even during 1950, the Kompressor could almost hold its own against the supercharged NSU twin, but by 1951 Germany was readmitted to the FIM, and with supercharging banned, the Kompressor's days were over.

With no replacement immediately available, Leonhard Ischinger adapted the existing Kompressor by removing the supercharger. Nicknamed *amputiert*, or amputated engine, an aluminum plate replaced the supercharger, and twin Fischer-Amal carburetors fed the engine (designation M250/2). While retaining the telescopic fork and the plunger rear end, as the power was 30 percent less and the engine had to rev higher, reliability suffered. But in the hands of BMW's new star rider Walter Zeller, the M250/2 took everyone by surprise to win the 1951 German championship.

To become competitive in international Grand Prix racing, BMW needed a more modern engine and chassis, and during 1951 a new Type 253 engine was introduced. Designed by Alfred Böning, and still with the 66x72mm bore and stroke and bevel gear-driven double-overhead camshafts, the Type 253 was more compact, with the bevel shafts driven by straight-cut gears from the front of the engine and angled to the cylinder heads instead of straight as on the Type 255. As the cylinders were offset, the bevel drive lined up with the exhaust camshaft on the right and the inlet on the left, the second camshaft coupled directly to the driven shafts. As the cams were close together, rockers were required to open the valves, resulting in a wide included valve angle of 82 degrees. The crankshaft also retained only two main bearings, ultimately a limiting factor in determining the maximum power. No power claim was made, but it was estimated to be close to 50 horsepower at 8,500 rpm.

Distinguishing the new engine was a more aerodynamic cylinder head with two bolts retaining the valve covers, and all 253 engines rotated counterclockwise, the opposite of other BMW engines (when viewed from the front).

↑ After Germany was allowed to re-enter international competition in 1951, BMW needed an unsupercharged racer, and the most expedient approach was to remove the supercharger from the existing Type 255 Kompressor. First raced by Walter Zeller in August 1950, although underpowered, Zeller still won the 1951 German championship on this Type 250/2. *Lothar Mildebrath*

← Three BMWs at the German championship race at Grenzlandring in September 1951. Zeller (No. 21) and Meier (No. 1) are on earlier Type 250/2s while Kraus has the new two-bolt Type 253. This had a special slab-sided gas tank with a telescopic fork and plunger rear suspension. *Lothar Mildebrath*

↑ During 1953 Noll and Cron rode a sidecar outfit based on the plunger frame two-bolt Type 253a. They finished sixth in the 1953 World Championship, this style leading them to become world champions in 1954 and 1956. *Lothar Mildebrath*

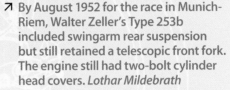

↗ By August 1952 for the race in Munich-Riem, Walter Zeller's Type 253b included swingarm rear suspension but still retained a telescopic front fork. The engine still had two-bolt cylinder head covers. *Lothar Mildebrath*

↑ The 1953 works Type 235c, now with an Earles Fork. This example has carburetors and it was common for riders to carry a spark plug wrench and racing plugs in spring clips to exchange after warmup. The rear fender was unsprung like the front. *Lothar Mildebrath*

Originally installed in an existing plunger frame with telescopic fork, Meier rode the first Type 253a in May 1951, and during the season Kraus rode it alongside Meier and Zeller on existing Type 250/2s.

BMW decided to take a break from racing for the early part of 1952, but development of the racing 500 continued, and when they returned midseason, the team consisted of the Meier brothers (Georg and Hans), Zeller, and Hans Baltisberger. A new frame provided a lower fuel tank position, allowing swingarm rear suspension, and this first appeared on Georg Meier's machine in July at Schotten. Known as the Type 253b, this initially included a crudely modified plunger frame with the driveshaft in the right fork leg and the rear brake integrated on the right. Shortly afterward, at the German Grand Prix in Solitude, Hans Baltisberger on the only factory entry provided BMW its first world championship points by finishing sixth. In August, for the race at Riem in Munich, Zeller had a more elegant purpose-built swingarm

frame, with straight downtubes, the Type 253b engine now featuring crankcases with the more usual BMW arrangement of twin lower-mounting bolts. The season culminated with Georg Meier setting a lap record of 123.70 miles per hour at the ultra-fast Grenzlandring.

Gerhard Mette joined the team for 1953 and development resulted in the most successful version, the R253c. A redesigned cylinder head featured a narrower included valve angle of 73 degrees, with four bolts fixing the rocker covers. With magnesium (Elektron) crankcases, carburetion was either by twin Fischer-Amal R2A30-mm carburetors or fuel injection. The suspension was either telescopic or a leading link Earles front fork, with the rear brake on the left side of the swingarm, the Earles fork ultimately gaining preference. BMW also tried three types of frame, A for Hockenheim, B for Baltisberger and Mette, and C for the Meier brothers and Zeller.

BMW was an early experimenter with fuel injection, in 1952 fitting Kraus-Huser's works sidecar 253b outfit with a Bosch injection

designed by Dr. W. Noack. This sprayed fuel through the sides of the inlet tracts with the injector nozzle between the flat throttle slide and the inlet valve. For the Isle of Man, Zeller's 253b featured a new mechanical Bosch injector system, the injector located upstream of the throttle, spraying axially into the air trumpets. After crashing on the second lap at the Isle of Man, Zeller won the German Grand Prix at the controversial Schotten circuit, but as all the foreign teams declined to race, the results were disallowed. Also during 1953, as well as the Kraus/Huser team, Wilhelm Noll and Friz Cron campaigned an unfaired sidecar with the earlier two-bolt 253 engine and a telescopic fork. Noll and Cron finished sixth and Kraus/Huser eighth in the Sidecar World Championship. After victory in the German 500cc championship, Georg Meier ended his great career. Although successful in German events, the BMW solo and sidecar racers still weren't making their mark on the international scene. All that would change in 1954.

1954

With BMW concentrating on development of the three-wheeled Isetta bubble car, the existing motorcycle range continued with only minor updates. The twins received full-width front brakes, new quieter torpedo-style mufflers, and a fully covered Knecht air filter, with the R68 and R51/3 also including alloy wheel rims. As a precursor to the 1955 Earles fork R69 and R50, all models received a new headlight bucket, complete with chrome and plastic key and triangular indicator lights. The singles remained popular, but as the German market for basic ride-to-work singles would die in the face of cheaper cars and mopeds, 1954 would be a peak production year for BMW, and one not replicated until 1977. This year's sales success also came on the back of racing achievement, particularly in the Sidecar World Championship, Noll and Cron winning the first of BMW's 19 Sidecar World Championships. BMW also returned to record breaking this year, with successful attempts at Montlhéry in May and October. Georg and Hans Meier, with Walter Zeller, set new eight- and nine-hour records on a faired RS54 in May, while in October Noll managed a new 10-kilometer sidecar record of 132 miles per hour.

THE RS54 AND RACING 1954–1955

During 1953, BMW prepared a production version of the works Type 253c, this initially titled the R53RS and displayed with a telescopic fork at Frankfurt in September. Hans Meier subsequently tested a second machine with an Earles fork, and it formed the basis of the production RS54 (Rennsport) of early 1954. At the time BMW was scaling back its official racing program, and with no more Type 253c development, the RS54 was renamed the Type 253/2. Twenty-two RS54s were dispatched, both solo and sidecar, through early 1955, mostly to privateers, dealers, and importers. The total produced through 1957 was 24 (or possibly 25), and they were so expensive to produce the factory lost almost as much on each machine as it made.

Originally all RS54s were identical, and although very similar to the factory Type 253 racer, the RS54 engine cases were aluminum (rather than Elektron), and Type 253 special parts like fuel injection and a five-speed gearbox weren't included. The basic engine architecture was unchanged from the 253, including the 66x72mm bore and stroke, 40 and 36mm valves set at 82 degrees, and four-ring 10:1 pistons. With a pair of Fischer-Amal 30mm R2A carburetors, the claimed power was 45 horsepower at 8,000 rpm, or 50 horsepower at 8,500 rpm with higher-octane gasoline. The RS54 frame was similar to Zeller's factory 253, with an oval section top tube, duplex loops, and a pivoted fork at both ends. At the front was an Earles-pattern leading-link type with the driveshaft enclosed in the right fork arm. The motorcycle had 19-inch wheels, the front brake a 200mm twin leading shoe front, and the dry weight was only 135 kilograms (298 pounds). Sidecar versions had a different frame, front fork, and brakes. The frame was no longer a double cradle, the front swingarm longer, with longer shocks, and the brakes were hydraulically actuated.

With the introduction of the RS54 available to selected privateers, the works team for 1954 included only Zeller on solos and Noll and Cron on sidecars. On the factory Type 253, the fuel injection was further developed for 1954, with long intakes and the fuel now pumped directly into the cylinder heads through nozzles opposite the spark plugs. High-domed pistons provided a 10.2:1 compression ratio and the safe maximum revs were 9,000 rpm. Carburetors were still favored on slower circuits, the abrupt nature of the fuel injection delivery also suiting sidecars more than solos. Zeller won the 1954 German championship but didn't achieve any spectacular international results. It was another story altogether in sidecar racing, and Noll and Cron demonstrated the flat-twin layout was ideal for sidecar racing, the low, wide engine facilitating safe drifting and the shaft drive an asset rather than a hindrance. Noll and Cron's works sidecar racer, sometimes with fuel injection, now featured streamlining,

and with three victories, they easily won the Sidecar World Championship.

In October 1954, Alex von Falkenhausen returned to head the competition department and the factory team was officially disbanded. Factory support did continue to selected riders in the form of motorcycles, engines, parts, and mechanics. Walter Zeller received the most support, with John Surtees riding at the German Grand Prix at the Nürburgring. Surtees retired, but Zeller finished second, BMW's best solo finish yet. Others to receive works assistance included Australian Jack Forrest and Dieter Riedelbauch (who finished sixth in the Italian Grand Prix at Monza). Carburetion was either by Dell'Orto carburetors or fuel injection, and Zeller not only won the German championship, but also finished 10th in the 500cc World Championship. This performance prompted von Falkenhausen to further develop the Type 253 and contest the

entire world championship the following year. In the Sidecar World Championship, BMW fielded three teams, winning every round. Although the basic racer was still an RS54 with a sidecar, the Steib sidecar was integrated into the large, wide fairing that incorporated two air scoops. The engines were now carburetted and retained a four-speed gearbox. Willy Faust and Karl Remmert took the championship ahead of Noll/Cron and Schneider/Strauss. Unfortunately, Faust and Remmert's success was blunted by tragedy, with Faust injured and Remmert killed in a practice crash at Hockenheim later in the year. Faust subsequently retired from racing, but in October 1955 Wilhelm Noll set a new absolute world sidecar speed record of 174 miles per hour in a special streamlined machine on the Munich-to-Ingolstadt autobahn.

↑ Walter Zeller was the only factory solo rider for 1954, and again he won the German championship. This is prior to a race at Hockenheim, the Type 253 with carburetors. For faster circuits, the 253 sometimes featured a dustbin fairing and fuel injection. *BMW Group Archives*

↖ Four new RS54s outside the works department in Munich in 1954 prior to dispatch. Two solo versions are flanked by sidecar examples. *Lothar Mildebrath*

← Wilhelm Noll and Friz Cron won BMW's first Sidecar World Championship in 1954. They came second in 1955, winning again in 1956 before retiring. *BMW Group Archives*

1955

R69, R50, R67/3, and R25/3

BMW finally moved beyond the prewar era with the release of two new twins, the R50 and R69. By 1955, the plunger frame was generally considered obsolete, replaced on most large-capacity machines by swingarm rear suspension, and BMW's telescopic was rudimentary at best. BMW already had swingarm suspension on its racing Type 253 and RS54, and as these models also featured an Earles fork front end, this was the path BMW followed with its new R69 and R50 models. At this stage the earlier 600cc plunger R67/3 continued, as did the R25/3 single. Unfortunately, the release of the R50 and R69 also coincided with a dramatic slump in motorcycle sales. As cars became more affordable, motorcycle sales suffered and many of BMW's competitors (Horex, Adler, Ardie, and DKW) vanished by the end of the decade.

BMW was actually fortunate to survive. The introduction of the expensive and unprofitable V-8 502, 503, and 507 cars stretched BMW's resources, and as motorcycle development stagnated after 1955, BMW was caught in a falling market. Although 23,531 motorcycles were produced during 1955, most of these were the older-style R25/3s.

R69

The higher performance R69 engine was almost identical that of the R68, including the barrel-shaped rear crankshaft roller bearing, five-ring pistons, 38mm and 34mm valves with 8mm stems, pointed cylinder fins, identical Bing 1 carburetors, and manual ignition control. The R69 had new connecting rods with sword-shaped shanks, but the engine was the model's only shared component. Behind the flat-twin engine was a new diaphragm spring clutch and three-shaft gearbox (instead of two-shaft) in a stronger housing and an improved input shaft shock absorber. There was no longer an external hand lever, and two sets of gearbox ratios were available, one for solo use and another for sidecars. The 1955 R69 included a paper Micronic air filter, with the earliest examples featuring the two-piece silver canister of the 1954 models. Also carried over from the 1954 R68 was the 6-volt electrical system and Noris magneto ignition with automatic advance unit.

The R69 frame was derived from the RS54 racer, and the front suspension was a development of the leading link swingarm type developed by Englishman Ernie Earles. While swingarm rear suspension was already widely accepted, except for sidecar use Earles-type forks were not as popular. Promoted by BMW for their smooth ride, Earles forks did possess the advantage of not diving under braking, but they also disadvantaged handling due to the

→ **The R69 replaced the R68 as BMW's sporting model for 1955 but was met with a lukewarm reception. For 1955 the taillight was still the earlier small, round Eber type, although larger accessory Hella units were available as an option. This example has an accessory swinging pillion seat.** *BMW Group Archives*

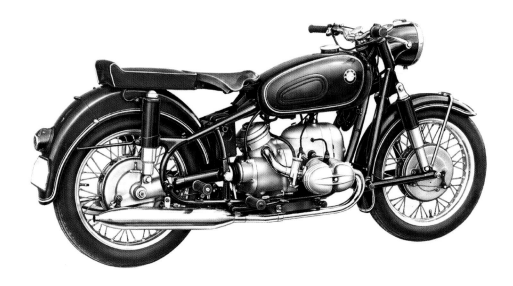

The R69's engine was carried over from the R68, but the clutch and gearbox were new. The also R69 retained the manual magneto control with cable entering the crankcase. Two-fin valve covers continued as an R68 and R69 trademarks. *BMW Group Archives*

↓ The Earles fork front suspension with twin Boge dampers and a friction steering damper. Unlike the RS54 Rennsport, the two support tubes were straight and nor curved. *BMW Group Archives*

1955–1960 R69 *(DIFFERING FROM THE R68)*

Engine designation	**268/2**
Power	**35 horsepower at 6,800 rpm**
Compression ratio	**7.5:1**
Frame designation	**245/1**
Front suspension	**Swingarm with twin shock absorbers**
Rear suspension	**Swingarm with twin shock absorbers**
Wheels	**3x18 front and rear (2.75Cx18 rear sidecar)**
Tires	**3.5x18 front and rear (4x18 rear sidecar)**
Wheelbase	**1,415mm (55.7 inches), 1,450mm (57 inches) sidecar**
Dry weight	**202 kg (445 lbs.), 320 kg (705 lbs.) with sidecar**
Engine numbers	**652001–654955**
Frame numbers	**652001–654955**
Numbers produced	**2,956**

increased unsprung weight and steering inertia. Manufactured by BMW under license from Earles, two tubes angled back from the steering head to behind the front wheel. Unlike on the RS54, these fork legs were straight rather than curved. A swingarm pivoted on a fixed-axle attached to these tubes, with two Boge hydraulic shock absorbers connecting the swingarm to the lower fork crown. There were two positions for the top shock attachment, one for solo, and a lower one for sidecar use, which increased the trail. The automotive-type Boge hydraulic shock absorbers were more advanced than those on the 1950–1954 twins, with progressively wound springs, and these were adjustable through integral short levers on the rear.

Tapered roller bearings were located both the front and rear swingarm pivots, and the driveshaft was now enclosed in the right side of the swingarm, with the universal joint moved to the gearbox end of the driveshaft to cope with the increased travel. Despite the addition of swingarm rear suspension, the frame still resembled the earlier plunger type, but with supports for the swingarm, steel cups locating the shock absorbers, and a slightly thicker central spine and steering head. The R69 had 18-inch wheels, with alloy rims front and rear, while the new rounded 17-liter gas tank included a locking toolbox beneath the left rubber kneepad. A larger 6.5-gallon tank was optional, this with a toolbox on top.

For many sporting enthusiasts, the R69 was a disappointing replacement for the handsome and elemental R68. The R69 was not only heavier and more cumbersome, but the Earles fork, while extremely suitable for a sidecar, provided idiosyncratic handling on a sporting solo motorcycle. But while the R69 wasn't particularly successful, with fewer than 3,000 built over six years, it proved popular with police forces and built an unequaled reputation for reliability.

R50

Just as the R69 replaced the R68, the R50 replaced the R51/3 for 1955. The R50 engine was basically that of the R51/3, but with four-ring (rather than five-ring) pistons providing a slightly higher compression ratio and new Bing carburetors. The previous I-section connecting rods now had sword-shaped shanks, and the power was slightly increased. As on the R51/3, the cast-iron cylinder fins were round, a feature that would characterize the 500 models until 1969. Shared with the R69 were the three-shaft gearbox, diaphragm-spring clutch, and earlier silver air filter canister. As the chassis was identical to the R69's, the cheaper R50 proved more popular, and while upholding BMW's tradition of quality and reliability, because the R50 had no sporting pretensions, the Earles fork wasn't considered an impediment.

R67/3

Created almost exclusively for the German market, the R67/3 was the final BMW twin to retain the plunger rear end, and with its larger rear tire was even more suitable for sidecar haulage. However, the new Earles fork models were more appropriate for a sidecar attachment, and although it was produced for two years, the R67/3 remained a relatively unpopular budget model.

↑ The R50 shared the R69's chassis with Earles fork front suspension and reshaped gas tank. The standard seat for 1955 was a solo Denfeld, with a rubber suspension block rather than a spring. *BMW Group Archives*

1955–1960 R50 (DIFFERING FROM THE R51/3 AND R69)	
Engine designation	252/2
Power	26 horsepower at 5,800 rpm
Compression ratio	6.8:1
Carburetion	2x Bing 1/24/45-1/24/46
Dry weight	195 kg (423 lbs.)
Engine numbers	550001–563515
Frame numbers	550001–563515
Numbers produced	13,510

1955–1956 **R67/3** *(DIFFERING FROM THE R67/2)*

Engine designation	**251/5**
Rear wheel	**4x18 (sidecar)**
Rear tire	**4x18 (sidecar)**
Engine numbers	**617001–617700**
Frame numbers	**617001–617700**
Numbers produced	**700**

↑ Produced alongside the new Earles fork models for 1955 and 1956, the R67/3 retained the telescopic front fork and plunger rear suspension and was more suited to sidecar use. Although primarily sold in Germany, this R67/3 is in Syria. *BMW Group Archives*

↑ The R60 replaced the R67/3 during 1956, ostensibly identical to the R50, but with only 28 horsepower, its performance was modest. New longer mufflers were fitted this year, but the taillight remained the smaller Eber type. This is a police version with a new Telefunken radio system. *BMW Group Archives*

1956

R69, R60, R50, and R26

With the R60 and R26 replacing the R67/3 and R25/3 during 1956, BMW's entire range now featured Earles fork front suspensions. But with motorcycle production slipping dramatically this year, to 15,500, updates to the existing models were minimal. In response to new German regulations requiring 82-decibel silencers after December 1955, longer, fatter, and quieter mufflers were fitted. Other updates included a sidestand lug on the R50 frame and an improved geared rack-and-pinion throttle.

R60

Basically an R50 with the R67/3 600cc engine, visually the R60 looked identical to the R50. With a higher rear-wheel ratio than the R50 and R69S, the R60 was a more relaxed touring bike, but only for those requiring leisurely performance. Smooth torque and a gentle power delivery made for a pleasant ride, but the R60 struggled to top 90 miles per hour.

1956–1960 **R60** *(DIFFERING FROM THE R67/3 AND R50)*	
Engine designation	**267/4**
Carburetion	**2 x Bing type 1/24/95–1/24/96**
Engine numbers	**618001–621530**
Frame numbers	**618001–621530**
Numbers produced	**3,530**

R26

Joining the twins with swinging arm suspension front and rear for 1956 was the R26 single. With 50 percent larger cooling fins, the cylinder head was no longer painted black, and a slightly higher compression ratio, larger carburetor, and more efficient air filter under the seat resulted in a small power increase. Originally the connecting rod was aluminum, the big end running directly in the rod journal, replaced later by the more usual steel con rod with roller big-end bearing.

The R26 chassis was very similar in layout to the R50, providing improved handling and comfort over the old plunger frame R25/3, and while motorcycle sales were generally extremely depressed during the latter half of the 1950s, the R26 proved surprisingly popular, particularly for export markets in Third World countries. More than half the motorcycle production between 1956 and 1960 comprised the R26.

1956–1960 R26 (DIFFERING FROM THE R25/3)	
Engine designation	226/1
Power	15 horsepower at 6,400 rpm
Compression ratio	7.5:1
Carburetion	1 x Bing type 1/26/46
Frame designation	226/1
Front suspension	Swingarm with twin shock absorbers
Rear suspension	Swingarm with twin shock absorbers
Wheels	2.15Bx18 front and rear
Wheelbase	1,390mm (54.7 inches)
Dry weight	158 kg (348 lbs.)
Engine numbers	340001–370242
Frame numbers	340001–370242
Numbers produced	30,236

↑ The R26 250cc single of 1956 also featured an Earles fork front end and swingarm rear suspension. As on the R50 and R60, the quieter muffler was longer and the taillight still the smaller type. *BMW Group Archives*

← More popular than the twins in the late 1950s, the R26 was also available with a Steib S250 sidecar. *BMW Group Archives*

BMW built a new short-stroke Grand Prix racer for 1956, the Type 253f. This had a bore and stroke of 70x64mm, a five-speed gearbox, and an exposed driveshaft positioned alongside the right side of the swingarm with a floating final drive and torque arm to the swingarm. The crankcases were magnesium, and with 11:1 Mahle pistons, 42mm and 37mm valves, and Bosch magneto ignition, the power was 60 horsepower at 9,000 rpm with fuel injection or 58 horsepower at 9,500 rpm with Dell'Orto SS32 carburetors. The frame continued with the Earles fork, now with straight tubes as on the production R50/R69, with 230mm cable-operated front brakes on each side and a hydraulically operated rear brake. BMW's most serious solo racer yet, Walter Zeller campaigned it in the 1956 500cc World Championship, managing fourth at the Isle of Man and following that with second places in Holland and Belgium. Although he failed to win a Grand Prix, Zeller finished second to John Surtees in the 500cc World Championship. That year former World Champion Fergus Anderson also rode the 253f, but was killed on it at Floreffe in Belgium, while Dieter Riedelbauch took the German championship.

Fritz Hillebrand and Manfred Grünwald replaced Faust and Remmert for 1956, and they won the first two sidecar Grands Prix on the new, lower sidecar racer. Along with a lower frame, and a reduction in wheel diameter from 18 to 16 inches, the sidecar was now BMW built with a fixed frontal fairing for the bike and platform. This lower, more integrated style would characterize sidecar racers until the end of the decade. Noll and Cron eventually won their second world championship, Noll then

retiring to pursue car racing.

With the Gilera fours back to full strength, the BMWs struggled in the 1957 500cc World Championship. Ernst Hiller and Zeller managed some respectable results, and although Hiller won the 500cc German championship, Zeller retired at the end of 1957. For 1958, Hiller, Geoff Duke, and Dickie Dale were provided works machines, but without official support. Dale achieved some reasonable results, finishing second in the Swedish Grand Prix and fourth

↑ Although he failed to win a Grand Prix, Walter Zeller came second in the 1956 500cc World Championship on the short-stroke Type 253f. The fairing this year left the hands exposed and enclosed the exhaust pipes, with the front brake cooled through a turbo wheel. *Lothar Mildebrath*

← The Type 253f of 1956 had a short-stroke engine, a five-speed gearbox, and a new chassis with straight fork legs. This is the 1958 version with a full fairing as required by new regulations outlawing the dustbin style. *Lothar Mildebrath*

Noll's retirement left the championship open for ex-Luftwaffe pilot Hillebrand and Grünwald for 1957. Despite Hillebrand's death in an accident in Spain before the season ended, they still won the world championship. There was only one supported team for the 1958 season, 1957 runners-up Walter Schneider and Hans Strauss. While the factory BMW dominated, it was put under considerable pressure from the private Swiss team of Florian Camathias and Hilmar Cecco, who won at Assen. It was a similar scenario during 1959, although the margin was closer as Camathias and Cecco won two Grands Prix. As the development of the racing sidecar proceeded toward lower outfits, only the BMW engine, driveline, and suspension would be retained, but its dominance would continue.

The R69 also managed some surprising racing results during 1959, with John Lewis and Bruce Daniels winning the Thruxton 500 production race at 66.88 miles per hour, ahead of a field of much more highly fancied British 650s. Two weeks later, Bruce Daniels teamed with Peter Darvill, riding the R69 to victory in the 24-hour Barcelona endurance race at the twisting Montjuïc circuit. In a race previously dominated by nimble 125s, this was another unlikely success, and a tribute to the R69's reliability.

overall in the world championship, while Hiller took the German championship for the second time. Duke never managed to come to terms with idiosyncratic BMW, riding one only seven times, but winning a nonchampionship race at Hockenheim in May. Dale rode the BMW again during 1959, now on an RS with curved fork tubes, finishing eighth in the world championship, while Hiller took his third German title. The Japanese rider Fumio Ito rode the BMW during 1960, but this was the end

for the RS in world championships. While the adherence to the Earles-type fork, with its high-steering inertia and idiosyncratic handling, always limited the RS's competitiveness as a solo racer, the great BMW rider Ernst Hiller remained unperturbed by it. After selling his private RS following a serious accident at Imola in 1960 where he fractured his spine, Hiller was back on an RS in 1962. At 34 years of age, he went on to win his fourth German 500cc championship.

↑ Legendary rider and four-time World Champion Geoff Duke rode the Type 253f during 1958, winning here at Hockenheim but generally struggling to come to terms with the idiosyncratic RS. As he often complained about the braking, the front brake included a large air scoop. *Lothar Mildebrath*

← English rider Dickie Dale was one of the few non-German riders who managed to come to terms with the difficult RS. Here at the Isle of Man in 1958, this year he finished fourth in the 500cc World Championship and eighth in 1959. The front brake included a large turbo wheel for improved cooling. This was an era where riders were lucky to survive and Dale was killed on a Norton at Nürburgring in 1961. *Lothar Mildebrath*

↑ Walter Schneider and Hans Strauss won the Sidecar World Championship in 1958 and 1959. They won three of the four races in 1958 but were pushed harder in 1959, winning two of the five races. This year BMWs filled the first 12 places in the world championship. *Lothar Mildebrath*

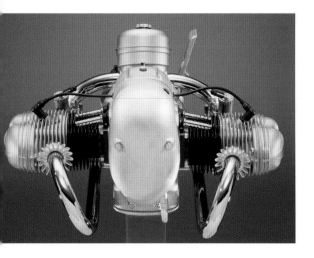

1957–1959

R69, R60, R50, and R26

Motorcycle production crumbled after 1956, with only 5,429 motorcycles built in 1957, most for export markets. As BMW was now concentrating on cars, updates to the motorcycle range between 1957 and 1959 were minimal. All models received the larger Hella taillight in 1957, and for 1958 the twins' air filter cover was more rounded. Black was still the only color available, and while models were still expensive, production increased slightly, to 7,156 motorcycles in 1958 and 8,412 in 1959. With the United States becoming the most important export market, distributors Butler & Smith promoted the BMW's reliability by sponsoring John Penton's coast-to-coast record run in June 1959. On a standard R69, Penton rode the 3,051 miles from New York City to Los Angeles in 52 hours, 11 minutes, and 1 second, bettering the previous record by more than 24 hours. Press enthusiasm remained guarded and unenthusiastic, *Cycle* magazine summing up the R60 in 1959 by saying: "The R60 can be considered tough, and absolutely reliable."

But spiraling losses from expensive cars saw BMW close to bankruptcy by the end of 1959, with management planning to sell the company to Daimler-Benz. The Austrian distributor Wolfgang Denzel, who had produced a 700cc prototype car based on the Isetta chassis and powered by a 697cc fan-cooled version of the boxer motorcycle engine, thwarted this. The 700 was positively received, with 25,000 advance orders, and at a shareholder meeting on December 9, 1959, Denzel forestalled a management decision to sell BMW to Daimler-Benz. Denzel found the development costs of the 700 had been illegally written off and didn't appear in the balance sheet. Subsequently, two shareholders managed to obtain 10 percent

↑ Similar to the R68, the R69 engine would not only last the decade, but would continue to power the R69S during the 1960s. *BMW Group Archives*

↓ All models received a larger taillight for 1957, and the more rounded air filter cover in 1958, but updates over the next few years were minimal. The R50/R60 always had the four-fin rocker covers. *BMW Group Archives*

of represented share capital to adjourn the meeting, and the deadline for the sale to Daimler-Benz elapsed.

With the fate of the company now in the hands of the shareholders, attention turned to the major shareholder Herbert Quandt. The Quandts were one of Germany's richest industrial families, but Herbert's interest in keeping BMW alive was more than financial. Impressed by the commitment shown by the smaller shareholders, workers, and dealers, he decided to personally supervise the restructuring of BMW. Entrusting his personal legal advisor Gerhard Wilcke with the responsibility, Wilcke sold the aircraft division and provided limited resources for the development of new products. And while motorcycles were lower on the priority than cars, the existing motorcycle range was improved and expanded.

↑ With the US market BMW's priority during the 1950s, Butler & Smith offered the R69 with a range of optional accessories, including a windshield, saddlebags, and lamp bracket. This R69 still has the handlebar-mounted manual spark control lever. *BMW Group Archives*

→ During the late 1950s, the United States was the primary export market for BMW twins. Here are a couple on R50s. *BMW Group Archives*

If you want to be happy for a day, drink.
If you want to be happy for a year, marry.
If you want to be happy for a lifetime, ride a BMW.

SEE YOUR NEAREST AUTHORIZED BMW DEALER, OR FOR INFORMATION WRITE TO:
EAST: BUTLER & SMITH, INC., 160 WEST 83RD STREET, NEW YORK, N.Y. 10024
WEST: FLANDERS COMPANY, 200 WEST WALNUT STREET, PASADENA, CALIF. 91103
CANADA: NORTHWEST MOTORS LTD., ONTARIO

After surviving near bankruptcy, BMW pinned its hopes on the success of the new 700 car and was well rewarded. By April 1960, 155 700s were rolling out of the factory in Munich every day, and by the end of the year, production numbered nearly 10,000. This provided the optimism for limited development of a range of motorcycles, and although the updated machines looked outwardly similar, improvements were introduced primarily aimed at increasing reliability.

1960–1961

R69S, R69, R60/2, R60, R50S, R50/2, R50, R27, and R26

The existing R69, R60, R50, and R26 continued into 1960, overlapping with their replacements, the R69S, R60/2, R50/2, and R27. While they looked visually similar to their predecessors, inside the engine for the S and /2 were new cam followers, a stronger crankshaft and camshaft, stronger bearing housings, and a new clutch. Although the design of the four-speed gearbox was unchanged for the /2, this now had closer ratios. The basic 6-volt electrical system was also unchanged, but new for the /2 were a Bosch magneto and generator. The wheels now had thicker chrome spokes, and the 18-inch wheel rims were sometimes chrome-plated steel in addition to aluminum. Production steadily increased, with 9,473 motorcycles built in 1960 and 9,460 in 1961. At this stage, BMW's motorcycles were still more profitable than its cars.

← BMW entered the 1960s emphasizing long-term enjoyment with its new range.

During this period, the factory rekindled its interest in off-road competition, with Sebastian Nachtmann winning a gold medal in the 1960 ISDT at Bad Aussee, Austria, on his factory R69S. BMW also established an unrivaled reputation for reliability when the imitable Danny Liska of Niobrara, Nebraska, rode his R60 from the Arctic Circle in northern Alaska to Tierra del Fuego on the tip of South America, the first person to do so on a motorcycle. Over a period of six months between 1960 and 1961, Liska covered 95,000 miles, later replicating this feat venturing from the northern most point of Europe to southern Africa, a distance of some 40,000 miles.

R69S and R50S

Other than higher compression three-ring pistons, larger inlet ports, and a larger volume air filter with a new canister, the general engine specifications for the R69S were similar to that of the R69. Both the R69S and R50S retained the two-rib valve covers and rockers operating in needle bearings. The crankcase ventilation was improved, with the S models receiving a rotary disc crankcase ventilator. The S models also had larger diameter exhaust tip on the less restrictive muffler, and the R69S was the most powerful production BMW twin yet. With the R50's slightly smaller 34mm and 32mm valves, but with thicker valve stems, and 26mm Bing carburetors, the R50S produced the same power as the earlier R69, but at a frenetic 7,650 rpm. The R69S no longer had the manual ignition control that the R69 inherited from the R68, and despite featuring a stronger rear spherical roller main bearing, both the S models initially suffered from unreliability.

While the general chassis specifications were unchanged from the previous R69, R60, and R50, the R69S and R50S incorporated a hydraulic steering damper cleverly activated by a knob on the steering head via a short linkage. The R69S was also the only model offered in alternative colors, and 6 percent were built in Alpine White. Other colors—red, blue gray, and green—were available by special order. These were also offered for the R60/2 and were generally for the US market. A wide variety of options were also available for the R69S, including larger gas tanks, single seats, fairings, crash bars, and a VDO tachometer.

Racing success continued for the R69S as René Maucherat and René Vasseur won the 1960 24-hour Bol d'Or at Montlhéry. Peter Darvill, again partnered with Bruce Daniels, narrowly failed to win the Barcelona 24-hour race at Montjuïc in 1960, but with factory assistance for their R69S, they repeated their 1959 success in 1961. This year they also won the Silverstone 1,000-kilometer race.

↑ Similar to the previous R69, the R69S was the most powerful BMW motorcycle to date. One of the new features was a hydraulic steering damper, and sometimes the wheel rims were chrome-plated steel, but with thicker spokes. This has a swinging pillion seat attached to the rider's saddle. *BMW Group Archives*

→ The R69S was very successful in endurance racing in the early 1960s. This factory-prepared R69S racer has a quick filler Georg Meier tank, abbreviated seat with small taillight, velocity stacks, and a racing exhaust system. *BMW Group Archives*

1960–1969 R69S *(DIFFERING FROM THE R69)*

Engine designation	268/3
Power	42 horsepower at 7,000 rpm
Compression ratio	9.5:1
Carburetors	2xBing 1/26/75-76
Frame designation	245/2
Engine numbers	655001–666320
Frame numbers	655001–666320
Numbers produced	1,270 (1960–1961), 10,314 (Total 01/1960–12/1969)

← R50Ss for the United States had a
higher handlebar, but apart from
the short twin-fin valve covers, little
distinguished it from the R69S.
BMW Group Archives

↓ Plagued by reliability issues, the short-
lived R50S was much less popular than
the R69S. This example has lighter
aluminum wheel rims and an optional
tire pump. The narrow Denfeld bench
seat was an option to the solo saddle.
BMW Group Archives

1960–1962 R50S *(DIFFERING FROM THE R50 AND R69S)*

Engine designation	252/3
Power	35 horsepower at 7,650 rpm
Compression ratio	9.5:1
Carburetors	Bing 1/26/71–72
Dry Weight	198 kg
Engine numbers	564001–565634
Frame numbers	564001–565634
Numbers produced	1,050 (1960–1961), 1,634 (Total 08/1960–08/1962)

↑ Still with the earlier rocker covers, the R60/2 and R50/2 were virtually indistinguishable from the R60 and R50. *BMW Group Archives*

↓ For the United States, the R60/2 and R50/2 received a higher handlebar. These basic versions were more popular than the expensive sporting examples. *BMW Group Archives*

R60/2 and R50/2

Replacing the R60 during 1960 was the R60/2, with the R50/2 supplanting the R50 from January 1961. Both these models looked virtually identical to the earlier versions, retaining the earlier friction steering damper, but shared the engine updates with the S models. New for the R60/2 and R50/2 were higher compression three-ring pistons, with all three hard-chromed piston rings above the wristpin, resulting in a slight increase in power for the R60/2. The R50/2 engine specifications were unchanged from the R50, and during 1961 it was the most popular model in the twin-cylinder lineup.

1960–1969 R60/2 *(DIFFERING FROM THE R60)*

Engine designation	267/5
Power	30 horsepower at 5,800 rpm
Compression ratio	7.5:1
Carburetors	2x Bing 1/24/125–1/24/126
Frame designation	245/2
Engine numbers	622001–630000 and 181001–1819307
Frame numbers	622001–630000 and 181001–1819307
Numbers produced	1,480 (1960–1961), 15,427 (Total 01/1960–12/1969)

1960–1969 R50/2 *(DIFFERING FROM THE R50)*

Compression ratio	7.5:1
Frame designation	245/2
Engine numbers	630001–649037
Frame numbers	630001–649037
Numbers produced	2,820 (1961), 18,635 (Total 01/1961–12/1969)

R27

During the restructuring of BMW in 1960, the R26 was updated, becoming the R27. Although fundamentally similar, the R27's engine had a higher compression ratio and new camshaft to produce slightly more power. The contact breaker was now positioned on the front of the camshaft, and the timing chain included a spring-loaded tensioner. The most significant update was incorporation of rubber engine mounts to quell the increased vibration. Four rubber mounts supported the engine and gearbox in the duplex frame, with a rubber cylinder head bracket and two fore and aft rubbers on the front and rear restricting longitudinal movement. In all other respects the chassis was identical to the R26. The R27 was intended to be the biggest seller in the revamped motorcycle range of the early 1960s, and while it began strongly in 1960 and 1961, sales soon tapered off as it was too expensive and still only offered barely adequate performance. The R27 would be the last single-cylinder BMW motorcycle until the F650 of 1993.

1960–1966 **R27** (DIFFERING FROM THE R26)	
Engine designation	**226/2**
Power	**18 horsepower at 7,400 rpm**
Compression ratio	**8.2:1**
Carburetors	**1 x Bing type 1/26/68**
Frame designation	**226/2**
Engine numbers	**372001–387566**
Frame numbers	**372001–387566**
Numbers produced	**6,394 (1960–1961), 15,364 (Total 01/1960–12/1966)**

↓ With its rubber-mounted engine, the R27 replaced the R26 for 1960, BMW initially expecting it to be their most popular model of the new range. *BMW Group Archives*

1962 PRODUCTION	
R69S	1,068
R50S	584
R60/2	700
R50/2	1,150
R27	800

↓ **Butler & Smith offered a number of optional extras, including a fairing and saddlebags, as on this R60/2 in New York.** *BMW Group Archives*

1962

R69S, R60/2, R50S, R50/2, and R27

As BMW concentrated on expanding its car production, moving from the Isetta and 700 to larger capacity cars, its motorcycle existing range continued unchanged. This year saw the beginning of a rather bleak era for motorcycles as production and development stagnated. With only 4,302 motorcycles manufactured, 1962 represented the lowest point since 1927. The unreliable R50S disappeared completely during 1962, while the R69S received pistons with shorter wrist pins and reinforced cylinders. The shorter piston pin was introduced to cure the problem of wrist pins floating loose, with the more substantial cylinders in response to reported engine failures following sustained periods of high revs.

Post-1961 frames had reinforcing gussets on the downtubes near the battery carrier, and during 1962 the R69S frame included small triangular frame gussets welded to the vertical tubes of the rear swingarm pivots. The swingarm pivot posts were also drilled to allow easier bearing lubrication, something that previously required removal of the entire swingarm. Setting the R69S apart by 1962 were R69S emblems on the rear fender, and German home-market models received Hella turn signals in the handlebar ends.

1963

R69S, R60/2, R50/2, and R27

Although production increased markedly, to 6,043 during 1963, most of this was due to increased demand for the R27 single. Apart from a cast-in vent plug for the R69S rear drive case designed to prevent oil seepage in hot weather, the twins continued unchanged.

1964

R69S, R60/2, R50/2, and R27

By 1964, BMW motorcycles were considered high-quality products for a conservative, discerning clientele, representative of an earlier era. Not intending to compete directly with the British twins—particularly Triumph, which was now bombarding America with more than 20,000 motorcycles a year—BMW preferred to maintain a status quo. A BMW was far removed from the flashy colors, bright chrome, small gas tank, and intense power (with associated vibration) that characterized the British twins, and improvements were only implemented when deemed necessary. It proved a moderately successful formula, with production increasing to 9,043 during 1964, the R50/2 now the most popular model.

One of the problems that became evident on the R69S was crankshaft flex at high rpm, and after September 1963 a rubber-mounted vibration damper was fitted on the front of the R69S crankshaft. This was a large steel disc mounted on a vulcanized ring and fitted on the crankshaft taper between the front engine cover and generator. Although it seemed a reasonable solution, unfortunately the frequent maintenance required to prevent the rubber core from disintegrating was a source of irritation. The lower front fork cross brace was now bulged to clear the vibration damper. To remedy occasional clutch slipping, the R69S and R60/2 also received reinforced springs after June 1964 (after R69S 658624 and R60/2 626401). Also after June 1964 (after R50/2 636591, R60/2 626361, and R69S 658624), a funnel-type grease fitting was installed to lubricate the front swingarm bearing on all twins.

↑ Still with the earlier rocker covers, The R69S received a number of evolutionary updates during 1962. This 1962 version doesn't have the vibration damper with a bulge on the front engine cover. *Ian Falloon*

1963 PRODUCTION	
R69S	825
R60/2	1,050
R50/2	1,468
R27	2,700

1964 PRODUCTION	
R69S	1,300
R60/2	1,955
R50/2	3,817
R27	1,971

1965 PRODUCTION

R69S	**1,581**
R60/2	**2,307**
R50/2	**2,131**
R27	**1,099**

↓ **A small number of R69Ss were produced in Alpine White. In 1962, German versions had turn signals in the handlebar ends.** *BMW Group Press*

1965

R69S, R60/2, R50/2, and R27

Production dipped to 7,118 this year, and the offerings were very much business as usual. Updates were minimal, the factory offering a stiffer spring for the Boge front shocks after February 1965, later installing this on the R50/2 (from 677018), the R60/2 (from 626401), and the R69S (from 658929). In July 1965, the R50/2 received longer pushrods (243.5mm instead of 242mm) to allow for a thicker gasket, lowering the compression ratio. All BMWs remained expensive, but because the R69S still provided excellent performance, it continued as the most popular model in America. *Cycle World* was extremely impressed with its test R69S, claiming, "The R69S is a near perfect machine."

↖ The R69S retained the earlier basic instrument layout with a speedometer mounted in the headlight shell. *BMW Group Press*

⇐ A vibration damper was fitted to the front of the R69S crankshaft from 1964, this requiring a new bulging front engine cover. *BMW Group Press*

← In 1962, the R69S had a model designation badge on the rear fender. *BMW Group Press*

↓ Strong and robust, Alpine White seemed to accentuate the R69S's solidity. This European version has the standard narrow bench seat. Only R69Ss had the hydraulic steering damper under the tank. This later example has the new tank badges. *BMW Group Press*

↓ In the United States, the R69S was available with an unusual Wixom fairing and hard saddlebags. *BMW Group Press*

1966 PRODUCTION	
R69S	1,416
R60/2	2,698
R50/2	2,557
R27	2,400

1966

R69S, R60/2, R50/2, and R27

This was the final year for the R27, and the 600 and 500cc twins continued for another year unchanged. While production increased to 9,071, the only update was a redesigned speedometer helical gear from October 1965 to eliminate oil leaks (after R50/2 640039, R60/2 727956, and R69S 660144).

1967

R69S, R60/2, and R50/2

After several years with minimal changes, the 500 and 600cc twins with their Earles fork were now appearing antiquated, particularly in the United States. BMW introduced a number of updates, and a new series of US models. Ostensibly the basic motorcycle was unchanged, and apart from the new US versions, there was little to indicate a 1967 model over a 1966 variant. One distinguishing feature was the new enamel gas tank emblems, and while the tanks (large and small) were unchanged, the BMW lettering was now without the earlier serif-style tails. Despite the introduction of the specific US types, production continued to slide, to only 7,896 motorcycles built this year.

Engine updates included rotating valves for all models, and during 1967 the bolt sleeves in the cylinder heads had larger bearing surfaces, with a consequent reduction in valve clearance. The crankshaft was also modified during 1967, receiving a wider central cheek. Despite reducing the endplay in the transmission shafts, smooth shifting remained a problem. Reducing shaft endplay was designed to reduce engine noise at idle on the R69S from 84 decibels to 78 decibels, and from 74 to 72 decibels for both the R60/2 and R50/2.

A number of carburetor updates appeared during 1967, and in June new float guides, short float ticklers, and revised main jets were introduced to improve starting and cure uneven idle. All models had new carburetors beginning in August, these including recalibrated main jets, offset fuel intake hoses, and black plastic tickler caps instead of metal. A Micro-Star paper air filter was standardized, and there were no longer sliding choke levers on the R50/2 and R60/2 air filter canisters. Models in 1967 also had new Magura handlebar levers, with notches and balls, these with nylon bushes in the pivots, while the switches were redesigned at this time to accept Hella bar-end turn signal indicators.

↑ Although the engine was continually updated, visually the R60/2 looked very similar to before, only the new tank badges setting the 1967 R60/2 apart from earlier versions. Still available with the Earles front fork, US examples like this had a higher handlebar. *BMW Group Archives*

↓ The R69S was also available to special order in colors other than black or white, with red quite popular in the United States. This 1967 version also has the new badges and the generally more favored solo seat. *Ian Falloon*

R69US, R60US, and R50US

A belated, and almost half-hearted, effort to update the /2 appeared from 1967 with three specific US market models, the R50US, R60US, and R69US. These US versions were similar in specification to their Earles fork brothers, but a front telescopic fork replaced the Earles leading link type. While it could have been construed as an endeavor to provide a more modern alternative to the rather staid Earles fork types, BMW claimed to introduce the three US versions because the telescopic fork was more suited to off-road use. Since 1963, BMW had successfully tested the telescopic fork on ISDT bikes, and the new fork provided soft springing and a considerable 8.4 inches of travel. The 36mm BMW-designed leading-axle telescopic fork was very sophisticated for its day. Providing progressive rebound and compression damping through a tapered hydraulic metering rod, it had a big advantage over the Earles fork because of a reduction in unsprung weight. The fork featured rubber gaiters and a new front fender with tubular-steel fork brace, while the 200mm front drum brake was identical, with the backing plate secured by a long aluminum brace. Because the steering head was higher, the overall height went up to 995mm (39.2 inches) for the R69US and 980mm (38.6 inches) for the other two models. The centerstand was also taller and the sidestand longer. The steering head angle was a relatively steep 26.5 degrees, providing improved high-speed action on bumpy roads, but at the expense of heavier low-speed steering. The R69US retained the hydraulic steering damper, but for those used to the Earles fork front end, dive under braking was disconcerting. From the steering head back, the US versions were basically unchanged from standard, but they received a larger rear tire, lower rear drive ratio, and aluminum wheel rims.

Cycle magazine found the suggestion that the R69US was suitable for off-road use "a trifle absurd." But went on to say that "for long-distance, high-speed touring, there is no better motorcycle on earth." But this attempt to bring the /2 into the 1970s was largely unsuccessful. The telescopic fork couldn't disguise the ancient ancestry, and the list price of $1,712.75 made the R69US the most expensive 600cc motorcycle available.

↓ **On the R60US, a telescopic front fork replaced the Earles fork. The steering head was higher and the sidecar lugs deleted, but otherwise the R60US was identical to the R60/2. This example is fitted with a large sport gas tank.** *BMW Group Archives*

↑ The new telescopic fork was robust and provided long travel, but as the R69US had an even higher steering head than the R60US and R50US, the proportions were unbalanced.
BMW Group Archives

1967–1969 **R60/2, R50/2** *(FROM AUGUST 1967)*

Carburetors	2x Bing 1/24/91–1/24/192 (R69S from 663245)
	2x Bing 1/24/125–1/24/126 (R60/2 from 1 814032)
	2x Bing 1/24/149–1/24/150 (R50/2 from 645590)

1967–1969 **R69US, R60US, R50US**
(DIFFERING FROM THE R69S, R60/2, R50/2)

Frame designation	245/3
Front suspension	**Telescopic fork**
Rear tire	4.00x18
Wheelbase	1,427mm
Dry weight	199 kg (R69US)

1967 PRODUCTION

R69S	1,420	
R69US	490	1,003 (01/1967–12/1969)
R60/2	2,615	
R60/US	708	1,879 (01/1967–12/1969)
R50/2	2,464	
R50US	199	401 (08/1967–08/1969)

↑ BMW buyers in the United States during 1968 were offered the choice of the telescopic fork US versions or the traditional leading-link Earles fork. From the left are the R69S, R60US, and R69US. *BMW Group Archives*

1968 PRODUCTION	
R69S	1,113
R69US	83
R60/2	1,830
R60US	728
R50/2	1,188
R50US	132

1968

R69S, R69US, R60/2, R60US, R50/2, and R50US

Despite the introduction of the three specific US models, demand for BMW motorcycles began to slide after 1967. Production declined to only 5,074 this year, and updates were minimal. The clunky gearshift continued to be a problem, and after July 1968, the cam plate radii were enlarged, accompanied by modifications to the output shaft shifting pegs. Also after July 1968, as on the US versions, all models were offered the option of a larger 4.00x18-inch rear tire.

In September 1968 Kurt Liebmann and Fred Simone took the victory in the Virginia International Raceway five-hour race on an R69US, with John Potter and William van Houten second on a similar machine. Amol Precision prepared both R69USs.

1969

R69S, R69US, R60/2, R60US, R50/2, and R50US

For their final year, in the United States only the telescopic fork versions were available, with more R69US models built this year than Earles fork R69Ss. With production dwindling to 4,701 in 1969, the viability of the motorcycle operation was now questionable. Car production was expanding and becoming increasingly profitable, and as a remnant of an earlier era, the /2, with its lavish attention to detail and finish, was expensive to produce. The engine, with its built up crankshaft, and gear camshaft drive, didn't lend itself to mass production, and even components such as throttle control and the rear brake linkage were unnecessarily complex. After subsidizing automotive losses in the early 1960s, the roles were now reversed, and it was motorcycle production that was unprofitable. The Munich plant was required for automotive expansion and motorcycles either had to finish, or move elsewhere. The final motorcycle was built in Munich on May 13, 1969, and after 46 years of production would move to a new factory in Berlin.

Although the /2 series was close to ending, a few small updates were still introduced. After September 1968, problems with inadequately cast cylinder heads were solved with new long-reach steel spark plug inserts and appropriate longer reach spark plugs. And even as late as

1969 PRODUCTION	
R69S	321
R69US	430
R60/2	792
R60US	443
R50/2	1,040
R50US	70

↓ **The R69US engine was identical to the R69S, still with the bulge for the vibration damper, but with more space around the engine.** *BMW Group Archives*

November 1969, BMW attempted to improve the gearshift by changing the diameter of the detent spring. All US versions had reflectors this year.

Although production during the 1960s never managed to replicate the boom years of the early 1950s, the /2 twins sold solidly until 1967. Never mainstream motorcycles, by the end of the 1960s, the Earles fork twins were generally considered antiquated and obsolete. Virtually unchanged for more than a decade, they were relatively heavy and the performance was sedate. Although the R69S was capable of around 108 miles per hour, the steering and handling characteristics were unusual and idiosyncratic. Their heavy frames and strong Earles forks were designed for sidecar attachment, and sidecars were now out of fashion. BMW reasoned that by simply grafting a telescopic fork onto the existing /2, it would gain a new lease of life. But this didn't happen, and the three US market models failed to generate much enthusiasm. And they looked ungainly, the combination of a high-mounted steering head with the existing low rear-loop frame failing to win the hearts of devotees. Although not especially rare, the /2 and R69S, in particular, exemplify the finest qualities of the pre-1969 twins. With its built-up crankshaft, predominance of ball and roller bearings, and gear-driven camshaft, the engine was a jewel, yet the R69S (and all /2s) remains an eminently practical and useable classic motorcycle. Alongside the R68, the R69S has justifiably earned a place as one of the most desirable postwar BMW motorcycles.

SIDECAR RACING DURING THE 1960S AND 1970S

From 1960, privateers began to match the factory effort, and Helmut Fath and Alfred Wohlgemuth surprised everyone by winning four races on their private entry to take the championship. Also Fritz Scheidegger's first kneeler outfit appeared this year, built in an attempt to offset the power differential between his and the factory engines. Although Scheidegger's outfit represented the next generation, he had to bow to the superior power of the factory outfit of Max Deubel and Emil Hörner. Their machine retained a conventional sitting position with the fuel tank above the engine, but they still won the world championship from 1961 through 1964.

Scheidegger's machine, on the other hand, was a generation removed. By 1962, each wheel had a disc brake, and for 1964, he fitted 10-inch magnesium Mini car wheels at the front and side. But it wasn't until the factory's withdrawal at the end of 1964 that he could prove his machine's superiority. Scheidegger and John Robinson won the 1965 world championship, repeating this in 1966. Scheidegger was killed following a brake failure at Mallory Park in March 1967, but Klaus Enders with Ralf Engelhardt took over and gave the BMW twin another world championship. They lost the title to Helmut

Fath and his URS in 1968, but returned the following year with renewed factory support. With Fath's ex-passenger Wolfgang Kalauch, and later Engelhardt, Enders again won the 1970 world championship and then decided to retire. After a rather unsuccessful season racing BMW cars, Enders returned to sidecars in 1972, and with Engelhardt, he went on to become the most successful sidecar racer ever, with 27 Grand Prix victories and six world titles. By 1974, his Dieter Busch–prepared RS produced 67 horsepower at 10,000 rpm. Two Dell'Orto carburetors fed the 70x64mm engine, now with a center bearing, and the sidecar outfit featured a wide rear car tire on an Enders-designed wheel, single strut rear suspension, and a very short steering column with a U-link pivoted front fork. With hydraulically operated drum brakes, including two heavily finned double leading shoe brakes on the front wheel, the 419-pound outfit was capable of more than 150 miles per hour.

After 21 years and 19 world championships, the RS monopoly ended and the two-strokes took over. Although not exceptionally powerful, the RS BMW engine proved incredibly reliable and ideally suited to sidecar racing. Ironically, its era ended just as BMW was entering a new age of profitability, but BMW wouldn't consider producing a two-stroke racer.

↑ Although he never won a world title, Swiss sidecar pilot Florian Camathias and his privately prepared BMW often threatened the factory and unofficial works teams. Here he is with Hilmar Cecco at the Isle of Man in 1959, and they nearly won the world championship that year. A crash in 1961 at Modena resulted in Cecco's death, but Camathias was back in 1962, finishing second to Deubel's factory BMW, repeating this in 1963. Camathias preferred the British style sidecar on the left, and in October 1965, at Brands Hatch, his outfit left the road and the popular Swiss driver was killed.
Lothar Mildebrath

← This R60US has the optional larger sport tank and extra-wide Denfeld dual seat with passenger grab handles. Nearly covering the rear fender, this large seat was also uncomfortable and not popular. *BMW Group Archives*

↑ With the retirement of Deubel, and tragic deaths of Scheidegger and Camathias, the field was open for promising new teams. One was Johann Attenberger, with passenger Josef Schillinger. Due to Attenberger's stiff left knee, their outfit had the sidecar on the left, and in only their second Isle of Man TT in 1968, they finished second, receiving a special trophy. Unfortunately Attenbeger and Schillinger's promise was unfulfilled, as they were both killed in a crash during the Belgian Grand Prix at Spa a month later. *BMW Group Press*

↑ Max Deubel was the most consistent sidecar racer of the 1960s, winning the world championship four times in succession, from 1961 to 1964. Teamed with Emil Hörner, they benefited from a factory engine, but Scheidegger narrowly beat them in 1965 and 1966. After two seasons in second place, Deubel and Horner called it quits, Deubel to manage his hotel and Horner to return to his trade as a mechanic. This is at Ballaugh Bridge on the Isle of Man in 1964. *Lothar Mildebrath*

↑ By far the most successful BMW sidecar racer was Klaus Enders, here with Ralf Engelhardt on his way to winning the 1969 World Championship. Prepared by Dieter Busch, the BMW engines were highly developed and by 1974 included a center main bearing. This year Enders' machine was entered as a Busch-BMW in several events, resulting in BMW not winning the official manufacturers' title. *BMW Group Press*

1970–1980
NEW GENERATION:
SUPERBIKES AND SUPER TOURERS

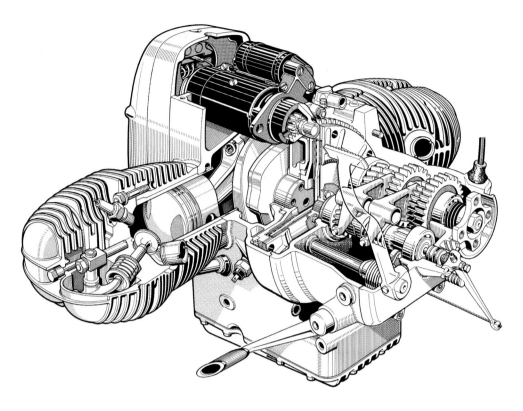

During the 1960s, the motorcycle market changed dramatically. Not only did the European motorcycle market collapse, but also the Japanese manufacturers began producing powerful, reliable, and sophisticated larger displacement machines. After nearly a decade of developmental stagnation and stumbling sales, and despite a pessimistic outlook, BMW's technical director Helmut Werner Bönsch managed to launch a new series of motorcycles. Although continuing the traditional two-cylinder boxer layout, both the engine and chassis represented a significant departure from the previous /2 and would remain in production until 1996.

Bönsch knew that for BMW to remain a viable motorcycle producer the company had to expand its market for quality luxury touring motorcycles and saw the future with a development of the traditional flat-twin. Marketed at the rider who placed a premium on comfort and convenience, the new /5 series was the most radical motorcycle design in BMW's history and would grow to become one of the most successful.

All that was needed for the production of the /5 was a suitable factory, and BMW decided to convert its repair and machine work facility in Spandau, West Berlin. Motorcycle production commenced at Spandau in September 1969 with the R60/5. A month later, the R75/5 joined it, and in November, the R50/5 completed the lineup. By the end of the year, 1,205 motorcycles had left the Spandau works.

1970

R75/5, R60/5, and R50/5

Hans-Günther von der Marwitz was entrusted with the /5's design, and as an enthusiastic motorcyclist, he continued the tradition initiated by Rudolf Schleicher and Alexander von Falkenhausen. Used to racing an AJS 7R, von der Marwitz was dismayed at the handling of the Earles-fork /2, and when assigned to the design of the next-generation BMW motorcycle, von der Marwitz wanted it to handle as well as a Manx Norton.

The engine design was all new, with three displacements offered: 498, 599, and 745cc, all sharing the same basic architecture. A number of significant design features set it apart from the earlier /2. Inside the one-piece aluminum, internally reinforced tunnel housing crankcase

↖ With its plain bearing crankshaft and electric start, the new engine represented a significant departure from BMW's established practice. *BMW Group Archives*

← No other motorcycle represented the style of the mid-1970s more than the R90S, and BMW exploited its sex appeal. *BMW Group Archives*

↓ The /5 was advertised as the fastest and sportiest BMW motorcycle ever.

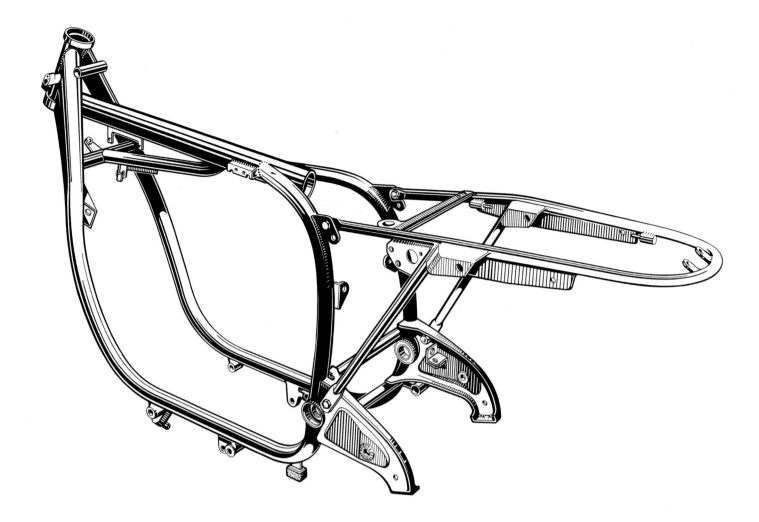

↑ Inspired by the Norton "featherbed,"
the new frame featured a double
cradle, but the weakness was always
the bolted-on rear subframe.
BMW Group Archives

↓ The early R50/5 was virtually
indistinguishable from the R60/5 and
R75/5. This is the 1970 US R50/5 with
higher handlebars.
BMW Group Archives

was a one-piece forged crankshaft (without a center bearing to minimize cylinder offset) running in plain bearings. The camshaft was situated underneath the engine, driven by a duplex chain from the front of the crankshaft, and many components came straight off the automotive production line, notably the three-layer plain bearings for the crank and con rods.

As the bearings required high-pressure lubrication, an Eaton trochoidal oil pump was fitted at the rear of the camshaft, while at the front was a three-phase 180-watt alternator powering the new 12-volt electrical system. Battery and coil ignition with an automatic advance replaced the earlier magneto, and above the engine (on the R60 and R75 and optional on the R50) was an electric starter motor.

Although the valve actuation system retained pushrods, as the pushrod tubes were now underneath the cylinders, the engine looked more modern. Aluminum, used extensively to minimize the effect of the heavy starting system, included alloy instead of steel-cylinder barrels, with a cast-iron sleeve bonded to the cylinder through the Al-Fin process.

The cylinder heads were also new, with a much shallower included valve angle of 65 degrees. The R75/5 had large 42mm and 38mm valves, and a more radical camshaft than the R50/5 and R60/5. The R60/5 valves were 38mm and 34mm, with the R50/5 receiving 34mm and 32mm valves. The R75/5 also had Bing Constant Velocity carburetors rather than the Bing concentric carburetors on the smaller versions. The /5 included a completely new air intake system, with the air filter incorporated inside the engine cases, with a rear facing air intake grille. As the air intake faced rearward, there was no ram air effect, but the air filter volume was 60 percent larger than that of the R69S. A four-speed three-shaft gearbox bolted on the rear of the engine. Although the gearbox shifted more smoothly than earlier BMW twins, it still wasn't flawless and many modifications to the shifting mechanism were made during the next few years.

New was the backbone-type, double-loop frame designed exclusively for solo riding. As the frame was constructed of variable section-tapered and oval tubing with a bolted-on rear subframe, the strength was questionable, but it remained essentially unchanged until 1996. Designer von der Marwitz was convinced too much frame stiffness was detrimental for a street motorcycle, the short swingarm also impeding stability, and criticism of the handling soon saw the /5 earning the unflattering nickname "rubber cow."

Suspension included the Fichtel & Sachs leading-axle telescopic fork of the earlier US /2, providing a generous 8.2 inches of travel, with twin Boge shock absorbers at the rear. Practical features extended to a large 24-liter (6.35-gallon) fuel tank and generously sized dual seat. With a host of lightweight features, including fiberglass fenders, the new /5 series models were also reasonably light for their class. The /5 BMW moved away from the company's decades-old tradition of primarily offering only plain black, although nearly all /5s for the United States were black in 1970 and 1971. Strangely, while the /5 represented a huge step in modernity in most respects, several archaic features remained, notably the primeval plunger ignition key and antique instrument cluster incorporated in the headlamp.

The /5 certainly vindicated Bönsch's optimism. The R75/5 was no longer a staid and stodgy motorcycle only for the initiated diehard. For a rider interested in long-distance, comfortable, high-speed travel, there was simply no other contender in 1969. Here was a motorcycle that could reliably cruise all day at 100 miles per hour, with all the conveniences expected of modern machinery. Offering respectable handling, and adequate performance, the new boxer, especially the R75/5—the first official 750cc twin since the military R75 of 1942–1944—was immediately successful. When it was released in August 1969, even the skeptics were impressed.

R60/5 production commenced at Spandau in September, with the R75/5 in October and the R50/5 in November. During 1970, 12,346 examples of the /5 series were sold. Motorcycle sales hadn't been as strong since 1955, and the future of the /5 was secure. The first US/5s appeared on the East Coast in January 1970 and the West Coast in February, and most of these were R75/5s. Only a few R50/5s were sold in the United States.

↑ The European R50/5 had a lower handlebar. The seat on the early /5s had chrome passenger handles and there were no side covers.
BMW Group Archives

1970 **R75/5**

Engine designation	**246**
Type	**Four-stroke, flat-twin, air-cooled**
Bore x stroke	**82x70.6mm**
Displacement	**745cc**
Power	**50 horsepower at 6,200 rpm**
Compression ratio	**9:1**
Valves	**Overhead-valve**
Carburetion	**2 x CV Bing 64/32/3–4**
Gears	**4-speed**
Ignition	**Battery and coil**
Frame	**Twin-loop tubular-steel**
Front suspension	**Telescopic fork**
Rear suspension	**Twin shock absorber**
Wheels	**1.85B19 and 1.85B18**
Tires	**3.25S19 and 4.00S18**
Brakes	**200mm drum front and rear**
Wheelbase	**1,385mm (54.5 inches)**
Wet weight	**210 kg (463 lbs.)**
Engine & frame numbers	**2970001–2970443 (1969) 2970444–2976486 (1970)**
Numbers produced	**540 (1969), 6,118 (1970)**
Colors	**Gray, White, Black, Green**

1970 **R60/5** *(DIFFERING FROM THE R75/5)*

Bore	**73.5mm**
Displacement	**599cc**
Power	**40 horsepower at 6,400 rpm**
Compression ratio	**9.2:1**
Carburetion	**2 x slide Bing 1/26/111–112**
Engine & frame numbers	**2930001–2930666 (1969) 2930667–2934690 (1970)**
Numbers produced	**666 (1969), 4,116 (1970)**

1970 **R50/5** *(DIFFERING FROM THE R75/5)*

Bore	**67mm**
Displacement	**498cc**
Power	**32 horsepower at 6,400 rpm**
Compression ratio	**8.6:1**
Carburetion	**2 x slide Bing 1/26/113–112**
Engine & frame numbers	**2900001–2900395 (1969) 2900396–2902443 (1970)**
Numbers produced	**399 (1969), 2,053 (1970)**

1971

R75/5, R60/5, and R50/5

Considering it was an all-new model, the /5 was surprisingly well sorted and there were only minor updates for 1971. A new centrifugal advance unit provided maximum advance at 3,000 rpm, and the R75/5 received new CV carburetors to quell low-speed running problems. In an effort to improve acceleration, the R75/5 final drive ratio was lowered. More careful assembly of the long travel front fork, with closer tolerances, also alleviated some of the criticism of head shaking and wobbles. The /5 may have alienated BMW purists, but it was successful in appealing to a wider clientele, with 1971 sales of 18,898, the most since 1955.

↑ The R60/5 was virtually unchanged for 1971; this is the US version with a higher handlebar. *BMW Group Archives*

1971 **R75/5** *(DIFFERING FROM 1970)*

Carburetion	**2 x CV Bing 64/32/9–10 (after 2977320)**
Engine & frame numbers	**2976487–2987130**
Numbers produced	**10,390**

1971 **R60/5** *(DIFFERING FROM 1970)*

Engine & frame numbers	**2934691–2941429**
Numbers produced	**6,645**

1971 **R50/5** *(DIFFERING FROM 1970)*

Engine & frame numbers	**2902444–2904189**
Numbers produced	**1,737**

← The controversial "toaster" chrome-plated panels appeared on the 1972 /5. The R75/5 was still the only version with Bing constant velocity carburetors.

↓ The 1972 R60/5 also received the chrome tank panels and side covers. The seat this year received a new passenger grab rail. *BMW Group Archives*

1972

R75/5, R60/5, and R50/5

New styling was the most evident update for the 1972 model year. This centered on the controversial 17-liter (4.6-gallon) "toaster" tank with chrome panels and chrome-plated battery panels. Primarily for the US market and so called because of its apparent similarity to a kitchen appliance, the toaster's radical styling wasn't universally accepted—it only lasted one year. This still didn't provide an impediment to sales, these increasing to 21,045 in 1972.

As the engine was already proving exceptionally reliable, updates were again minimal, but in February 1972 the crankshaft was strengthened, with new bearing shells, and new rocker shaft supporting brackets and hardened steel shims reduced noise.

One of the more significant updates for 1972 was to the front fork, a three-piece floating damper nozzle replacing the earlier fixed bushing, allowing the piston to move more freely. Although the tire sizes remained unchanged, from October 1971 on, all /5s received a wider WM3 2.15Bx18-inch rear wheel rim. A wider selection of colors was also available for 1972, and most United States 1972 models were black, blue, or silver, with chromed panels.

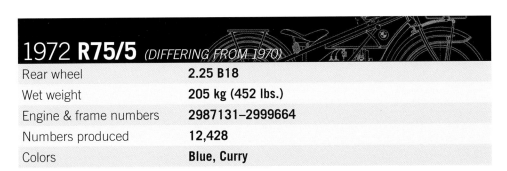

1972 R75/5 *(DIFFERING FROM 1970)*

Rear wheel	**2.25 B18**
Wet weight	**205 kg (452 lbs.)**
Engine & frame numbers	**2987131–2999664**
Numbers produced	**12,428**
Colors	**Blue, Curry**

1972 R60/5 *(DIFFERING FROM 1971 R75/5)*

Engine & frame numbers	**2941430–2947999**
Numbers produced	**6,564**

1972 R50/5 *(DIFFERING FROM 1971 R75/5)*

Wet weight	**200 kg (44 lbs.)**
Engine & frame numbers	**2904190–2906324**
Numbers produced	**2,130**

↑ A longer swingarm improved stability, and new rubber carburetor intakes provided more foot room.
BMW Group Archives

↓ The single dial instrumentation and plunger ignition key was an anachronism by 1973.
BMW Group Archives

1973

R75/5, R60/5, and R50/5

For its final year, the /5 continued with a number of significant updates, primarily to the chassis, the most important a longer swingarm introduced from January 1973. Engine updates included a new inner rotor for the oil pump, a new camshaft, and another centrifugal advance unit.

A return to conservative styling meant the 24-liter tank with rubber kneepads was standard, with an optional smaller 17-liter tank, now with rubber pads rather than chrome-plated panels. The battery covers were also optional, but these were now painted black or blue in addition to chrome-plated. The longer swingarm lengthened the wheelbase 50mm (1.97 inches), significantly improving the straight-line stability, reducing wobbles, enhancing handling through better weight distribution, and allowing room for a larger 16 Ah battery.

Many of the features that made motorcycles of the early 1970s so appealing also characterized the /5. With exceptional finish for a mass-produced motorcycle, over its four-year lifespan, the /5 series more than lived up to expectations, with 68,956 produced. Not only did it continue the BMW motorcycle tradition of offering unparalleled touring comfort and reliability, the /5 (particularly the R75/5) also provided acceptable performance. Although the skeptics initially criticized the lighter frame design with its bolt-on rear subframe, it was soon evident that the /5 provided better handling than any previous BMW motorcycle. But in some respects the /5 still remained outdated, and by 1973 disc brakes had arrived, as had closer ratio five-speed gearboxes. On July 28, 1973, only three days after the 500,000th BMW motorcycle (an R75/5) came off the production line, the last /5 left Spandau.

1973 **R75/5** *(DIFFERING FROM 1972)*

Wheelbase	**1,435mm (56.5 inches)**
Engine & frame numbers	**2999665–3000000 4000001–4008371 4009001–4010000**
Numbers produced	**8,894 (Total 1969–1973: 38,370)**
Colors	**Metallic Blue, Red, Green**

1973 **R60/5** *(DIFFERING FROM 1972 R75/5)*

Engine & frame numbers	**2948000–2952721**
Numbers produced	**4,730 (Total 1969–1973: 22,721)**

1973 **R50/5** *(DIFFERING FROM 1972 R75/5)*

Engine & frame numbers	**2906324–2907865**
Numbers produced	**1,546 (Total 1969–1973: 7,865)**

↟ A pair of 1973 /5s, both with the smaller gas tank. The R75/5 on the left is without side covers while the R60/5 on the right has chrome-plated covers. *BMW Group Archives*

↖ After the radical 1972 "toaster," BMW reverted to a more conservative look for 1973. Most /5s had the larger gas tank this year. *BMW Group Archives*

↑ The smaller gas tank remained an option, now with rubber kneepads. Not all 1973 /5s had battery side covers. *BMW Group Archives*

Although the R69S had isolated success in long-distance racing during the 1960s, the R75/5 proved more suitable for racing. The R69S was difficult to set up and required a specific riding approach, and while von der Marwitz may not have succeeded totally in creating a motorcycle that handled as well as a Manx Norton, it was admirably close. During 1970 and 1971, Helmut Dähne achieved some good results in production racing in Germany, while Hans-Otto Butenuth rode a special racer in the 1971 production TT, finishing a creditable fourth. Dähne repeated this in 1972 and 1973. With the advent of Formula 750 in 1972, Butenuth, Dave Potter, and Dähne rode F750 machines in the Imola 200. Dähne finished 13th, also campaigning the F750 bike during 1973, finishing 14th in the Imola 200.

On the other side of the Atlantic, Butler & Smith decided to build on their earlier success in the Virginia five-hour race, sponsoring an entry in the 1970 event. Service manager Helmut Kern spent 92 hours blueprinting the 750cc engine in time for the race in September, and Kurt Liebmann, partnered by Chuck Dearborn, won convincingly, three laps ahead of the second-place Honda 750.

At the end of 1970, factory representative Volker Beer organized for the factory to supply many racing components already tested by Dähne in Germany. Four racing frames and a variety of engine parts were supplied to Udo Gietl so he could build two F-750 racing bikes for the 1971 season. In conjunction with AMOL Precision, Gietl built one racer for Liebmann, with another later in the year for Justus Taylor. A third F-750, with a production R75/5 frame, was built for Charles Dearborn, along with a production racer for Liebmann. While the F-750 bikes had limited success that year, Liebmann (with John Potter) again won the Danville five-hour production race.

Butler & Smith opened a West Coast office in Compton, California, in 1971, and

↑ Helmut Dähne on his way to fourth place in the 1972 Isle of Man 750cc Production TT. *BMW Group Press*

↓ Butler & Smith's first race was an entry in the 1970 Virginia International Raceway five-hour endurance race, won by Kurt Liebmann and Charles Dearborn. *Udo Gietl*

with R75/5 sales stagnant, Reg Pridmore was provided a R75/5 to ride in the 1972 West Coast Production series. Eventually, this became a highly developed production racer, Pridmore managing 15 wins from 23 starts, winning the 1973 AFM production class championship.

During 1972 and 1973, Udo Gietl's F-750 GP bikes were basically outclassed and had limited success, and at the end of 1973, frame builder Rob North was asked to provide a frame similar to those of his highly successful Triumph and BSA 750cc triples. Developed over a two-and-half-year period, at 335 pounds ready to go, the Butler & Smith racer was lighter than the Yamaha and Suzuki two-strokes and capable of around 165 miles per hour. But they were always underpowered, especially at high-horsepower tracks like Daytona. Where the F-750 GP machines were more effective was in regional road racing, the high point a magnificent 1-2 victory at Summit Point, West Virginia, in April 1974, Justus Taylor leading home Kurt Liebmann in the Open Expert GP.

Gary Fisher was drafted alongside Pridmore for 1975, and in the final race for the F-750 BMWs, Fisher put the bike, now with monoshock rear suspension, on the front row at Laguna Seca. He diced with Kenny Roberts until the monoshock failed. Pridmore also proved the F-750 BMW's potency by out accelerating the Yamaha 700s at Road Atlanta. Often top 10 finishers in AMA Nationals, and faster than the once-dominant Harley V-twins, the B&S GP racers remain an impressive testament to the craftsmen and engineers involved in Butler & Smith's 1970s racing program.

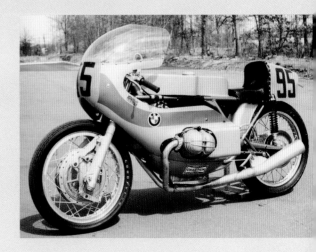

↑ Kurt Liebmann astride the Rob North–frame R75/5 racer at Daytona, 1974. Although beautifully presented, the four-stroke twin was no match for the two-stroke Yamahas. *Ian Falloon*

← The final Daytona appearance for the North-framed GP 750 was in 1975. This is Liebmann, who failed to finish. *Ian Falloon*

→ Built by Udo Gietl, the 1971 Butler & Smith GP racer had a 250mm Fontana brake, narrow frame, and one-off fairing. This is Kurt Liebmann's 1972 Pocono 50-mile road race winning machine. *Udo Gietl*

↑ With its small fairing and distinctive silver smoke colors, the R90S was a groundbreaking model for BMW. The 1974 version featured a number of differences from later examples, including solid front disc rotors, earlier Hella handlebar switches, aluminum-bodied turn signals, white ring on the instruments, kick-start, and tape pinstriping. Some R90Ss received the older-style enameled (cloisonné) gas tank badges instead of the newer thin metal type. *Mac Kirkpatrick*

1974

R90S, R90/6, R75/6, and R60/6

Even when the R75/5 was released, the market for motorcycles was changing. In 1969, Honda rewrote the rules with its astounding CB750, a 67-horsepower overhead camshaft four-cylinder motorcycle that was fast, reliable, and affordable. While Dr. Helmut Bönsch encouraged the development of the R75/5, he now declared that it would be unfortunate if BMW followed the path of producing larger and more powerful motorcycles. So the development of the /6 series initially proceeded along similar lines to the /5.

The release of the /6 series in October 1973 marked the end of the /5, and while the /6 was very much a continuation of the /5 concept, the new sporting R90S saw a significant change in direction for BMW. Not only did the R90S boast innovative styling, it provided class-leading performance. For the first, and only, time in the history of BMW's production motorcycles, the performance was comparable to that of any motorcycle produced in Japan, Italy, or England. The R90S was the first BMW Superbike, and with it BMW's image of conservatism was quashed. Production also increased this year, to 23,160.

R90S

Even after Bönsch retired, BMW was reluctant to embrace the idea of a larger displacement, sporting boxer, and this was where Bob Lutz intervened. An ex-US Marine fighter pilot and motorcycle enthusiast, Lutz was executive vice president of BMW Sales at that time and a member of the BMW board. He encouraged the development of a sporting motorcycle and allowed the enlisting of stylist Hans A. Muth for the task. Muth's small fairing with integral instrumentation, elegant gas tank, luxurious saddle, and individual air-brushed smoke black paint was enough to create one of the most memorable bikes of the 1970s, and the R90S was arguably most significant postwar production BMW motorcycle yet.

Creating a Superbike out of the rather staid R75/5 was not an easy proposition. A twin-cylinder motor could never match a four-cylinder in outright horsepower so BMW decided to emphasize all-around performance. Additionally, BMW was ideologically committed to maintenance-free shaft final drive, deciding to interpret the Superbike in a unique manner.

The tunnel-style engine housing was carried over from the final series R75/5, but strengthened around the front crankcase aperture. The front crankshaft bearing was now in a closed seat, and all the /6 series shared a new outer alternator and ignition cover. This included three air vents and vertical ribbing instead of the earlier smooth cast type. Inside the engine were only minor updates—the crankshaft were balanced for the pistons with 90 percent tungsten plugs inserted in the crank webs and the cylinders were painted black for improved heat dissipation.

Inside the cylinder head were larger (40mm) exhaust valves, the rocker arms pivoted in needle roller bearings, instead of bronze bushes, and the R90S had a different aluminum air filter housing with larger intakes. Setting the R90S apart from all other BMW motorcycles were the pair of Italian 38mm Dell'Orto PHM concentric carburetors. Indicative of the performance image BMW desired, the PHM Dell'Orto was relatively new, incorporated an accelerator pump, and was hence nicknamed the "pumper."

New for the R90S (and /6) was a long-awaited five-speed gearbox. The die-cast housing was new, lighter, and smaller than the previous four-speed unit, and the three-shaft design provided improved shifting over the /5. However, there remained room for improvement and 1974 transmissions were problematic. All /6s received an updated electrical system, with larger 25-Ah battery. But while the other /6s received a 280-watt three-phase Bosch alternator, the R90S' smaller diameter 240-watt alternator provided more clearance at higher rpm when crankshaft whip was more evident.

The R90S frame was a development of the R75/5, with some additional gussets around the steering head. The bolt-on rear subframe was new, but the strength of the entire structure was

← **No other motorcycle represented the style of the mid-1970s more than the R90S, and BMW exploited its sex appeal.** *BMW Group Archives*

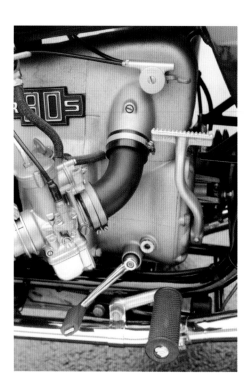

↑ **Only the R90S received Dell'Orto "pumper" carburetors. In 1974, R90Ss also retained a kick-start, this becoming optional in 1975.** *Mac Kirkpatrick*

still questionable as there was little rigidity provided by triangulation. The 36mm telescopic fork was internally identical to that of the R75/5, but with sporty fork cups instead of the traditional ribbed gaiters. The Boge shock absorbers were new for the R90S and /6 series and provided the R90S with a plush ride. Road irregularity was well insulated from the rider, but the soft suspension and extra long travel did compromise ultimate sporting ability. BMW was showing that the R90S was a real world sporting motorcycle, one that could be ridden hard and fast in comfort, on all manner of roads. Acknowledging that high-speed stability wasn't perfect, BMW fitted a three-way adjustable double-acting Stabilus hydraulic steering damper under the steering head.

Along with Weinmann light alloy wheels, the R90S had twin front stainless-steel disc brakes, gripped by floating single-piston (38mm) ATE calipers, with the master cylinder located underneath the fuel tank. A Bowden cable connected the master cylinder to the handlebar-mounted brake lever. Although the individual MotoMeter speedometer and tachometer was shared with all /6s, the R90S also received a clock and voltmeter mounted in the small Muth-designed fairing. In 1974 a standard clock was almost revolutionary, not appearing as standard equipment on a motorcycle since the wind-up eight-day clock on the Ariel Square Four 30 years earlier. Muth's styling makeover not only included the fiberglass fairing, but also extended to the steel 24-liter fuel tank and Denfeld saddle. The R90S sold for a heady $3,430 in 1974, somewhat more than the $2,950 for an R90/6 and the $2,075 for a Kawasaki 900cc Z1. But there was no doubt that there was more than $500 in extra equipment over an R90/6, even if the disparity to the Z1 was more difficult to justify.

All BMW motorcycles of this period were characterized by superb quality control, each bike assembled by one technician with 86 inspectors checking various components and the motorcycles before they left the factory in Spandau. The high price ensured the R90S earned celebrity status, finding a place in the garages of racing car champions Emerson Fittipaldi and Hans Joachim Stuck, and motorcycle enthusiast King Hussein of Jordan.

The R90S astonished the press when it was released. *Cycle* magazine said, "Without question this is one of the top three motorcycles in the world. It has Superbike performance. Double disc brakes stop it in 130 feet from 60 miles per hour. The engine is quiet and frugal, the cruising range is almost 300 miles, and comfort at highway speeds is astonishing."

1974 R90S *(DIFFERING FROM THE R75/5)*

Engine designation	**247**
Bore	**90mm**
Displacement	**898cc**
Power	**67 horsepower at 7,000 rpm**
Compression ratio	**9.5:1**
Carburetion	**2 x Dell'Orto PHM 38 AS-AD**
Gears	**5-speed**
Tires	**3.25H19 and 4.00H18**
Front brakes	**Dual disc 260mm**
Wheelbase	**1,465mm (57.7 inches)**
Wet weight	**215 kg (474 lbs.)**
Engine & frame numbers	**4070001–4075054 (09/1973–08/1974)** **4950001–4951005 USA (01/1974–07/1974)**
Numbers produced	**986 (1973), 4,067 (1974), 1,005 (USA 1974)**
Color	**Silver Smoke**

R90/6, R75/6, and R60/6

Celebrating the boxer's 50th anniversary, three other /6 models joined the R90S in the 1974 model lineup. Now with a five-speed gearbox, the /6 replaced the /5, and there was no longer a 500cc twin. The three models were outwardly similar, and in 1974 they featured many /5 components (such as the handlebar switches and enamel tank badges). All /6s were offered with a smaller (18-liter) gas tank and touring saddle with larger chrome handrail. They also kept the gaiters on the fork legs, but included the separate instruments and warning light console.

R90/6

Heading the 1974 touring lineup, the R90/6 shared much with the R90S, but a lower compression ratio and a pair of 32mm Bing carburetors contributed to a reduced power output. With its single front disc brake, the R90/6 looked visually similar to the R75/6, and the performance was quite brisk for a touring motorcycle, the R90/6 not far behind the R90S. The R90/6 proved especially successful in the United States, and by the end of its production in 1976, it had established itself as the most popular BMW motorcycle ever until that time, with nearly 10,000 sold.

As with the /5, uniformity of many engine components marked the /6 series. The new stronger crankcases were shared with the R90S, as was the crankshaft. Considering the performance differential between the four new models, the similarity in engine specification was striking and an example of clever model rationalization. The R90/6 also received the R90S cylinder heads (with larger exhaust valves), and the rockers now pivoted in needle roller bearings. Details setting the R90/6 apart from the R90S included lower compression pistons, plain aluminum cylinders, and 32mm Bing constant vacuum carburetors (also on the R75/5).

Model rationalization continued with the frame, rear subframe, swingarm, and rear brake shared with the R90S. The R90/6 (and R75/6) front fork provided for a single front disc brake only, and the standard fuel tank was 18 liters (4.3 gallons), with a larger 22-liter (5.8-gallon) tank optional. The /6 instrument layout with separate speedometer and tachometer with five warning lights was shared with the R90S.

↑ Three outwardly similar /6s joined the R90S for 1974. The R60/6 on the right has the standard smaller gas tank, while the R90/6 and R75/6 have their optional larger tanks. *BMW Group Archives*

1974 **R90/6** *(DIFFERING FROM THE R90S)*

Power	**60 horsepower at 6,500 rpm**
Compression ratio	**9.0:1**
Carburetion	**2 x CV Bing 64/32/11–12**
Front brakes	**Single disc 260mm**
Wet weight	**210 kg (463 lbs.)**
Engine & frame numbers	**4040001–4044971 (09/1973–08/1974)** **4930001–4932218 USA (01/1974–07/1974)**
Numbers produced	**3,049 (1973), 1,922 (1974), 2,218 (USA 1974)**
Colors	**Red, Green, Blue, White, Black, Curry**

R75/6

Apart from the new crankcases and rockers pivoting on needle roller bearings, the R75/6 engine specification was unchanged from the R75/5, while the chassis was identical to that of the R90/6.

↓ The R90/6 was particularly popular in the United States. The front brake was a single disc and this 1974 model has metal-bodied turn signals. *Ian Falloon*

1974 **R75/6** *(DIFFERING FROM THE R75/5 AND R90/6)*

Engine & frame numbers	**4010001–4012831 (09/1973–08/1974)** **4910001–4911097 USA (0/1974–07/1974)**
Numbers produced	**1,203 (1973), 1,628 (1974), 1,097 (USA 1974)**

R60/6

Now the smallest in the /6 lineup, the R60/6 engine was very similar in specification to that of the previous R60/5, carburetion still by two slide-type Bing 26mm carburetors with accelerator pumps. BMW didn't think the R60/6 needed a disc brake to slow it down, and it retained the earlier twin leading shoe front drum brake. Otherwise the chassis was as on the R75/6.

↑ For 1974, the R60/6 was the smallest boxer twin. This retained the Bing slide carburetors and drum front brake. Unlike the /5, the gas tank didn't have rubber kneepads. *BMW Group Archives*

1974 **R60/6** *(DIFFERING FROM THE R60/5 AND R75/6)*

Engine & frame numbers	2910001–2911677 (07/1973–08/1974) 4900001–4900827 USA (01/1974–07/1974)
Numbers produced	448 (1973), 1,229 (1974), 827 (USA 1974)

1975

R90S, R90/6, R75/6, and R60/6

As the /6 series represented a significant development, updates for 1975 centered on refinement. New colors were added; brake discs were perforated, instruments, levers and switches modernized, and seats redesigned. Production continued to climb, with sales of 25,566 motorcycles this year.

R90S

While the R90S proved virtually trouble free from the outset, it continued to evolve through its production cycle, and this year saw the kick-start optional and a new crankshaft, front main bearing, flywheel, and stronger flywheel retaining bolts. The weakest component, the five-speed transmission, also came in for some updates with new first and second gear shifting forks. As the kick-start was now optional, the Bosch starter motor was more powerful.

The basic chassis was also unchanged, but 1975 models received new fork legs, a new front hub, and a larger diameter (17mm) axle to tighten the handling. During the year, the front fork also received new dampers, these providing more compression damping, stiffening the suspension, and reducing the fork travel to 200mm (7.9 inches). To improve wet weather braking performance, the twin stainless-steel disc rotors were drilled.

For 1975, the R90S (and /6) finally shed some of the obsolete links with the earlier /5 series. All the handlebar controls were updated, with black dogleg Magura levers and new Hella handlebar switches, and the Hella turn signals now featured low reflective black plastic bodies rather than aluminum ones. Also new for 1975 was the seat cover, and the R90S was available in an additional color, Daytona Orange.

Although the production numbers for the 1975 model year were similar to those of 1974, R90S production now peaked. It was evident many of the updates were designed to make the R90S more appealing for the US market. The Daytona Orange color scheme wasn't greeted so enthusiastically in Europe, where it was considered garish, but it appealed to Americans. The result was that more than a quarter of the 1975 R90S production run went to the United States, where considerably more were sold than in 1974.

↑ The R90S cockpit was further refined for 1975, with new MotoMeter instruments and improved Hella switches. *BMW Group Archives*

← New for the 1975 model, the R90S had perforated front disc rotors. *Ian Falloon*

↓ The R90S has rightfully earned its place as one of the 1970s' motorcycle icons. *BMW Group Archives*

1975 **R90S** *(DIFFERING FROM 1974)*

Engine & frame numbers	4080001–4084675 (06/1974–09/1975)4900001–4980001–4981738 USA (07/1974–08/1975)
Numbers produced	1,376 (1974), 3,299 (1975), 677 (USA 1974), 1,061 (USA 1975)
Color	**Daytona Orange**

↑ **The 1975 R60/6 retained the front drum brake.** *BMW Group Archives*

R90/6, R75/6, and R60/6

Updates in 1975 for the /6s mirrored those of the R90S. These included the new crankshaft, gearbox shifting forks, optional kick-start, and more powerful starter motor. The /6s also featured the 17mm front axle, new seat, turn signals, handlebar switches, and the R90/6 and R75/6 had a perforated front brake disc. Curry was deleted from the /6 color range, and this year the /6 was offered with an optional touring package that included a windshield and the larger fuel tank, or a touring luxury package, with a wider range of accessories.

1975 **R90/6** *(DIFFERING FROM 1974)*	
Engine & frame numbers	4050001–4053311 (06/1974–08/1975) 4960001–4964263 USA (08/1974–08/1975)
Numbers produced	984 (1974), 2,327 (1975), 1,802 (USA 1974), 2,461 (USA 1975)

1975 **R75/6** *(DIFFERING FROM 1974)*	
Engine & frame numbers	4020001–4023688 (08/1974–08/1975) 4940001–4942087 USA (08/1974–08/1975)
Numbers produced	1,198 (1974), 2,490 (1975), 962 (USA 1974), 1,125 (USA 1975)

1975 **R60/6** *(DIFFERING FROM 1974)*	
Engine & frame numbers	2920001–2923868 (08/1974–08/1975) 4920001–4921103 USA (08/1974–07/1975)
Numbers produced	1,575 (1974), 2,293 (1975), 593 (USA 1974), 510 (USA 1975)

↓ Although the 1976 R90S looked little changed from 1975, it had a number of updates, including larger brake calipers and stronger engine and transmission cases. *Mac Kirkpatrick*

1976

R90S, R90/6, R75/6, and R60/6

By 1976, development of the /7 series for 1977 was well underway, and the existing /6s continued, looking visually analogous to 1975. But hiding underneath the similar exterior were a considerable number of updates and improvements, introduced as an overture for the /7 series. In many respects the 1976 /6s signified the end of an earlier era. This was certainly true in regard to quality of finish, and the improvements provided a link between the old and the new. For some, 1976 represented the year of the quintessential air-head boxer—one with the more pleasing earlier engine aesthetics but incorporating significant technical improvements. Although 1976 was a bridging year, 28,209 motorcycles were sold this year.

R90S

Visually, it was difficult to tell the 1976 and 1975 R90S apart, but hiding within the engine were many unseen updates. With the development of the 980cc /7 already well underway, most of these engine modifications were a precursor to this uprated design and shared with other 1976 /6s. Although the specifications were unchanged, new engine components included the crankcases, reinforced to accept larger cylinder spigots; cylinders (sealed by an O-ring instead of base gasket); pistons; and cylinder heads. The oil sump pan was 10mm deeper, while the cylinder heads included shorter rocker arms and hollow pushrods to reduce valve clatter. Gearbox updates included strengthened cases and a new gearshift cam plate and detent spring to improve shifting, while chassis improvements included a new swingarm and larger piston (40mm) ATE front brake calipers. These modifications didn't seem like much, and despite the daunting $3,965 price, they contributed to the 1976 R90S representing the consummate archetype of the genre. With its bold styling, stunning colors, and high-performance engine, the R90S elevated BMW into the world of the Superbike. After Steve McLaughlin led home Reg Pridmore in the 1976 Daytona Superbike race, Daytona Orange took on a new meaning, and the R90S became the classic BMW motorcycle of the 1970s.

1976 **R90S** *(DIFFERING FROM 1975)*	
Engine designation	**247/76**
Engine & frame numbers	**4090001–4093724 (08/1975–06/1976)** **4990001–4991260 USA (08/1975–06/1976)**
Numbers produced	**912 (1975), 2,812 (1976),** **584 (USA 1975), 676 (USA 1976)**

RACING THE R90S

At about the same time as the R90S was unveiled, BMW prepared a factory R90S for the 1973 Bol d'Or 24 Hour endurance race at Le Mans. Ridden by Dähne and Gary Green, the bike finished third, covering 3,200 kilometers. Dähne then continued to develop his older R75/5 racer for production events. With the production TT capacity limit now 1,000cc, he installed a new 900cc engine with five-speed gearbox and dual-disc front end on the R75/5 chassis, finishing third.

The 1975 Production TT was a 10-lap handicap race with two riders, and Dähne teamed with Werner Dieringer. After two laps Dähne was in the lead by a minute, when he knocked a hole in the right side cylinder head cover, losing oil and seizing the engine. Dähne finished ninth in the Open Classic TT on the same bike later in the week, the first four-stroke home. His lap of 101.89 miles per hour was the first 100-mile-per-hour lap by a BMW at the Isle of Man.

Dähne returned to the Isle of Man in 1976, this time determined not to suffer from the ground clearance problems of the previous year, shorter con rods trimming an inch off each side. Teamed with Hans-Otto Butenuth, Dähne led the 10-lap 1976

Production TT from start to finish, averaging 98.82 miles per hour. However, under the handicap system, they were credited with fifth, the first time the fastest finishers didn't win a TT. Dähne's fastest lap of 102.52 miles per hour remains the best ever lap of the Isle of Man by a pushrod boxer twin.

The release of the R90S also coincided with the expansion in production and production-based racing in America. As Reg Pridmore and the Butler & Smith R75/5 were the most competitive combination in West Coast production racing during 1973, it was no surprise to see them on the leader board with the new R90S during 1974. Pridmore continued to ride the production R90S (now Daytona Orange) during 1975, finishing fourth in the Daytona production race, but as production racing evolved into Superbike racing, so did the R90S.

By 1976, two-strokes had driven the four-strokes out of open class racing, but as they bore no relationship to street motorcycles, the AMA created the Superbike series to woo the fans back. Rules required the machines to look stock, but underneath the street bodywork they were highly developed racers, and in the first year of Superbike, only Butler & Smith exploited the Superbike regulations to the full.

↑ Reg Pridmore's R90S Superbike had dual shock rear suspension at Daytona, and Pridmore went on to win the 1976 AMA Superbike Championship.
BMW Group Archives

↓ Dähne and Butenuth rode took the R90S to victory in the 1976 Unlimited Production TT at the Isle of Man. The engine had shorter cylinders to improve ground clearance.
BMW Group Archives

Team manager Udo Gietl, with Todd Schuster, Kenny Augustine, AMOL Precision, and West Coast executives Helmut Kern and Matt Capri, worked tirelessly to create the R90S Superbikes, arguably the most spectacular BMW racing motorcycles ever built.

When they lined up at the inaugural Superbike race at Daytona in March 1976, the Butler & Smith R90Ss produced 92 horsepower at the clutch. During the season, it was continually developed, eventually producing 102 horsepower at 8,600 rpm. Gietl reworked the swingarm to incorporate a single, semi-horizontal Koni F1 racing car shock absorber and prepared three R90S Superbikes. Gary Fisher and Steve McLaughlin rode monoshock versions, and Pridmore was on a twin shock. In the first AMA Superbike race Fisher led before retiring, McLaughlin assumed the lead, and on the final lap Pridmore led, but McLaughlin drafted past across the finishing line to win by 3 inches. Pridmore was initially credited with

victory, but the photo finish equipment later proved McLaughlin the winner. It was one of the closest race finishes ever at Daytona, and the race average was 99.8 miles per hour. So dominant were the BMWs that they made the rest of the field look second rate.

Pridmore went on to win the 1976 AMA Superbike Championship, and with the PR job done, Butler & Smith decided to pull the plug on the expensive program. As monoshock rear suspension was banned for 1977, Butler & Smith only entered one R90S, Pridmore finishing fourth at Daytona.

But the original R90S Superbikes refused to die, with victories by Ron Pierce at Loudon in 1977 and Harry Klinzmann at Laconia in 1978. John Long ended the 1978 AMA Superbike season with a points tie for the championship and was credited with second overall. For a privately entered pushrod twin to succeed so well in a field of factory-prepared fours was an astonishing achievement.

↑ The three Butler & Smith R90Ss dominated the 1976 Daytona Superbike race, running in formation most of the race. Here Pridmore leads McLaughlin and Fisher. *BMW Group Archives*

↓ Steve McLaughlin on the monoshock R90S was the eventual winner of the first Daytona Superbike race. *Ian Falloon*

R90/6, R75/6, and R60/6

Although the 1976 model /6 also looked visually identical to that of 1975, underneath were a number of updates that also characterized the R90S this year. The R90S's new stronger engine housing was shared with the R90/6 and R75/6, while R60/6 featured a new crankcase specific to that model. All versions now had the deeper sump oil pan and new cylinders sealed by an O-ring, and cylinder heads with new rockers. The R75/6 and R90/6 now featured a 40mm front brake caliper, but still a single disc.

Although overshadowed by the more spectacular R90S, the /6 series were excellent motorcycles, and justifiably popular. They were well built, extremely reliable, and the R90/6 and R75/6 provided outstanding touring performance for the day. Although the R60/6 remained underpowered, the R90/6 and the R75/6 epitomized the finest aspects of the boxer twin: quality, aesthetics, smoothness, and performance.

1976 R90/6 (DIFFERING FROM 1975)

Engine & frame numbers	4060001–4063018 (08/1975–06/1976) 4970001–4973316 USA (09/1975–06/1976)
Numbers produced	716 (1975), 2,302 (1976), 2,012 (USA 1975), 1,304 (USA 1976)

1976 R75/6 (DIFFERING FROM 1975)

Engine & frame numbers	4030001–4035306 (08/1975–06/1976) 4945001–4947578 USA (09/1975–06/1976)
Numbers produced	1,955 (1975), 3,351 (1976), 1,166 (USA 1975), 1,412 (USA 1976)

1976 R60/6 (DIFFERING FROM 1975)

Engine & frame numbers	2960001–2965122 (08/1975–06/1976) 4925001–4925914 USA (09/1975–05/1976)
Numbers produced	2,012 (1975), 3,110 (1976), 643 (USA 1975), 271 (USA 1976)

→ This 1977 R100RS has wire-spoke wheels and the optional sporting solo seat. The brake calipers were anodized blue this year. *BMW Group Archives*

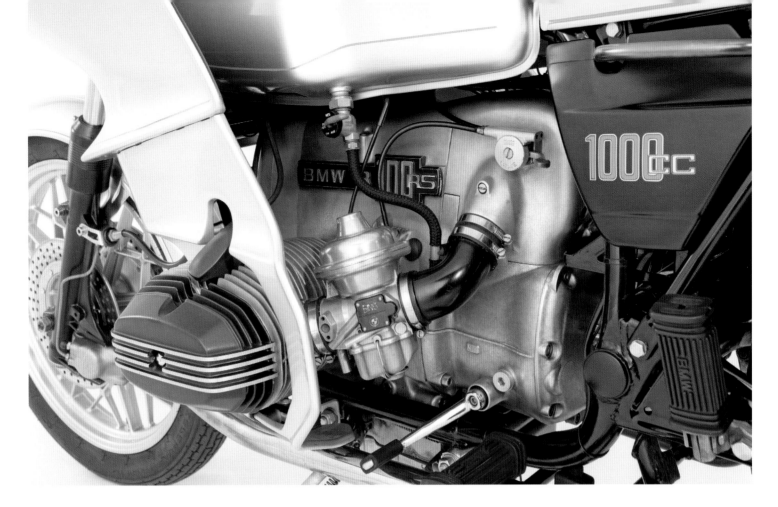

1977

R100RS, R100S, R100/7, R75/7, and R60/7

Although the R90S changed the perception of BMW motorcycles as staid and boring machines, it still wasn't perfect. The R90S was both a styling triumph and a high-performance motorcycle, and while the handling was acceptable, there was some criticism of high-speed instability. As this was possibly due to a combination of frame flex and the high steering inertia caused by the handlebar-mounted fairing, the next development of the top-of-the-line BMW motorcycle centered on a more aerodynamic and integrated frame-mounted fairing. The result was the R100RS, *Rennsport* or Racing Sport, harking back to the bevel-drive double-overhead camshaft racers of 1954. When it was released in August 1976, the R100RS didn't really bear any relationship to those magnificent racers, but it caused a sensation similar to that of the R90S three years earlier. And with it, BMW created another classic motorcycle, just as distinctive as the R90S, and functionally superior. Today integrated full fairings are de rigueur for motorcycles, and the R100RS was the pioneer.

Alongside the R100RS for 1977 was a completely new range, the /7 series. Now comprising five models, the top models had displacement that jumped to the 980cc of the R100RS. The 900cc models were discontinued, and initially the 750 and 600cc versions were much as before, in updated form. As in the past, a high degree of model uniformity and parts interchangeability distinguished the series, with all /7s sharing much with the more expensive R100RS, and sales increased this year, to 31,515.

R100RS

Following the success of the R90S, Hans Muth was asked to style a motorcycle emphasizing rider protection and aerodynamic function. Again he was successful, and the R100RS was the first production motorcycle to offer a fully integrated fairing that not only provided outstanding weather protection, but it also contributed to the stability of the motorcycle. Even nearly 40 years later, the R100RS fairing remains a benchmark in motorcycle fairing design efficiency. Because of the larger frontal area, the top speed was less than that of the R90S, but the high-speed handling was superior, as was rider comfort. Although the R90S continued as

↑ Unlike the R90S, the R100RS carburetors were the more usual Bing CV. Angular rocker covers were new this year. *BMW Group Press*

↓ The R100RS pioneered wind tunnel–designed aerodynamic fairing. This has cast-alloy wheels, but most 1977 examples were fitted with wire-spoke wheels. *BMW Group Press*

the R100S, it was now relegated down in the lineup. True to form, the R100RS also set a new price benchmark, selling for a staggering $4,595 in 1977.

Many of the engine developments for the R100RS, and its /7 series stable mates, were introduced on the R90S and /6 for the 1976 model year. The most noticeable update was the increase in capacity, although the cylinders had thicker and shorter cooling fins to reduce noise and were no longer painted black. Inside the cylinder head were larger, 44mm inlet valves, with new angular black anodized rocker covers, with polished fins. Instead of the R90S's concentric Dell'Orto carburetors, the R100RS received Bing 40mm constant vacuum carburetors.

Although the /7 frame and swingarm was essentially unchanged from the final 1976 version, a second transverse tube was added between the front double downtubes and the frame tubing was a thicker section, with additional gusseting around the steering head. Most 1977 R100RSs were fitted with spoked wheels with the usual aluminum rims, but with two blue pinstripes on each rim. Italian FPS cast-alloy snowflake-pattern wheels were listed as an option for the R100RS only, the rear a 2.50x18-inch, but weren't generally available during 1977 due to supply problems. Also setting the RS off were blue anodized brake calipers.

A much narrower, almost clip-on style, handlebar distinguished the R100RS from other sporting BMWs. Short enough to fit completely inside the fairing, the flat handlebar provided a very aggressive riding position, making the R100RS more suitable for high, rather than low, speed touring duties. By far the most innovative feature of the R100RS was the wind tunnel–designed injection-molded fiberglass fairing, claimed to reduce air resistance by 5.4 percent, front wheel lift by 17.4 percent, and side yawing by 60 percent over the R90S.

Standard on all /7s, including the R100RS, was the stylish 24-liter (6.3-gallon) steel fuel tank of the R90S, with a flush-mounted lockable filler cap, and the R100RS was offered with a choice of two seats: the R90S-style dual seat and a solo (almost one and a half) sport seat.

1977 R100RS (DIFFERING FROM THE 1976 R90S)

Bore	**94mm**
Displacement	**980cc**
Power	**70 horsepower at 7,250 rpm**
Carburetion	**2 x Bing 94/40/105–106**
Frame designation	**247/77**
Wet weight	**230 kg (507 lbs.)**
Engine & frame numbers	**6080001–6085159 (03/1976–06/1977)** **6180001–6181263 USA (05/1976–06/1977)**
Numbers produced	**1,418 (1976), 3,741 (1977),** **542 (USA 1976), 721 (USA 1977)**
Color	**Silver**

R100S, R100/7, R75/7, and R60/7

Although relegated in its status in the new lineup, the R100S continued the style of its illustrious predecessor, the R90S, and all /7s incorporated many of the updates introduced on the R100RS. Although it lacked the R90S mystique, the R100S was an improved motorcycle and arguably the strongest performer in the 1977 lineup. This was vindicated in production racing, with Kenny Blake and Joe Eastmure taking the victory in the 1977 Australian Castrol Six-Hour race for stock production bikes on a R100S.

As with the /6 series, each model of the /7 series represented a slightly different variation on the engine Typ 247/76 theme. There was fundamentally little difference in the engine specifications of the R60/7 and the R75/7 and their respective /6 variants, while the R100/7 was also quite similar to the R90/6. The R100S engine was identical to that in the R100RS, although the power output was slightly less due to a more restrictive exhaust system. All featured the new angular rocker covers and plain aluminum cylinders. The carburetion was ostensibly carried over from the previous models, except the R100S now used Bing 94 carburetors similar to those on the R100RS. All /7s featured the new frame with additional strengthening, and as on the /6, all the wheels for 1977 /7s and R100Ss were wire spoked with aluminum rims. All /7s had a single front disc brake this year (including the R60/7), the R100S retaining dual-perforated front discs. Ostensibly the /7 was very similar to the /6, but all models shared the R90S-style sporting front fender and 24-liter fuel tank with flush-mounted cap. Although the R75/7 and R60/7 weren't officially listed after the 1977 model year, a small number were produced into 1978 and 1979, and even a few R60/7s in 1980.

↑ Replacing the R90S for 1977, the R100S was no longer the range leader, but as it shared the R100RS engine, it still provided impressive performance. *BMW Group Archives*

↓ The basic touring model in the 1977 1,000cc lineup was the 100/7, now with the R90S-style gas tank and more sporting front fender. *BMW Group Archives*

→ The R60/7 had a front disc brake
instead of the R60/6's drum.
BMW Group Archives

↓ The /7 instrument panel. The top triple
clamp was still a flat-steel unit, and the
front master cylinder operated by a
Bowden cable. New this year on all /7s
was the flush-mounted fuel filler.
BMW Group Archives

1978

R100RS, R100S, R100/7, R80/7, and R60/7

The 1978 model year was one of transition for BMW. Replacing the short-lived R75/5 was the similar R80/7, and this was effectively the final year for the R60/7 before the new-generation R65 replaced it. This year also saw a variety of additional official, police, and touring models: the R60/7 T, the R80/7 T, and R80/7 N. In the United States, the strong deutschmark had a detrimental effect, forcing up prices and reducing sales. It was rumored that up to 8,000 motorcycles sat in dealers' showrooms, and at $5,295, only 1,092 examples of the flagship R100RS were sold in the United States this year.

In the United States, noise, emission controls, and the introduction of lower octane low-lead fuel were also hurting the air-cooled boxer engine, requiring complicated engine breather systems and a general lower state of tune. In the face of cheaper and higher performing Japanese fours, the expensive boxers struggled to find a market, although they continued to maintain a loyal following in Europe. And with production falling to 29,580 motorcycles built during 1978, the future of the BMW motorcycle looked uncertain. In an effort to stem a downward spiral, a R100RS was prepared for an attempt on a series of long-distance records at Nardo in southern Italy. A team of four riders (Dähne, Cosutti, Milan, and Zanini) set four new world records, including an average speed of 220.711 kilometers per hour (137.14 miles per hour) over 100 kilometers.

1977 R100S *(DIFFERING FROM THE R100RS AND R90S)*

Power	**65 horsepower at 6,650 rpm**
Carburetion	**2 x Bing 94/40/103–104**
Wet weight	**220 kg (485 lbs.)**
Engine & frame numbers	**6060001–6063149 (05/1976–06/1977)** **6160001–6161385 USA (05/1976–06/1977)**
Numbers produced	**1,461 (1976), 1,643 (1977),** **841 (USA 1976), 544 (USA 1977)**
Color	**Metallic Red**

1977 R100/7 *(DIFFERING FROM THE R100S AND R90/6)*

Carburetion	**2 x Bing 64/32/19–20**
Wet weight	**215 kg (474 lbs.)**
Engine & frame numbers	**6040001–6043414 (05/1976–06/1977)** **6140001–6142451 USA (05/1976–06/1977)**
Numbers produced	**1,771 (1976), 3,741 (1977),** **1,587 (USA 1976), 864 (USA 1977)**
Colors	**Blue, Orange, Black**

← The R100RS was available in gold for 1978. The brake calipers were now anodized silver and all wheels were cast aluminum. *BMW Group Archives*

↓ A sporting solo seat was still optional, but new this year was a rear disc brake and a wider wheel rim. *BMW Group Archives*

1977–1979 R75/7 *(DIFFERING FROM THE R100/7 AND R75/6)*

Carburetion	**2 x Bing 64/32/13–14**
Engine & frame numbers	**6020001–6024507 (05/1976–06/1977)** **6220001–6220278 (08/1977–04/1978)** **6222001–6333005 (01/1979)** **6120001–6121474 USA (07/1976–06/1977)**
Numbers produced	**1,533 (1976), 2,974 (1977), 1,315 (USA 1976),** **159 (USA 1977), 107 (1977 for 1978 model year),** **171 (1978), 5 (1979)**

1977–1980 R60/7 *(DIFFERING FROM THE R100/7 AND R60/6)*

Carburetion	**2 x Bing 1/26/123–124**
Front brake	**Single disc 260mm**
Engine & frame numbers	**6000001–6011412 (05/1976–01/1978)** **6015001–6015382 (09/1978–14/1980)** **6100001–6100407 USA (07/1976–05/1977)**
Numbers produced	**2,207 (1976), 3,310 (1977), 296 (USA 1976),** **111 (USA 1977), 263 (1978), 350 (1979), 56 (1980)**

R100RS

Only detail changes distinguished the 1978 R100RS, including a new camshaft, advanced 6 degrees, and a new timing chain case. An external linkage was fitted to the gearshift to further improve the action and reduce effort, and only cast-alloy wheels were fitted this year, the rear 18-inch wheel now including a wider, 2.75-inch rim and incorporating a drilled 260mm Brembo disc brake instead of the Simplex drum brake.

The most noticeable updates were to the MotoMeter instruments, now with black faces with green numerals, the tachometer and the quartz clock now electric. In 1978, the first of several series of special editions was released, with 200 Motorsport coming off production lines, available with matching white Krauser saddlebags and some with dark blue seat upholstery.

↑ The Motorsport special edition R100RS was built in limited numbers during 1978. *BMW Group Archives*

R100S, R100/7, R80/7, and R60/7

Replacing the R75/7 was the slightly larger R80/7, and this would become one of the more popular standard models. A lower-compression 50-horsepower version was also produced, but not sold in the United States. As the R60/7 was proving unpopular, only a small number were built toward the end of 1977, as 1978 models.

Most 1978 /7 chassis updates were also shared with the R100RS, including the new instruments. While the first 1978 R100S had wire-spoked wheels, R100RS alloy wheels with a Brembo rear disc brake soon replaced them. The R100/7, R80/7, and R60/7 continued with the spoked wheels and a rear drum brake. All US R100/7s, R80/7s, and R60/7s included a single front disc brake, while European R100/7s and R80/7s featured a second front disc. On European /7s, the cast-alloy wheels and rear disc brake (of the R100RS and R100S) were also an option this year.

For the United States, in addition to the R100RS Motorsport Special Edition, R100S Sport and Touring versions were offered, the R100S Touring with higher handlebars and no fairing. A third special edition was the R100/7 Special, in red or black with the alloy wheels and a rear drum brake; a R80/7 Avus Special Edition also was available.

1978 **R100S** *(DIFFERING FROM 1977)*	
Rear wheel	**2.75 B18**
Rear brake	**260mm Brembo disc**
Engine & frame numbers	**6065001–6068753 (04/1977–07/1978)** **6162501–6163870 USA (07/1977–07/1978)**
Numbers produced	**752 (1977), 3,003 (1978), 963 (USA 1977), 407 (USA 1978)**
Color	**Red Smoke Metallic**

1978 R100/7 *(DIFFERING FROM 1977)*

Engine & frame numbers	**6045001–6047995 (04/1977–08/1978)** **6145001–6148196 USA (07/1977–07/1978)**
Numbers produced	**898 (1977), 2,185 (1978), 2,565 (USA 1977),** **631 (USA 1978)**
Colors	**Red Metallic, Black (R100/7 Special), Havana Gold (US only)**

1978 R80/7 *(DIFFERING FROM THE R100/7 AND R75/7)*

Bore	**84.4mm**
Displacement	**798cc**
Power	**55 horsepower at 7,250 rpm** **(or 50 horsepower at 7,000 rpm)**
Compression ratio	**9.2:1 (or 8.2:1)**
Carburetion	**2 x Bing 64/32/201–202**
Engine & frame numbers	**6025001–6028787 (04/1977–07/1978)** **6200001–6201985 R80/7N (08/1977–07/1978)** **6122501–6124909 USA (04/1977–07/1978)**
Numbers produced	**2,323 (1977), 3,658 (1978), 1,813 (USA 1977),** **596 (USA 1978)**
Colors	**Gloss Black (Avus), Havana Gold (US only)**

1978 R60/7 *(DIFFERING FROM 1977)*

Engine & frame numbers	**6007001–6011412 (07/1977–01/1978)** **6101001–6101158 USA (08/1977–11/1977)**
Numbers produced	**3,035 (1977), 1,391 (1978), 158 (USA 1977)**
Color	**Black only**

↑ For 1978 the R80/7 replaced the R75/7. These retained wire-spoke wheels with a rear drum brake. US versions like this only had a single-front disc brake. *Ian Falloon*

1979

R100RT, R100RS, R100S, R100T, R100/7, R80/7, R65, and R45

In the wake of the serious sales slump, BMW replaced virtually the entire motorcycle division management team. Dr. Eberhard Sarfert took over as general manager, and the boxer lineup was considerably expanded and revised for 1979, the engine including numerous updates to the camshaft drive, ignition, and driveshaft. All 1,000cc models had the higher output "S" engine, with 40mm carbs.

As BMW had been left without a small-capacity entry-level model since the end of 1973, the company introduced the new series R45 and R65 and increased the 1,000cc twin range to five models. The R100T filled a void, as a touring machine between the sporting R100S and basic R100/7, while supplanting the R100RS, with the highest price and most equipment, was the full-touring R100RT. As it was aimed at the fickle US market, the R100RT began life precariously, but ultimately established a successful formula, lasting through 1996. With 24,415 motorcycles manufactured during 1979, production was the lowest since 1974.

↑ One of the color options for the 1979 R100RT was Metallic Brown and silver, with gold hue wheels. Some in this color combination had a white seat. *Ian Falloon*

↓ New for 1979 was the R100RT tourer. Identified by the large fairing, with built-in air vents, this provided exceptional touring comfort, but the R100RT was considerably overpriced. *Ian Falloon*

R100RT

Based on the R100RS and designed to compete against the Harley-Davidson FLH-80 Classic, the lavishly equipped R100RT came standard with an aerodynamically developed fairing and excellent detachable Krauser-built saddlebags. The boxer engine was shared with the R100RS (without the 1979 model oil cooler), as was the basic chassis.

Both the R100RT and R100RS received new crankcases, not shared with other /7s, but all /7s included a new crankshaft with riveted counterweight material to the inner surfaces of the crank webs instead of tungsten plugs. All /7s also received a new camshaft drive with a single-row chain, including a spring-loaded hydraulically damped tensioner. One of the main updates was to the ignition. Although retaining a Bosch contact breaker system, a rotary trigger was separately enclosed in a housing within the timing chain cover, resulting in more stable ignition timing. Another effective modification was to the driveshaft, this now incorporating a torsional hydraulic damper. The transmission case also received external vertical cross ribbing for additional strength and heat dissipation.

The R100RT's wind tunnel–designed fairing included an adjustable screen, automotive-style adjustable air vents, and two large lockable storage compartments. As it was considerably lighter than comparable full-dress tourers, the R100RT provided superior on-the-road performance with outstanding rider protection. But the list price of $6,345 made it the most expensive bike generally available and was ultimately an impediment to sales.

1979 R100RT *(DIFFERING FROM THE R100RS)*

Wet weight	234 kg (516 lbs.)
Engine & frame numbers	6155001–6157982 (06/1978–08/1979) 6190001–6190004 USA (04/1978–04/1978) 6195001–6196039 USA (08/1978–07/1979)
Numbers produced	1,029 (1978), 3,055 (1979), 628 (USA 1978), 656 (USA 1979)
Colors	Red, Brown/Silver

R100RS, R100S, R100T, R100/7, and R80/7

All /7s shared the engine and driveline updates of the R100RT, while the R100RS now featured a standard oil cooler. The R100S also included the R100RS engine, with the same Bing carburetors and 40mm exhaust header pipes. This year saw several transitory variations on the /7 theme, some specifically for the US market, such as the R100S Touring and R100T. R100T specification also varied between markets, and in the United States, it included standard chrome saddlebag brackets and engine protection bars, voltmeter, quartz clock, and an electrical accessory outlet. But despite the high specification and keen pricing ($1,415 less than the R100RT), the R100T only sold in very limited numbers. The older-style fork gaiters were absent from all /7s this year, and the R100T, R100/7, and R80/7 included cast-alloy wheels with the Simplex drum brake.

↑ The R100RS received a standard oil cooler for 1979, this located in a new, solid front fairing panel. As before, a sporting solo seat was an option. *BMW Group Archives*

↓ The R100RS for 1979 was available in this very attractive blue and silver color scheme. The engine also included a number of significant updates this year. *BMW Group Archives*

1979 **R100RS** *(DIFFERING FROM 1978)*

Engine & frame numbers	6095001–6097007 (06/1978–08/1979) 6185001–6185421 USA (08/1978–07/1979)
Numbers produced	704 (1978), 2,303 (1979), 209 (USA 1978), 223 (USA 1979), 628 (USA 1978 R100RST), 656 (USA 1979 R100RST)
Colors	**Blue/Silver**

↗ Dark Red Metallic was a new color for the 1979 R100S, this now receiving the high-horsepower R100RS engine. The side covers were black this year.
BMW Group Archives

↓ Effectively replacing the R100/7 for 1979, the R100T generally had standard engine protection bars and chrome saddlebag brackets.
BMW Group Archives

1979 R100S *(DIFFERING FROM 1978)*

Power	**70 horsepower at 7,250 rpm**
Carburetion	**2 x Bing 94/40/105–106**
Engine & frame numbers	**6070001–6070651 (06/1978–07/1979)** **6165001–6165104 USA (08/1978–11/1978)**
Numbers produced	**224 (1978), 645 (1979),** **102 (USA 1978), 2 (USA 1979)**
Color	**Dark Red**

← The US R100T had higher handlebars. The front brakes were now dual disc and the wheels cast alloy, with a rear drum brake. *BMW Group Archives*

1979 R100T AND R100/7 *(DIFFERING FROM 1978)*

Power	**65 horsepower at 6,600 rpm**
Carburetion	**2 x Bing 94/40/103–104**
Rear wheel	**2.50 B18**
Front brakes	**Dual disc 260mm**
Engine & frame numbers	**R100/7 6050001–6051293 (06/1978–08/1979)** **R100/7 USA 6170001–6170414 (09/1978–08/1979)** **R100T 6115001–6115002 (07/1978)** **R100T 6150001–6150173 (11/1978–07/1979)**
Numbers produced	**R100T: 58 (1978), 307 (1979); R100/7: 393 (1978), 1,553 (1979), 202 (USA 1978), 723 (USA 1979)**
Colors	**Red/Silver, Blue (R100T)**

1979 R80/7 *(DIFFERING FROM 1978)*

Rear wheel	**2.50 B18**
Front brakes	**Dual disc 260mm (single disc USA)**
Engine & frame numbers	**50 HP 6205001–6205392 (06/1978–08/1979)** **55 HP 6030001–6030973 (06/1978–08/1979)** **6126001–6126113 USA (08/1978–07/1979)**
Numbers produced	**545 (1978), 2,271 (1979), 103 (USA 1978), 73 (USA 1979)**

R65 and R45

Endeavoring to widen the boxer's appeal, BMW released two new smaller twins for 1979, theoretically paving the way for the future. But although functionally superior in some respects, the smaller boxers never really endeared themselves with buyers. They may have been narrower and more stylish, with better handling than their larger brethren, but they remained expensive, underpowered, and relatively heavy.

The engine architecture was similar to the larger boxers, but one of the advantages of the short-stroke engine was that it allowed shorter cylinders, con rods, and pistons, reducing overall engine width by 2.6 inches. New features shared with the larger twins included the single-row cam chain and ignition points in a separate housing. The smaller twins also included a lighter flywheel and smaller diameter clutch. Vibration was also a problem on the R65, particularly in top gear at around 55 miles per hour, the recently introduced speed limit in America.

↗ The R65 was fitted with dual-front disc brakes for most markets, these with a new type of ATE twin-piston caliper. *BMW Group Archives*

↓ The R65 was too expensive and didn't offer enough performance to make it popular in the United States. US versions in 1979 only had a single-front disc brake. *Ian Falloon*

Although similar to that of the larger twins, retaining the bolted-on rear subframe, the simpler frame no longer had oval section tubing or additional gussets, and the swingarm was 2 inches shorter. The front fork was a Fichtel & Sachs 36mm center-axle type, and completing the more sporting profile were a pair of 18-inch cast-alloy wheels. The single-disc front brake caliper was an improved double-piston ATE type.

Hans Muth designed the new angular 22-liter (5.8-gallon) fuel tank. It was an attractive design but didn't rival the elegance of the /7 tank. On the road, the R65 and R45's combination of a shorter wheelbase, less suspension travel, and increased cornering clearance contributed to considerably sharper handling than their larger counterparts. Unfortunately, as the weight wasn't significantly less than that of the 1,000cc twins, the performance was barely adequate, and the R45 was particularly anemic. Although the R65 was a competent and classy middleweight, its timing couldn't have been worse in the United States, as at $3,445 it was competing with 1,000cc Japanese motorcycles. You really had to desperately want a BMW twin to buy one.

1979 R65

Engine designation	**248**
Type	**Four-stroke, twin-cylinder, flat-twin**
Bore x stroke	**82x61.5mm**
Displacement	**650cc**
Power	**45 horsepower at 7,250 rpm**
Compression ratio	**9.2:1**
Valves	**Overhead-valve**
Carburetion	**2 x CV Bing 64/32/2030–2040**
Gears	**5-speed**
Ignition	**Battery and coil**
Frame	**Twin-loop tubular-steel**
Front suspension	**Telescopic fork**
Rear suspension	**Twin shock absorber**
Wheels	**1.85B18 and 2.50B18**
Tires	**3.25H18 and 4.00H18**
Brakes	**Single front disc 260mm, 200mm drum rear**
Wheelbase	**1,400mm**
Wet weight	**205 kg (452 lbs.)**
Engine & frame numbers	**6340001–6345303 (01/1978–08/1979)** **6380001–6381576 USA (07/1978–08/1979)**
Numbers produced	**11,975 (1978–1980)**
Colors	**Silver-Beige, Red, Charcoal**

1980

R100RT, R100RS, R100S, R100T, R100/7, R80/7, R65, and R45

As most developmental resources were now directed toward the new K series and dual-purpose G/S, the existing range was ostensibly unchanged for 1980. BMW still faced many problems in the United States. Not only were there further price increases, the R100RT now listing at a staggering $7,195, the venerable boxer engine was struggling to meet noise and emission requirements while maintaining a respectable power output. As the price continued to climb in America, and the performance diminished, sales stagnated to such an extent that only 3,866 1,000cc models were sold in the United States during 1979 and 1980. But despite a flat US market, sales elsewhere remained strong, and production increased to a healthy 29,260 motorcycles.

Apart from US versions, the specifications for 1980 were similar to those of 1979. BMW struggled in 1978 and 1979 in the United States as the company endeavored to sell premium motorcycles in the wake of a falling dollar. With America accounting for one third of sales, the future looked bleak, but evolutionary development of the existing boxer engine continued, notably improved lubrication to the camshaft and main bearings.

1979 R45 *(DIFFERING FROM THE R65)*

Bore	**70mm**
Displacement	**473cc**
Power	**35 horsepower at 7,250 rpm (27 horsepower at 6,500 rpm)**
Compression ratio	**8.2:1 (27 horsepower)**
Carburetion	**2 x CV Bing 64/28/203–204 (64/26/204–204 27 HP)**
Engine & frame numbers	**6300001–6304884 (01/1978–08/1979)** **R45N 6320001–6325645 (03/1978–08/1979)**
Numbers produced	**15,905 (1978–1980), including 6,430 35 horsepower**

To allow US models to run on low lead or unleaded regular gasoline, but also to enable the engine to pass more stringent EPA requirements, the compression ratio for all US bikes was lowered to 8.2:1, but for other countries, the engine specifications were unchanged. The lower compression ratio was claimed to only slightly reduce the power output, and all the US R100s received new pistons, cylinder heads, and a twin snorkel air intake with a flat air filter.

A special edition R100S Exclusive Sport, with a triple-tone blue Walter Maurer paint scheme, joined the lineup for 1980. Including chrome shock absorber springs and polished aluminum fork legs, this was greeted disapprovingly by BMW traditionalists and very short-lived. Also offered this year was a sport version of the R100T, which included a low handlebar and fairing, while the R100/7 and R80/7 were essentially unchanged, with the US R80/7 now the 50-horsepower version. Also receiving lower compression pistons, further denting performance, was the US R65. By 1980, the price had climbed to $4,230, the power was down, and it needed a revamp.

By 1980, the 1,000 and 800cc boxers in their current form had inevitably run their course. As the company had done a decade earlier, BMW needed to adapt to market demands. In addition to ever-increasing Japanese competition, BMW had to meet new noise and emission laws, and the next decade would see a change in direction, with the water-cooled K series. But this didn't signal the end of the boxer, as it would receive a reprieve in 1981, evolving into what would become one of BMW's most successful series: the G/S.

↑ **One of the less successful boxer renditions was this Walter Maurer special edition R100S. Featuring chrome shock absorber springs and polished aluminum fork legs, this version was short lived.**
BMW Group Archives

1980 **R100RT** *(DIFFERING FROM 1979)*

Power	**67 horsepower at 7,000 rpm (USA)**
Compression ratio	**8.2:1 (USA)**
Engine & frame numbers	**6157983–6169354 (09/1979–07/1980)** **6196040–6196851 (USA 09/1979–07/1980)**
Numbers produced	**2,270 (1980), 567 (USA 1980)**

1980 **R100RS** *(DIFFERING FROM 1979 AND THE 1980 US R100RT)*

Engine & frame numbers	**6097008–6100000 (09/1979–06/1980)** **6223001–6223330 (06/1980–07/1980)** **6185422–6185519 USA (11/1979–06/1980)**
Numbers produced	**2,323 (1980), 87 (USA 1980), 567 (USA 1980 R100RST)**
Color	**Silver Beige**

1980 **R100S** *(DIFFERING FROM 1979 AND THE 1980 US RT100RT)*

Engine & frame numbers	**6070652–6071951 (08/1979–07/1980)** **6165105–6165152 USA (03/1980–07/1980)**
Numbers produced	**1,082 (1980), 48 (USA 1980)**

The R100RS was virtually unchanged for 1980, but was now available in silver/beige. *BMW Group Archives*

1980 **R100T AND R100/7** *(DIFFERING FROM 1979 AND 1980)*

Engine & frame numbers	R100/7 6051294–6053635 (09/1979–07/1980)
	R100/7 USA 6170415–6171344 (11/1979–07/1980)
	R100T 6150174–6150396 (08/1979–07/1980)
Numbers produced	R100T: 31 (1980); R100/7: 1,689 (1980), 419 (USA 1980)

1980 **R80/7** *(DIFFERING FROM 1979)*

Engine & frame numbers	50-HP 6205393–6206315 (09/1979–07/1980)
	55-HP 6030974–6032475 (09/1979–07/1980)
	6126114–6126349 USA (09/1979–07/1980)
Numbers produced	2,278 (1980), 173 (USA 1980)
Colors	Brown, Dark Blue

1980 **R65** *(DIFFERING FROM 1979)*

Compression ratio	8.2:1 (US)
Carburetion	2 x CV Bing 64/32/3030–3040
Engine & frame numbers	6345304–6349336 (09/1979–07/1980)
	6381577–6382459 USA (09/1979–07/1980)

1980 **R45** *(DIFFERING FROM 1979)*

Carburetion	2 x CV Bing 64/28/301–302 (64/26/301–302 27 HP)
Engine & frame numbers	6304885–6306430 (09/1979–07/1980)
	R45N 6325646–6329475 (09/1979–07/1980)

1981–1992
GELÄNDE STRASSE
AND THE K SERIES:
OUT WITH THE OLD, IN WITH THE NEW

In October 1980, BMW North America took over US distribution from Butler & Smith, this coinciding with a significantly updated boxer lineup. In the wake of the R90S and R100RS's success, for 1981 BMW created another milestone motorcycle, the R80G/S. Like its illustrious predecessors the R80G/S (Gelände Strasse, or woods/street), rewrote the rulebook, pioneering a new category. This class, the all-purpose large-capacity leisure motorcycle, was immediately successful and initiated a path that continues to serve BMW well today. Although now dwarfed by the latest incarnations, when it was released, the R80G/S was the world's largest dual-purpose motorcycle. Aimed at the explorer or adventurer rider, for a dirt bike the R80G/S was big and heavy, but for a street motorcycle, the weight and size were moderate. Off-road performance was compromised, but as the weight was less than the pure street R100 and R80 versions, the byproduct was exceptional street capability. The R80G/S was the only boxer twin to survive the advent of the K series unscathed, and it formed the basis of the final series of air-head twins.

↖ **As it was intended for dual-purpose use, the R80G/S had a 21-inch front wheel and long travel suspension.** *BMW Group Archives*

← **Laszio Peres in the 1978 German off-road championship on a prototype GS80.** *BMW Group Archives*

1981

R80G/S, R100RS, R100RT, R100CS, R100, R65, and R45

Continual refinement of the 1,000cc boxer engine resulted in its quintessential development this year. Within the factory walls, the death knell may have already sounded for the large capacity boxer twin, but this saw the culmination of a development of the classic design, resulting in an increase in production to 33,120. While not immediately popular in the United States, the R80G/S was considerably successful in Europe. Apart from police versions, the R80G/S was now the only 800cc model generally available, and the smaller R65 and R45 also received a makeover this year.

R80G/S

The impetus for the R80G/S came from BMW's increasing success in off-road racing with modified boxer twins. This began back in 1970, with Herbert Schek winning the over 500cc German off-road championship three times in succession between 1970 and 1972 on a modified R75/5. Schek also won gold medals in the 1971 and 1973 ISDT events, but generally the BMW's struggled against the lighter Maico two-strokes.

The introduction of an over 750cc class in 1978 encouraged an official return to off-road racing, and BMW produced the GS80. On this specialized 872cc competition model, Richard Schalber won the 1979 German off-road championship. In 1980, Werner Schütz had even better results, winning the German championship, and Rolf Witthöft captured the European championship.

While the factory team was proving the capability of the boxer twin in off-road competition, work was also progressing on a production dual-purpose model. When new management members were appointed in the beginning of 1979, they sanctioned the development of two new models. One was the K series, intended to replace the R100, while the other was an enduro boxer, designed to supplement the existing range. With limited developmental time available, the enduro intentionally drew on existing designs. Rüdiger Gutsche headed the project, and as Gutsche was an ISDT veteran on his own special R75/5-based enduro, this undoubtedly sped the development. Only 21 months after the project got the go-ahead, the R80G/S was officially presented and sold more than 6,000 in its first year of production.

Unlike the 1,000cc models, there was only one specification R80G/S engine. US and European versions used essentially the same engine as the earlier R80/7, but with a lower compression ratio, Galnikal cylinders, 10-pound lighter clutch and flywheel, Bosch electronic ignition, and a plastic airbox with flat air filter. The R80G/S included a kick-start as standard, although electric start was an option (standard in the United States) and featured a new pressure die-cast final drive housing.

The R80G/S frame was similar to that of the R65, without an additional strengthening tube in the backbone. The bolted-on rear subframe was new, as was the special single-sided swingarm, or Monolever. Also incorporating the driveshaft, the Monolever was claimed to provide 50 percent greater torsional rigidity than the normal double-sided type. The 36mm front fork was similar in internal design to that of the R65, but was a leading-axle type with provision for dual-disc brakes.

↑ The R80G/S pioneered the Monolever swingarm and single rear shock absorber. More rigid and 4 pounds lighter, this soon found its way to the rest of the BMW motorcycle range. *BMW Group Archives*

→ The R80G/S had very basic instrumentation. *BMW Group Archives*

1981 R80G/S

Engine designation	**247**
Type	**Four-stroke, twin-cylinder, flat-twin**
Bore x stroke	**84.4x70.6mm**
Displacement	**797.5cc**
Power	**50 horsepower at 6,500 rpm**
Compression ratio	**8.2:1**
Valves	**Overhead-valve**
Carburetion	**2 x CV Bing 64/32/305–306 (321–322 US)**
Gears	**5-speed**
Ignition	**Bosch electronic**
Frame	**Twin-loop tubular steel**
Front suspension	**Telescopic fork**
Rear suspension	**Monolever swingarm**
Wheels	**1.85B21 and 2.15B18**
Tires	**3.00x21 and 4.00x18**
Brakes	**Single disc 260mm and Simplex drum 200mm**
Wheelbase	**1,465mm (57.7 inches)**
Wet weight	**186 kg (410 lbs.); electric start 192 kg (423 lbs.)**
Engine & frame numbers	**6250001–6255161 (05/1980–08/1981)** **6362001–6362750 USA (06/1980–08/1981)**
Numbers produced	**21,864 (1980–1987)**
Color	**White**

↑ The R80G/S engine pioneered significant updates that would soon be featured across the range. These included Nikasil cylinders, electronic ignition, and a lighter flywheel to improve clutch action.
BMW Group Archives

→ The R100RT received a pair of self-leveling Nivomat rear shock absorbers for 1981. *BMW Group Archives*

↓ Although the engine included a number of significant updates, the R100RT's fairing and general style was unchanged. *BMW Group Archives*

R100RT, R100RS, R100CS, and R100

A rationalization of the lineup coincided with the introduction of the improved A10 engine for 1981. The R100RT and R100RS continued much as before, and the R100S evolved into the R100CS, with the R100 the only basic model in the range. As before, all US examples had the lower 8.2:1 compression ratio.

Engine updates included strengthened crankcases, modified oil passages, a deeper sump, and lighter Galnikal cylinders. Experience with the smaller R65 had shown the benefits of a lighter clutch and flywheel, especially in combination with the driveshaft shock absorber, and this was included on the A10 engine. Completing the updates was a new black plastic airbox with flat paper filter and a stronger pressure die-cast final drive housing similar to that of the monoshock R80G/S. All R100s received an updated electrical system, including a more powerful Bosch 280 Watt alternator, a more powerful Bosch starter motor, and Bosch electronic ignition.

Although the cast aluminum snowflake wheels looked similar to before, the front wheel on all R100s was now a wider 2.15Bx19-inch one. Unlike the R100S with its rear disc brake, the R100CS shared a narrower rear wheel with a rear drum brake with the R100, and some R100CSs also featured the earlier narrower rim wire-spoked wheels. New brakes also distinguished all R100s for 1981, including twin-piston Brembo front brake calipers with a handlebar-mounted Magura master cylinder. The front fork received new springs and dampers, and the R100RT this year included a pair of self-leveling Nivomat rear suspension units. Optional for other R100s, although they suffered from seal failure, these were extremely effective and were the most advanced suspension available for a touring motorcycle in 1981. A special edition R100RS this year was the John Player, released to celebrate the success of the racing 6 series JPS cars.

1981 R100RT (DIFFERING FROM 1980)

Power	70 horsepower at 7,000 rpm
Carburetion	2 x Bing 94/40/111–112 (113–114 US)
Ignition	Bosch electronic
Front wheel	2.50Bx19
Front brakes	2x Brembo twin-piston calipers
Wet weight	234 kg (516 lbs.)
Engine & frame numbers	6230001–6232899 (08/1980–08/1981) 6240001–6241232 USA (06/1980–08/1981)
Numbers produced	1,140 (1980), 2,910 (1981), 729 (USA 1980), 1,292 (USA 1981)
Color	Green

↖ As with all 1981 1,000cc boxer twins, the R100RS received an improved front braking system, with twin Brembo brake calipers. *BMW Group Archives*

↙ A distinctive feature of post-1980 boxer twins was the plastic airbox. All R100CSs had a rear drum brake. *BMW Group Archives*

↓ Continuing the R90S style, some R100CSs had wire-spoked wheels for 1981. *BMW Group Archives*

1981 R100RS *(DIFFERING FROM 1980 AND THE 1981 R100RT)*

Engine & frame numbers	6075001–6078595 (06/1980–08/1981) 6225001–6225628 USA (09/1980–08/1981)
Numbers produced	1,073 (1980), 3,907 (1981), 256 (USA 1980), 860 (USA 1981)
Colors	Graphite, Red, Silver, Black and Gold (JPS)

1981 R100CS *(DIFFERING FROM THE 1980 R100S AND 1981 R100RT)*

Power	66.6 horsepower at 7,000 rpm
Rear wheel	2.50Bx18
Rear brake	200mm drum
Engine & frame numbers	6135001–6136503 (06/1980–08/1981) 6188001–6188162 USA (09/1980–05/1981)
Numbers produced	516 (1980), 1,530 (1981), 126 (USA 1980), 38 (USA 1981)
Color	Black

R65 and R45

For 1981, the R65 and R45 incorporated many of the R100's improvements: the engine (designated A20), a lighter clutch, Nikasil cylinders, flat air filter, and an electronic ignition system. The engine included a larger oil pan and an additional crossover pipe in the exhaust to broaden the powerband. To redress the R65's lack of power, the R65 received larger (40mm and 36mm) valves, and US versions retained the lower (8.2:1) compression ratio. The driveshaft received additional cushioning and a lighter pressure die-cast final drive housing.

Apart from revised steering geometry, and a stronger 10mm longer swingarm, the general chassis layout was unchanged. A new, lower seat improved comfort, and for the United States a dual-disc front end was now standard on the R65. All these improvements contributed to the R65 becoming an extremely competent middleweight, but compared to the latest Japanese offerings, it was still expensive and underpowered.

↑ The basic R100 was a very competent motorcycle. The wheels were cast aluminum, but still with a rear drum brake. *BMW Group Archives*

↘ The R65 was updated for 1981. The engine was more powerful and the seat redesigned. *BMW Group Archives*

1981 **R65** *(DIFFERING FROM 1980)*

Power	**50 horsepower at 7,250 rpm**
Carburetion	**2 x CV Bing 64/32/307–308**
Ignition	**Bosch electronic**
Brakes	**Twin front disc (US)**
Engine & frame numbers	**6310001–6315471 (06/1980–08/1981)** **6385001–6386264 USA (06/1980–08/1981)**
Numbers produced	**16,859 (08/1980–09/1985)**
Colors	**Blue, Black, Turquoise**

1981 **R45** *(DIFFERING FROM 1980 AND THE R65)*

Engine & frame numbers	**27HP 6260001–6262890 (06/1980–08/1981)** **35HP 6270001–6271535 (08/1980–08/1981)**
Numbers produced	**11,343 (08/1980–07/1985), including 5,540 35 HP**

1982

R80G/S, R100RS, R100RT, R100CS, R100, R65LS, R65, and R45

With most developmental resources going into the forthcoming K series, there were few updates to the existing boxer twins for 1982. New this year was the controversial R65LS, and the R80 continued for official and police use. In the United States, price remained an impediment and overall sales were down to 30,398 for 1982.

R80G/S and R100s

R80G/S updates were minimal. An electric start was now standard and the rear wheel rim was wider. A blue version with a black seat was also available this year. R100s received a new frame and centerstand, and the gearbox included revised helical input gears and fifth gear. While it still continued in Europe, the R100CS was dropped from the US lineup for 1982 (and 1983), although a few trickled in through 1984. Two versions of the R100 replaced the R100CS: the R100 Touring and Sport. The Sport came standard with the CS sport fairing and narrow handlebar, while the Touring was fitted with standard saddlebags.

↑ Released for 1982, the R100 Touring included standard saddlebags. *BMW Group Archives*

1982 **R80G/S** *(DIFFERING FROM 1981)*

Rear wheel	2.50B18
Engine & frame numbers	6255162–6257665 (09/1981–08/1982) 6362751–6362785 USA (10/1981–08/1982)
Color	Blue

1982 **R100RT** *(DIFFERING FROM 1981)*

Engine & frame numbers	6232900–6236060 (09/1981–08/1982) 6241233–6242332 USA (09/1981–08/1982)
Numbers produced	2,512 (1982), 549 (USA 1982)

1982 **R100RS** *(DIFFERING FROM 1981)*

Engine & frame numbers	6078596–6392801 (09/1981–08/1982) 6225629–6226208 USA (09/1981–08/1982)
Numbers produced	3,748 (1982), 215 (USA 1982)
Colors	Metallic white, Black (RSR)

1982 **R100CS** *(DIFFERING FROM 1981)*

Engine & frame numbers	6136504–6138122 (09/1981–08/1982) 6188163–6188166 USA (08/1981–06/1982)
Numbers produced	1,276 (1982), 4 (USA 1982)

1982 **R100** *(DIFFERING FROM 1981)*

Engine & frame numbers	6037529–6040000 (09/1981–06/1982) 6175594–6176210 USA (09/1981–06/1982)
Numbers produced	2,394 (1982), 598 (USA 1982)

→ Another Hans Muth creation was the R65LS, but its rather extreme style wasn't a success. *BMW Group Archives*

R65LS, R65, and R45

In an effort to provide a more sporting image, Hans Muth created the radical R65LS. Underneath the rather extreme styling was a stock R65, but the R65LS incorporated some unique features. While combining the instrument nacelle and headlight, the fork-mounted spoiler was claimed to reduce front-end lift by 30 percent. Complementing this nosepiece was a new seat, with molded passenger grab rails and increased storage capacity. Sporting features extended to the fiberglass front mudguard and lower handlebars, while the R65LS's wheels were designed to provide the elasticity of wire-spoked wheels with the rigidity of cast wheels. The styling was accentuated in black, including the handlebars and flat black plasma-sprayed exhaust system. This may have looked racy, but it was poorly finished and not particularly durable. The ostentatious style extended to garish colors, and this radical makeover did little to endear the R65LS to BMW traditionalists. For many it was ugly, and as the performance was identical to the R65, the R65LS found few friends.

1982 R65LS *(DIFFERING FROM THE R65)*

Front wheel	**2.15B18**
Brakes	**Twin front disc 260mm, 220mm drum rear**
Wet weight	**207 kg (456 lbs.)**
Engine & frame numbers	**6350001–6353756 (03/1981–08/1982)** **6370001–6371146 USA (07/1981–08/1982)**
Numbers produced	**6,389 (1981–1985)**
Colors	**Silver, Red**

1982 R65 *(DIFFERING FROM 1981)*

Engine & frame numbers	**6315472–6320000 (09/1981–08/1982)** **6386265–6386974 USA (09/1981–08/1982)**

1982 R45 *(DIFFERING FROM 1981)*

Engine & frame numbers	**27HP 6262891–6264939 (09/1981–08/1982)** **35HP 6271536–6273393 (09/1981–08/1982)**

1983

With the K series release delayed another year, two new 800cc versions joined the existing flat-twin lineup: the R80ST and budget R80RT. This still wasn't enough to boost sales in a cost-sensitive US market, with production declining to 28,053.

R80ST

Joining the R80G/S was a pure street version, the R80ST. Sharing the R80G/S engine and Monolever chassis, the R80ST included a few more street accouterments. The front fork was similar to the R65 and the wire-spoked front wheel a 19-inch, while the lower seat, street tires, and light weight added to the street cred. Instrumentation also included a tachometer, but the chrome-plated high-level exhaust system looked incongruous. Although on paper the R80ST seemed to have all the qualifications for the perfect street motorcycle, the reality was that it was a parts bin special. The performance was only moderate for the daunting price of $4,190.

1983 R80ST (DIFFERING FROM THE R80G/S)	
Front wheel	**1.85B19**
Tires	**100/90H19 and 120/90H18**
Wheelbase	**1,446mm (56.8 inches)**
Wet weight	**198 kg (437 lbs.)**
Engine & frame numbers	**6054001–6058260 (04/1982–08/1983)** **6207001–6207753 USA (10/1982–08/1983)**
Numbers produced	**5,963 (1982–1984), including 980 in USA**
Colors	**Red, Silver-Gray**

↑ In 1983 BMW released the R80ST, a street version of the successful R80G/S, but unfortunately it promised more than it delivered. *Ian Falloon*

PARIS-DAKAR SUCCESS

In 1981, BMW entered three machines in the Paris-Dakar race, billed as the toughest rally in the world. Prepared by HPN Motorradtechnik, a small tuning firm in southern Bavaria, these had strengthened chassis and long-range fuel tanks. Hubert Auriol rode to an easy victory, repeating this in 1983 on a 980cc 70-horsepower version. Three-time World Motocross Champion Gaston Rahier joined the team for the 1984 event, winning ahead of Auriol, repeating this in 1985. Following the death of rally promoter Thierry Sabine during the 1986 rally, BMW disbanded its official works team. However, HPN continued to develop Paris-Dakar machines for privateers, and a 1,000cc HPN R80G/S was available in limited quantities for privateers in 1987.

↑ Hubert Auriol won the Paris-Dakar rally in 1981 and 1983. In 1984 he was second on the R100GS. *BMW Group Archives*

← Auriol and Gaston Rahier celebrating Rahier's victory in the 1984 Paris-Dakar Rally. *BMW Group Archives*

R80RT

R100RT sales never achieved expectations, particularly in United States, and in an attempt to address this, a cheaper R80RT joined the R100RT for 1983. An amalgam of the R80G/S engine with the R100 twin shock chassis and R100RT fairing, the R80RT offered a similar touring experience for only $5,490. Missing many of the R100RT's luxury touring accruements, the R80RT provided excellent value as long as ultimate performance wasn't a consideration. But the large frontal area of the touring RT fairing taxed the mildly tuned engine to the limit, and acceleration and top speed were leisurely.

Unlike the 1,000cc models, there was only one specification R80RT engine, all versions featuring the R80G/S and R80ST engine. Shared with the R100RT was the touring fairing that still included an adjustable windshield but lacked a voltmeter and clock. Luggage was nonstandard, but available as an option, while the brakes and wheels were shared with the R100 rather than the R100RT, with a narrower rear rim and drum brake. The rear suspension was also the standard R100 Boge twin shock absorbers, with the Nivomat an option.

1983 **R80RT** (DIFFERING FROM THE R80G/S AND R100RT)	
Carburetion	**2 x CV Bing 64/32/323–324 (US)**
Rear wheel	**2.50B18**
Rear brake	**200mm drum**
Wet weight	**234 kg (516 lbs.)**
Engine & frame numbers	**6420001–6424026 (06/1982–08/1983)** **6172001–6173121 USA (08/1982–07/1983)**
Numbers produced	**1638 (1982), 632 (USA 1982),** **2539 (1983), 967 (USA 1983)**
Colors	**Blue, Red**

R100RT, R100RS, R100CS, R100, R80G/S, R65LS, R65, and R45

Only minor updates were included on the rest of the 1983 lineup. R100s incorporated further gearbox modifications, including an improved gear selector cam plate, with deeper detents to eliminate false neutrals. And proving there was still life left in the venerable R100 boxer, Stuart Beatson won "the Battle of the Twins" racing series, finishing on the podium in all 11 races. What was more impressive was that Beatson covered 6,000 miles commuting to each race meeting on his R100CS.

1983 **R100RT** (DIFFERING FROM 1982)	
Engine & frame numbers	**6236061–6237429 (09/1982–08/1983)** **6242333–6243216 USA (09/1982–08/1983)**
Numbers produced	**909 (1983), 1,284 (USA 1983)**
Color	**Silver**

1983 **R100RS** (DIFFERING FROM 1982)	
Engine & frame numbers	**6392802–6395561 (09/1982–08/1983)** **6226209–6226731 USA (09/1982–08/1983)**
Numbers produced	**2,263 (1983), 772 (USA 1983)**
Color	**Alaska Blue**

← The basic R100 continued for 1983, and in the United States was the R100 Touring. *BMW Group Archives*

1983 R100CS *(DIFFERING FROM 1982)*

Engine & frame numbers	**6138123–6138797 (09/1982–08/1983)** **6188167–6188171 USA (08/1982–08/1983)**
Numbers produced	**493 (1983), 3 (USA 1983)**

1983 R100 *(DIFFERING FROM 1982)*

Engine & frame numbers	**6400001–6401588 (06/1982–08/1983)** **6176211–6176735 USA (07/1982–08/1983)**
Numbers produced	**594 (1983), 673 (USA 1983)**

1983 R80G/S *(DIFFERING FROM 1982)*

Engine & frame numbers	**6257666–6259654 (09/1982–08/1983)** **6362786–6362858 USA (09/1982–05/1983)**

1983 R65LS *(DIFFERING FROM 1982)*

Engine & frame numbers	**6353757–6354224 (09/1982–08/1983)** **6371147–6371357 USA (09/1982–08/1983)**

1983 R65 *(DIFFERING FROM 1982)*

Engine & frame numbers	**6410001–6412113 (08/1982–08/1983)** **6386975–6387434 USA (09/1982–08/1983)**
Color	**Silver**

1983 R45 *(DIFFERING FROM 1982)*

Engine & frame numbers	**27HP 6264940–6265356 (09/1982–08/1983)** **35HP 6273394–6274615 (09/1982–08/1983)**

↑ Initially the new K series was available as the faired K100RS (left) and basic K100 (right). *BMW Group Press*

↓ The K100 double-overhead camshaft horizontal liquid-cooled fuel-injected flat-four engine owed much to automotive technology and represented a huge departure from tradition for BMW motorcycles. *BMW Group Press*

1984

K100RT, K100RS, K100, R100RT, R100RS, R100CS, R100, R80G/S, R80G/S Paris-Dakar, R80ST, R80RT, R65LS, R65, and R45

Even when the groundbreaking R100RS was released in 1976, it was evident that the venerable air-cooled boxer engine couldn't sustain BMW forever. At 980cc and 70 horsepower, the boxer was at the limit of performance and reliability, but already the market demanded more power. By the end of the 1970s, four cylinders were considered the optimum layout for higher horsepower with acceptable reliability, but BMW wanted a different solution to the ubiquitous air-cooled transverse four. As Honda's Gold Wing had taken BMW's preferred flat-four layout, BMW went for a longitudinal four-cylinder engine, with horizontal cylinders, patented as the Compact Drive System. Development concentrated on a pair of engines: a 1,000cc four and 750cc triple.

Despite a six-week metal workers' strike, production of motorcycles rose to 34,001 during 1984, and to accommodate this increase in production, new manufacturing machinery and robots were installed at the Spandau works in Berlin.

K100, K100RS, and K100RT

When BMW embarked on the K series project, it was a huge step to take, the elegant simplicity of two air-cooled cylinders with pushrod-operated overhead valves and twin carburetors making way for a liquid-cooled overhead camshaft three and four, with electronic fuel injection. Almost dimensionally cubical, the K100's horizontal engine layout provided a low center of gravity, with exceptional access to the valve gear and crankshaft. As ultimate horsepower wasn't a consideration, only two valves per cylinder (34mm and 30mm) were set at a shallow included angle of 38 degrees, with twin overhead camshafts driven by a single roller chain.

To quell the inherent vibration of an inline four-cylinder engine, and the characteristic BMW sideways pitch, the output shaft was positioned underneath the crankshaft, meshing directly and rotating in the opposite direction. The dry clutch fed directly from the rear of this secondary shaft, rather than the crankshaft as in the boxer twins, and completing the engine specification was Bosch electronic fuel injection and liquid cooling. The compact drive system also included a Monolever swingarm pivoting on the gearbox housing rather than the tubular-steel space frame, with the engine and drivetrain as a stressed member. The 41.4mm center-axle front fork was considerably more substantial than on the boxer twins, and at the rear was a single gas-filled Boge shock absorber.

When the K100 was released during 1983, there were initially two models: the basic K100 and the faired K100RS. On the K100RS, the frame-mounted fairing continued the form of the R100RS, but wind tunnel testing resulted in a smaller structure, incorporating the mirrors with turn signals, and an adjustable aerofoil to deflect air over the rider's helmet, and increasing the top speed to 137 miles per hour. During 1984, a full-touring K100RT joined the K series lineup. With the fundamental engine and chassis of the K100, this came with higher handlebars and a larger fairing than the K100RS. Although the largest ever BMW motorcycle, compared to full-dress touring motorcycles from Japan, the K100RT was svelte.

Although still not mainstream motorcycles, the K100 and K100RS were immediately successful. The K100RS was arguably the finest sport touring motorcycle available at the time. It received an enthusiastic reception and was voted motorcycle of the year in five European countries.

1984 K100

Type	Four-stroke, horizontal inline four-cylinder, liquid-cooled
Bore x stroke	67x70mm
Displacement	987cc
Power	90 horsepower at 8,000 rpm
Compression ratio	10.2:1
Valves	Double-overhead camshaft
Carburetion	Bosch LE-Jetronic
Gears	5-speed
Ignition	Electronic Bosch VZ-51 L
Frame	Tubular space frame with the engine as a stressed member
Front suspension	Telescopic fork
Rear suspension	Monolever swingarm
Wheels	2.50x18 and 2.75x17
Tires	100/90V18 and 130/90V17
Brakes	Dual front 285mm disc and single 285mm rear disc
Wheelbase	1,516mm (59.7 inches)
Wet weight	239 kg (527 lbs.)
Engine & frame numbers	(Engine numbers no longer matching for all K series) 0000001–0006879 (05/1982–08/1984) 0030001–0031105 USA (03/1984–10/1984)
Numbers produced	12,871 (1983–1990)
Colors	Red, Silver

↑ Joining the K100 and K100RS during 1984 was the touring K100RT. *BMW Group Press*

1984 K100RS *(DIFFERING FROM THE K100)*

Wet weight	249 kg (549 lbs.)
Engine & frame numbers	0010001–0020000 (05/1983–09/1984) 0040001–0041170 USA (04/1984–09/1984)
Numbers produced	34,804 (1983–1993)
Colors	Silver, Blue

1984 K100RT *(DIFFERING FROM THE K100RS)*

Wet weight	253 kg (558 lbs.)
Frame numbers	0020001–0022786 (10/1983–08/1984) 0050001–0050631 USA (04/1984–08/1984)
Numbers produced	22,335 (1984–1989)
Colors	Red, Gray

→ Several series of R100RS final editions were built during 1984. This numbered Series 500 with matching panniers was available outside the United States. The fairing came with a small numbered plaque on the side, and the seat was thicker, with different upholstery. *Ian Falloon*

R100RT, R100RS, R100CS, R100, R80RT, R80G/S, R80G/S Paris-Dakar, R80ST, R65LS, R65, and R45

Responding to the success in the Paris-Dakar rallies of 1981, 1983, and 1984, a special Paris-Dakar version of the R80 G/S became available during 1984. While the engine and chassis were unchanged, setting the Paris-Dakar apart was an 8.3-gallon gas tank complete with Paris-Dakar rally winner Gaston Rahier's signature. This allowed for 300 miles between fuel stops. The R80G/S had a new remote reservoir gas-charged rear shock absorber and was voted West Germany's enduro of the year for the fourth year in a row.

Although the K100 was envisaged as a replacement for the 247 series, the R100 continued for one more year in its traditional twin-shock form. As BMW intended to retain the boxer only in smaller capacities, to celebrate the end of the 247, several final editions were produced during 1984. These included the R100CS Motorsport and R100RS final editions in separate series for Europe and the United States. A numbered R100RS series 500 was available outside the United States, while the 250 US R100 final editions were white, with thin red, orange, and blue pinstripes, and included a "Last Edition" plaque on the side covers. For the United States, there was also a small run of limited-edition R100CSs and R100RTs, and California received a specific version with slightly different pinstripes. These final series were intended to be the end of the line for the 247 series, but pressure from enthusiasts saw the R100 resurrected only two years later in Monolever form. This year also saw the end of the R80ST, a model that never really succeeded.

1984 R100RT *(DIFFERING FROM 1983)*

Engine & frame numbers	6237430–6237516 (09/1983–10/1984) 6243217–6244165 USA (09/1983–09/1984)
Numbers produced	45 (1984), 291 (USA 1984)

1984 R100RS *(DIFFERING FROM 1983)*

Engine & frame numbers	6395562–6396033 (09/1983–11/1984) 6226732–6337337 USA (09/1983–10/1984)
Numbers produced	42 (1984), 284 (USA 1984)

1984 R100CS *(DIFFERING FROM 1983)*

Engine & frame numbers	6138798–6138864 (09/1983–10/1984) 6188172–6188174 USA (04/1984–09/1984)
Numbers produced	49 (1984), 3 (USA 1984)
Color	Dark Blue (Motorsport)

← A Paris-Dakar version of the R80 G/S was available for 1984, the larger gas tank adorned with Paris-Dakar rally winner Gaston Rahier's signature. *BMW Group Press*

1984 **R100** *(DIFFERING FROM 1983)*

Engine & frame numbers	6401589–6401795 (09/1983–10/1984) 6176736–6177382 USA (09/1983–09/1984)
Numbers produced	193 (1984), 237 (USA 1984)

1984 **R100RT** *(DIFFERING FROM 1983)*

Engine & frame numbers	6424027–6425163 (06/1983–11/1984) 6173122–6186230 USA (09/1983–12/1984)
Numbers produced	986 (1984), 553 (USA 1984)

1984 **R80GS, PARIS-DAKAR** *(DIFFERING FROM 1983)*

Carburetion	2 x CV Bing 64/32/349–350 (351–352 US)
Wet weight	205 kg (451 lbs.)
Engine & frame numbers	6259655–6282801 (09/1983–08/1984) 6362859–6363056 USA (09/1983–07/1984)

1984 **R80ST** *(DIFFERING FROM 1983 AND THE R80G/S)*

Engine & frame numbers	6058261–6058984 (10/1983–10/1984) 6207754–6207980 USA (09/1983–10/1984)

1984 **R65LS** *(DIFFERING FROM 1983)*

Engine & frame numbers	6354225–6354496 (09/1983–08/1984) 6371358–6371669 USA (09/1983–08/1984)

1984 **R65** *(DIFFERING FROM 1983)*

Engine & frame numbers	6412114–6412907 (09/1983–08/1984) 6387435–6387985 USA (09/1983–08/1984)

1984 **R45** *(DIFFERING FROM 1983)*

Engine & frame numbers	27HP 6265357–6265842 (09/1983–08/1984) 35HP 6274616–6274994 (09/1983–08/1984)

↑ All K series, including this K100RT, received a solid rear disc for 1985, but were otherwise very similar.
Ian Falloon

1985

K100RT, K100RS, K100, R80G/S, R80G/S Paris-Dakar, R80RT, R80, R65LS, R65, and R45

Although the new generation water-cooled K series replaced the 1,000cc twins for 1985, the flat-twin remained in the lineup in the existing 450, 650, and 800cc guises, with two additional R80s this year. Motorcycle production continued to increase, with 37,104 machines built. This year, 1985, would be the peak production year of the decade.

K100, K100RS, and K100RT

The K100 received a few updates for 1985. To reduce vibration, the front three gearbox-mounting points were changed from rubber-bushed to solid mount, and the footpeg mounts were shortened and solidly mounted. This was intended to shift the resonant points to make the vibration tolerable. Also this year a solid rear disc brake rotor was added, and the K100RS included a redesigned windshield and air deflectors to flow more over the engine instead of the rider's legs.

1985 **K100** *(DIFFERING FROM 1984)*

Engine & frame numbers	0006880–0008853 (09/1984–08/1985)
	0031106–0031518 USA (11/1984–11/1985)
Color	**Blue**

1985 **K100RS** *(DIFFERING FROM 1984)*

Engine & frame numbers	0080001–0086896 (09/1984–08/1985)
	0041171–0042854 USA (09/1984–08/1985)
Color	**Red**

1985 **K100RT** *(DIFFERING FROM 1984)*

| Engine & frame numbers | 0022787–0030000 (09/1984–09/1985) |
| | 0050632–0053502 USA (09/1984–08/1985) |

R80 and R80RT (Monoshock)

While the K100 represented a radical departure for BMW, the new R80 harked back to the roots initiated with the R32. This revamped twin was the antithesis of most mid-1980s motorcycles, and instead of emphasizing engine performance through increased complexity without any consideration to weight saving, the new boxer twin reiterated the traditional formula. Simplicity, agility, and lightness were placed ahead of ultimate size and horsepower. Looking remarkably similar to the pre-1984 twins, the new R80 offered improved brakes and handling, but was no match in performance to the earlier R100.

All 800cc engines now included updates aimed at reducing noise, with silicon-rubber plugs fitted between the cooling fins and a quieter rocker arm assembly. US versions retained the SAS secondary air injection system. The new 800s also featured a more efficient exhaust system, with a large welded pre-muffler interconnecting the left and right exhaust pipes before the twin mufflers. Also new was a lighter and more substantial K series final drive assembly.

A combination of R80ST and K series components comprised the chassis of the revamped boxer. The frame was shared with the R80ST, with a Monolever swingarm, while the wheels brakes and suspension had more in common with the K series. Front suspension was by a stouter center-axle 38.5mm fork. With a single gas-charged Boge shock absorber at the rear, this mounted on the rear-axle housing (like the K series) rather than on the swingarm. The front and rear cast-alloy 18-inch wheels were also K series derived and accommodated tubeless tires. The R80RT specification was also upgraded slightly, the fairing now incorporating a clock and voltmeter.

↑ All boxer twins after 1985 were based on this 800cc version. *BMW Group Press*

↓ While the Monolever R80RT looked similar to its predecessor, the front fork was stronger and the 18-inch wheels were similar to those on the K series. *Ian Falloon*

1985 R80, R80RT *(DIFFERING FROM 1984)*

Carburetion	Bing V64/32/353–354 (357–358 US)
Rear suspension	Monolever swingarm
Wheels	MTH 2.50x18 front and rear
Tires	90/90x18 and 120/90x18
Front brakes	Single disc 285mm (Twin disc US 1985 only)
Wheelbase	1,447mm (57 inches)
Wet weight	210 kg (462 lbs.)
Engine & frame numbers	(Engine numbers no longer matching for Monoshock twins) 6440001–6443233 (03/1984–07/1985), R80 6480001–6480542 USA (07/1984–08/1985), R80
Numbers produced	13,815 (1984–1995), 497 (1984), 10 (USA 1984), 3,637 (1985), 794 (USA 1985)
Colors	Red, Blue

1985 R80RT *(DIFFERING FROM THE R80)*

Wet weight	227 kg (499 lbs.)
Frame numbers	6470001–6472957 (07/1984–08/1985) 6490001–6490812 USA (07/1984–07/1985)
Numbers produced	22,069 (1984–1995), 446 (1984), 10 (USA 1984), 3,638 (1985), 1,224 (USA 1985)
Colors	Red, Blue

R80G/S, R80G/S Paris-Dakar, R65LS, R65, and R45

In 1984, a team of factory R80G/Ss was triumphant in the Baja 1000 off-road race, winning the Class 30 competition, and this led to renewed interest in the R80G/S in America for 1985. Ostensibly unchanged since 1981, the R80G/S now incorporated the engine developments of the rejuvenated R80 series. For 1985, final drive assembly and casting was also new, while the unpopular smaller R65 and R45 series were now in their final year, due to be replaced for 1986.

1985 **R80G/S, PARIS DAKAR** (DIFFERING FROM THE R80 AND 1984 R80G/S)	
Engine & frame numbers	6282802–6285641 (09/1984–08/1985)
	6363056–6363167 USA (09/1984–07/1985)

1985 **R80LS** (DIFFERING FROM 1984)	
Engine & frame numbers	6354497–6354679 (09/1984–03/1985)
	6371670–6371713 USA (09/1984–02/1985)

1985 **R65** (DIFFERING FROM 1984)	
Engine & frame numbers	6412908–6413588 (09/1984–07/1985)
	6387986–6388255 USA (09/1984–04/1985)

1985 **R45** (DIFFERING FROM 1984)	
Engine & frame numbers	27HP 6265843–6266303 (09/1984–07/1985)
	35HP 6274995–6275540 (09/1984–07/1985)

1986

K100RT, K100RS, K100, K75S, K75C, R80G/S, R80G/S Paris-Dakar, R80RT, R80, and R65

BMW's commitment to the K series continued for 1986 with the release of two three-cylinder K75 models, and the company rationalized the boxer range by introducing an R80-based R65 twin. The reliance on the K series was a dubious move. While technologically and functionally superior, the K100 lacked the boxer's charisma. The K100 chassis was more rigid and the handling superior, but the four-cylinder engine vibrated disconcertingly and the design was deemed too far outside the mainstream to woo a new clientele. Motorcycle production gradually began to decline over the next few years, and only 32,054 motorcycles were built during 1986.

K75S and K75C

The K75 was a result of the building-brick principle and designed to complement the larger K100. The engine was basically three K100 cylinders, but in a slightly higher state of tune. The three-cylinder crankpins were spaced at 120 degrees, and the chassis was very similar to the K100's. Both initial K75s had a fairing, the K75S with a more discreet frame-mounted sporting fairing than the K100RS and the basic K75C a handlebar-mounted cockpit fairing. For 1986, US K75Ss also received a lower cowling that was fitted closely underneath the engine, and after this won a prize in the Stuttgart Design Centre, it later appeared on all versions. With less

↑ Arguably the best-handling BMW motorcycle yet, price and performance handicapped the K75S.
BMW Group Press

weight and a smoother engine, the K75 offered a surprising, and cheaper, alternative to the K100, while the K75S was arguably the best-handling BMW motorcycle yet.

But one of the problems faced by the K75C and K75S was at that time the 750cc category was targeted by the Japanese with lightweight high-performance racing-style motorcycles. While the K75 appealed to conservative buyers, it was still more expensive, heavier, and less powerful than the Japanese 750s. However, like the K100, the K75 managed to garner a following independent of this fashion-led Japanese incursion, and 20,000 examples were produced in the first three years.

↑ The K75's three-cylinder Compact-Drive arrangement was very similar to the K100's. *BMW Group Press*

↓ The K75C included a small handlebar fairing and offered an attractive alternative to the larger K100. *Ian Falloon*

1986 K75S AND K75C

Type	Four-stroke, horizontal inline three-cylinder, liquid-cooled
Bore x stroke	67x70mm
Displacement	740cc
Power	75 horsepower at 8,500 rpm
Compression ratio	11.0:1
Valves	Double-overhead camshaft
Carburetion	Bosch LE-Jetronic
Gears	5-speed
Frame	Tubular space frame with the engine as a stressed member
Front suspension	Telescopic fork
Rear suspension	Monolever swingarm
Wheels	2.50x18 and 2.75x17 (2.75x18 K75C)
Tires	100/90V18 and 130/90V17 (120/90x18 K75C)
Brakes	Dual front 285mm disc and single 285mm rear disc (200mm drum K75C)
Wheelbase	1,516mm (59.7 inches)
Wet weight	235 kg (518 lbs.), K75S; 228 kg (503 lbs.), K75C
Frame numbers	0110001–0115417 (06/1985–08/1986), K75C 0130001–0131562 USA (07/1985–08/1986), K75C 0100001–0103964 (10/1985–08/1986), K75S 0150001–0150452 USA (05/1986–08/1986), K75S
Numbers produced	18,649 K75S (1985–1995); 9,566 K75C (1985–1990)
Colors	Red (K75S), Silver (K75C)

K100, K100RS, and K100RT

Updates to the K100 included a redesigned seat, inherited from the K75, with grab handles incorporated in the rear of the seat base and fuel tank knee guards.

1986 K100 *(DIFFERING FROM 1985)*

Engine & frame numbers	0008854–0009656 (09/1985–08/1986) 0031519–0031522 USA (02/1986–10/1986)

1986 K100RS *(DIFFERING FROM 1985)*

Engine & frame numbers	0086897–0141769 (09/1985–08/1986) 0042855–0043435 USA (09/1985–08/1986)

1986 K100RT *(DIFFERING FROM 1985)*

Engine & frame numbers	0090001–0093533 (09/1985–08/1986) 0053503–054375 USA (09/1985–10/1986)

R65, R80, R80RT, R80G/S, and R80G/S Paris-Dakar

For 1986, the R80-based R65 replaced the earlier twin-shock smaller twins (R45, R65, and R65LS). Except for a smaller capacity engine, the R65 was identical to the R80, and for 1986 all R80s and R80RTs had a standard single front disc brake. The R80G/S and Paris-Dakar were unchanged this year.

↑ For 1986 the R80-based R65 replaced the earlier twin-shock smaller twins and was identical to the R80, except for a smaller capacity engine.
BMW Group Archives

1986 R65 *(DIFFERING FROM THE R80)*

Bore x stroke	82x61.5mm
Displacement	649cc
Power	48 horsepower at 7,250 rpm (27 horsepower at 5,500 rpm)
Compression ratio	8.7:1 (8.4:1)
Carburetion	Bing V64/32/359–360 (V64/26/317–318)
Wet weight	205 kg (452 lbs.)
Frame numbers	6073001–6074774 (06/1985–08/1986)
Numbers produced	8,260 (1985–1993)
Colors	Polaris, Red, Blue

1986 R80G/S, PARIS DAKAR *(DIFFERING FROM 1985)*

Engine & frame numbers	6285642–6289356 (09/1985–08/1986) 6363168–6363350 USA (09/1985–04/1986)

1986 R80 *(DIFFERING FROM 1985)*

Engine & frame numbers	6443234–6445826 (09/1985–08/1986) 6480543–6480906 USA (09/1985–08/1986)
Numbers produced	2,180 (1986), 313 (USA 1986)

1986 R80RT *(DIFFERING FROM 1985)*

Engine & frame numbers	6472958–6475887 (09/1985–08/1986) 6490813–6491267 USA (09/1985–08/1986)
Numbers produced	2,382 (1986), 215 (USA 1986)

1987 K SERIES

K100LT, K100RT, K100RS, K100, K75S, K75C, K75, K75T, R100RS, R80G/S, R80G/S Paris-Dakar, R80RT, R80, and R65

Despite some market resistance, the K series range expanded to include the full-dress touring K100LT and a basic K75 (and US K75T). Also released this year was an R80-based 1,000cc boxer twin, the R100RS, initially available as a special edition. But while the basic range was largely unchanged, the big news was the option of ABS (antilock braking) on the K100 faired models. Unfortunately, this announcement was a little premature as BMW decided to undertake more testing and it would be nearly a year and a half before ABS appeared on production models. Sales, however, continued to decline, with motorcycle production of 27,508, a return to 1970s levels.

K100LT, K100RT, K100RS, K100, K75S, K75C, K75, and K75T

Aimed at the US market, the opulent K100LT included Nivomat self-leveling rear suspension, a factory-installed alarm system, and a radio installation kit built into the fairing (with speakers, antenna, and wiring, and an optional stereo). With the K100LT, BMW finally began to make some inroads into the full-dress tourer market, and its success would eventually lead to larger, and even more luxurious, versions. By 1987, sales of the standard K100 were considerably slower than the sporting and touring variants and it was deleted from the US range. The K100RS was available in a Pearl White Motorsport version and received the K75Ss stiffer suspension, while the K100RT continued unchanged, as did the K75S and K75C. New this year in the triple range was a basic unfaired K75, this offered in the United States as the K75T with a windshield and stepped seat. Two special editions of the K75S were also available this year, one black with a beige seat and the other silver with a black seat.

↑ Rear suspension on the K100LT was by a Nivomat self-leveling unit and optional was BMW's first version of ABS. *BMW Group Press*

↓ With the K100LT, BMW successfully entered the full dress tourer market. *BMW Group Press*

1987 **K100LT** *(DIFFERING FROM 1986 AND THE K100RT)*	
Wet weight	**263 kg (580 lbs.)**
Frame numbers	**0170001–0172466 (07/1986–08/1987)** **0180001–0180524 USA (07/1986–05/1987)**
Numbers produced	**14,899 (1986–1991)**
Colors	**Bahama Bronze**

1987 **K100** *(DIFFERING FROM 1986)*

Frame numbers	0009657–0010000 (09/1986–12/1987)
Colors	**Red, Black, Silver, Gray, Blue**

1987 **K100RS** *(DIFFERING FROM 1986)*

Frame numbers	**0141770–0146025 (09/1986–08/1987)** **0043436–0044139 USA (09/1986–08/1987)**
Colors	**Red, Black, Silver, Gray, Blue**

1987 **K100RT** *(DIFFERING FROM 1986)*

Frame numbers	**0093534–0095988 (09/1986–08/1987)** **0054376–0054497 USA (03/1987–08/1987)**
Colors	**Red, Black, Silver, Gray, Blue**

1987 **K75S, K75C, K75T, K75** *(DIFFERING FROM 1986)*

Frame numbers	**0115418–0116037 (09/1986–08/1987), K75C** **0131563–0132294 USA (09/1986–09/1987), K75C & K75T** **0103965–0106038 (09/1986–08/1987), K75S** **0150453–0151658 USA (09/1986–08/1987), K75S** **0120001–0120187 (07/1985–06/1987), K75**
Colors	**Red, Black, Silver, Gray**

↑ The K100LT's high level of equipment included color-coordinated panniers and trunk and an optional radio and stereo system. *BMW Group Press*

1987 BOXERS

R100RS

As a prelude to a full reintroduction in 1988, BMW released a special edition of the classic R100RS. Initially intended as a batch of 1,000, production continued through 1987 beyond this number. Now based on the R80 and required to meet impending emission regulations, the new 1,000cc engine was designed to provide more relaxed power over a wider rev range. Inside the cylinder head were the smaller R80 42mm inlet valves, while the exhausts went up to the 40mm of the 1984 980cc engine. Although on-the-road performance was similar at legal speeds, the new R100RS was noticeably down on top speed compared to its predecessor. Underneath the RS bodywork was the R80 Monolever chassis, with a 38.5mm front fork, single Boge rear shock absorber, 18-inch wheels, twin front disc brakes, and a rear drum brake. Although many enthusiasts bemoaned the lower performance of the new R100RS, the special edition's success ensured the viability of its full reintroduction in 1988.

1987 **R100RS** *(DIFFERING FROM THE R80)*

Bore	**94**
Displacement	**980cc**
Power	**60 horsepower at 6,500 rpm**
Compression ratio	**8.4:1**
Carburetion	**Bing V64/32/363–364**
Front brake	**Twin disc 285mm**
Wheelbase	**1,447mm (57 inches)**
Wet weight	**229 kg (505 lbs.)**
Frame numbers	**0160001–0161642 (07/1986–07/1987)**
Numbers produced	**435 (1986), 1,206 (1987)**
Colors	**White, Red**

R80G/S, R80G/S Paris-Dakar, R80RT, R80, and R65

Now in its final year, the R80G/S was offered as before, but no longer available in the United States. Updates included new colors and a reshaped seat, while all other boxer twins were unchanged.

↑ During 1987 BMW released a special edition of the classic R100RS. Initially intended as a batch of 1,000, underneath the RS bodywork was an R80 Monolever chassis and it proved so successful it went into regular production for 1988.
BMW Group Archives

1987 R80G/S, PARIS DAKAR *(DIFFERING FROM 1986)*

Engine & frame numbers	6289357–6292522 (09/1986–07/1987)
Colors	Red/White, Blue/White (R80G/S)

1987 R80RT *(DIFFERING FROM 1986)*

Frame numbers	6475888–6478620 (09/1986–08/1987) 6491268–6491452 USA (09/1986–04/1987)
Numbers produced	3,274 (1987), 3 (USA 1987)

1987 R80 *(DIFFERING FROM 1986)*

Frame numbers	6445827–6447156 (09/1986–08/1987) 6480907–6481120 USA (09/1986–07/1987)
Numbers produced	1,155 (1987), 3 (USA 1987)
Color	Silver

1987 R65 *(DIFFERING FROM 1986)*

Frame numbers	6074775–6118807 (09/1986–08/1987)
Color	Silver

↑ For 1988, the base K75 was offered with an optional lower seat and higher handlebars. *Ian Falloon*

1988

K100LT, K100RT, K100RS, K100, K75S, K75C, K75, R100RT, R100RS, R100GS, R80GS, R80RT, R80, and R65

After seven years, with sales of more than 20,000, a second-generation Paralever R100GS and R80GS replaced the Monolever R80G/S. Designed to eliminate shaft drive reaction under load, the double joint swingarm Paralever was an extremely successful design and would eventually filter to other models. The boxer lineup was also rejuvenated with the addition of a new R100RT alongside the R100RS, while the K series continued with minor updates. Production continued to decline, to only 23,817 this year.

1988 K Series

K100LT, K100RT, K100RS, K100, K75S, K75C, and K75

For 1988, the K100LT included more equipment, now with three accessory power outlets, a larger rear top box capable of holding two crash helmets, and an additional high-mounted instrument panel with a coolant temperature gauge. Both this and the K100RS Special were finally offered with optional ABS. The basic K100 and K75 also received a facelift, both with a lower seat and higher handlebars, while the K75S was updated with more aggressive styling. The K75T was dropped from the US lineup this year, with the K100RT discontinued and the K100LT effectively replacing it.

1988 K100 *(DIFFERING FROM 1987)*

Weight	240 kg (529 lbs.)
Frame numbers	6308101–6308863 (10/1987–08/1988)

1988 K100RS *(DIFFERING FROM 1987)*

Frame numbers	0146026–0148133 (09/1987–08/1988) 0044140–0044500 USA (04/1988–08/1988)
Colors	Red, Black, Silver

← The K75S received an aggressive new graphics treatment for 1988, with midnight black engine cases, drivetrain, and wheels. The sport handlebar was also wider this year. *BMW Group Press*

1988 K100RT *(DIFFERING FROM 1987)*

Frame numbers	0095989–0097829 (09/1987–07/1989) 0054498–0054503 USA (05/1988–05/1988)
Colors	**Red, Gray, Blue**

1988 K100LT *(DIFFERING FROM 1987)*

Frame numbers	0172467–0174567 (09/1987–08/1988) 0180525–0180968 USA (10/1987–08/1988)

1988 K75S, K75C, K75 *(DIFFERING FROM 1987)*

Frame numbers	0116038–0116424 (09/1987–06/1988), K75C 0132295–0133142 USA (02/1988–03/1990), K75C 0106039–0107022 (09/1987–08/1988), K75S 0151659–0151946 USA (09/1987–08/1988), K75S 0120188–0120457 (09/1987–08/1988), K75
Colors	**Red, Black (K75C); Red, Silver, Black (K75S)**

→ The dual-purpose R100GS was the most successful of all the resurrected boxers. In addition to the Paralever rear suspension, the front fork was stronger and the new cross spoke wheels allowed for tubeless tires. *BMW Group Press*

↓ BMW's engineering breakthrough for 1988 was Paralever rear suspension. This reduced the shaft-drive torque reaction by routing the torque forward from the shaft to the frame. *BMW Group Press*

1988 Boxers

R100RT, R100RS, R100GS, R80GS, R80RT, R80, and R65

Joining the R100RS for 1988 was the R100RT, this effectively replacing the R80RT, but it was the new R100GS that stole the limelight. With a similar R80-based 60-horsepower engine to the R100RS and R100RT, the European R100GS had 40mm carburetors and a slightly higher compression ratio. US versions retained the R100RS 32mm carbs, with a slight reduction in power. In addition to the Paralever rear suspension, the front fork was a beefier, longer travel, 40mm Marzocchi with aluminum triple clamps, the frame reinforced with oval tubes, while the new cross-spoke wheels allowed for tubeless tires. Although the Paralever R80GS replaced the R80G/S, the earlier version lived on as the unpopular R65GS, specifically for the German market. The R100RS and R100RT may have appealed to the traditionalist, but it was the dual-purpose R100GS that sustained the life of the "air-head" twin until the advent of the R259 oil-head boxer. Price was always an issue for increased sales in the United States, and the R100RS and R100RT sold for a heady $7,750, although this was still significantly less than the K100RS and K100RT.

1988 R100GS, R80GS *(DIFFERING FROM THE R100RS AND R80G/S)*	
Power	58 horsepower at 6,500 rpm (US R100GS)
Compression ratio	8.5:1 (R100GS)
Carburetion	2 x CV Bing 94/40/123–124 (64/32/351–352), R100GS United States and R80GS
Rear suspension	Paralever swingarm
Wheels	1.85x21 MT and 2.50x17 MT
Tires	90/90x21 and 130/80x17
Brakes	Single disc 285mm and Simplex drum 200mm
Wheelbase	1,513mm (60 inches)
Wet weight	210g (463 lbs.)
Frame numbers	6276001–6331661 (12/1986–08/1988), R100GS 6152001–6152908 USA (01/1987–08/1988), R100GS 6245001–6248020 (01/1987–08/1988), R80GS
Numbers produced	34,007 (1987–1996), R100GS; 11,373 (1987–1996), R80GS
Colors	White, Black, R100GS; Red, R80GS

1988 **R100RS** *(DIFFERING FROM 1987)*

Frame numbers	0161643–0162358 (08/1987–08/1988) 6247001–6247548 USA (08/1987–03/1988)
Numbers produced	407 (1987), 860 (1988), 402 (USA 1987), 395 (USA 1988)

1988 **R100RT** *(DIFFERING FROM THE R100RS)*

Wet weight	**234 kg (516 lbs.)**
Frame numbers	6016001–6017067 (07/1987–08/1988) 6292601–6293172 USA (07/1987–08/1988)
Numbers produced	689 (1987), 570 (1988), 402 (USA 1987), 395 (USA 1988)
Color	**Bermuda Blue**

1988 **R80RT** *(DIFFERING FROM 1987)*

Frame numbers	6478621–6483775 (09/1987–08/1988)
Numbers produced	1,914 (1988)

1988 **R80** *(DIFFERING FROM 1987)*

Frame numbers	6447157–6448032 (09/1987–08/1988)
Numbers produced	761 (1988)

1988 **R65** *(DIFFERING FROM 1987)*

Frame numbers	6118808–6131123 (09/1987–10/1988)

↑ New for 1988 was the R100RT, very similar to the R80RT and effectively replacing it. *BMW Group Press*

↓ The R100RS went into regular production during 1988, also in white in addition to red. As it was based on the R80, the performance wasn't comparable to earlier R100RSs. *BMW Group Archives*

↑ The K1 was BMW's most radical design yet and initially proved very popular.
Ian Falloon

1989

K1, K100LT, K100RS, K100, K75S, K75, R100RT, R100RS, R100GS, R80GS, R80RT, and R80

By the end of the 1980s, the Japanese had rewritten the rule for Superbikes. High-horsepower engines, excellent handling, and full-coverage fairings were standard fare, but all the Japanese offerings featured chain drive. BMW decided the time was ripe for a shaft drive Superbike, one considerably more performance focused than the K100. When it was first displayed at the Cologne Show at the end of 1988, the K1 shattered the perception of BMW producing only conservatively styled touring and sport-touring motorcycles. As the K1 represented a significant K series update, the existing model range was unchanged, but production increased slightly, to 25,761 this year.

K1, K100LT, K100RS, K100, K75S, and K75

Emulating the classic R90S, BMW's first Superbike, the K1 continued an aerodynamic path initiated with Ernst Henne's record-breaking 500 Kompressor of 1937. Following the release of the K100, stylist Karl-Heinz Abe created a sports machine called "Racer," for the Time Motion exhibition of 1984. This model inspired the prototype K1, but underneath the dramatic styling was a significantly developed K100. BMW not only wanted the K1 stand out, but the company hoped its performance would be class leading.

As BMW was committed to the voluntary 100-horsepower limit for motorcycles sold in Germany, aerodynamic efficiency played a large part in the design. With its large enveloping two-piece front fender almost mating to the leading edges of the seven-piece fairing through to its large tail with miniature pannier, the drag coefficient was a remarkable 0.34 with the rider prone, by far the lowest of any production motorcycle. The K1 engine was also considerably updated, the cylinder head incorporating four valves per cylinder, with two 26.5mm inlet and two 23mm exhaust valves, the twin overhead camshafts acting directly on bucket tappets without adjustment shims. The engine also included higher compression pistons, lighter con rods and crankshaft, and a digital Motronic injection and ignition system similar to that on BMW cars.

← At the heart of the K1 was a new four-valve cylinder head, but as the horsepower was voluntarily restricted, the K1's potential was never unleashed. *BMW Group Press*

↓ With its all-enveloping bodywork, the K1 was the most aerodynamic motorcycle available in 1989. *BMW Group Press*

The chassis was also considerably updated, with a stronger frame, Paralever swingarm, wider Italian FPS wheels, a 41.7mm Marzocchi front fork, and a state-of-the-art Brembo braking system. ABS was standard in the United States. Although designed for high-speed use, even once the lurid colors and unique styling were accepted, the K1 failed in its quest to offer leading Superbike performance. Certainly the lighter steering and tighter suspension and brakes placed the K1 closer to the Japanese Superbikes, but the weight was intimidating and the engine not powerful enough. While the Paralever provided a vast improvement in overcoming the inherent deficiencies of shaft drive for a sporting motorcycle, it still couldn't disguise the considerable unsprung weight. The K1 may have been the best handling and strongest performing BMW motorcycle to date, but the true nature of the machine was lost in a confusion of purpose. The first deliveries of the K1 were in May 1989, and it was initially popular, winning many industry awards. Yet after producing nearly 4,000 during 1989, sales stalled and the K1 never recovered.

After six years in production, the K100 range was stabilized and largely unchanged. A lower seat was an option for the K100RS, and a special version with a black engine and drivetrain in white and blue was also available. The K100LT received an optional higher windshield, and the K75C was discontinued.

1989 **K1** *(DIFFERING FROM THE K100)*

Power	**100 horsepower at 8,000 rpm**
Compression ratio	**11:1**
Valve control	**Double-overhead camshaft, four valves per cylinder**
Carburetion	**Bosch Motronic**
Rear suspension	**Paralever swingarm**
Wheels	**3.50x17 and 4.50x18**
Tires	**120/70VR17 and 160/60VR18**
Brakes	**Dual front 305mm discs with 4-piston calipers and single 285mm rear disc**
Wheelbase	**1,560mm (61.4 inches)**
Wet weight	**258 kg (569 lbs.)**
Frame numbers	**6372001–6373211 (08/1988–08/1989)** **6365001–6365002 USA (01/1989–07/1989)**
Numbers produced	**6,921 (1988–1993)**
Colors	**Red, Blue**

1989 **K100** *(DIFFERING FROM 1988)*

Frame numbers	**6308864–6309422 (09/1988–07/1990)**

1989 **K100RS** *(DIFFERING FROM 1988)*

Frame numbers	**0148134–0149896 (09/1988–10/1989)**
	0044501–0044906 USA (09/1988–07/1989)
Colors	**White/Blue**

1989 **K100LT** *(DIFFERING FROM 1988)*

Frame numbers	**0174568–0177580 (09/1988–08/1989)**
	0180969–0181119 USA (03/1989–07/1989)
Colors	**Blue, Green**

1989 **K75S, K75** *(DIFFERING FROM 1988)*

Frame numbers	**0107023–0108502 (09/1988–08/1989), K75S**
	0151947–0151948 USA (09/1988–06/1989), K75S
	0120458–0120615 (09/1988–12/1988), K75
Colors	**Blue (K75S), Silver (K75)**

↑ The K100RS continued for 1989 with new colors and a blacked-out engine and drivetrain. *BMW Group Press*

↓ The R80GS continued as a popular alternative to the R100GS in Europe. *BMW Group Press*

1989 Boxers

R100RT, R100RS, R100GS, R80GS, R80RT, and R80

All boxers continued unchanged for 1989, and while the 48-horsepower R65 was discontinued, the R65 remained in production in 27-horsepower guise for Germany until 1993.

1989 **R100GS, R80GS** *(DIFFERING FROM 1988)*

Frame numbers	**6331662–6334434 (09/1988–08/1989), R100GS**
	6152909–6153378 USA (09/1988–09/1989), R100GS
	6248021–6250000 (09/1988–02/1990), R80GS

1989 **R100RS** *(DIFFERING FROM 1988)*

Frame numbers	**0162359–0163754 (09/1988–08/1989)**
	6247549–6247599 USA (09/1988–09/1989)
Numbers produced	**890 (1989), 1 (USA 1989)**

1989 **R100RT** *(DIFFERING FROM 1988)*

Frame numbers	**60170681–6018000 (09/1988–09/1989)**
	6293173–6293399 USA (09/1988–09/1989)
Numbers produced	**1,181 (1989), 2 (USA 1989)**
Colors	**Gray, Red**

↑ A four-valve K100RS was available for 1990, now with a Paralever swingarm and the K1's improved wheels and brakes. *BMW Group Press*

1989 **R80RT** *(DIFFERING FROM 1988)*

Frame numbers	6483776–6486351 (09/1988–08/1989)
Numbers produced	**2,107 (1989)**

1989 **R80** *(DIFFERING FROM 1988)*

Frame numbers	6448033–6448814 (09/1988–08/1989)
Numbers produced	**797 (1989)**

1990

K1, K100RS, K100LT, K75RT, K75S, K75, R100RT, R100RS, R100GS, R100GS Paris-Dakar, R80GS, R80RT, and R80

It was inevitable the four-valve engine and Paralever chassis would eventually find its way to the K100, and this happened less than a year after the K1's release on the revamped K100RS. Although BMW no longer competed in the Paris-Dakar rally, the introduction of the celebratory Paris-Dakar R100GS also wasn't unexpected. Motorcycle production increased considerably this year, to 31,589.

1990 K Series

K1, K100RS, K100LT, K75RT, K75S, and K75

Whereas the K1 struggled in its quest to be a Superbike, the new K100RS was more successful in that it made no pretensions as to its intended function. Featuring the K1's four-valve engine, reinforced chassis with Paralever swingarm, cartridge-style Marzocchi front fork, three-spoke FPS 17- and 18-inch wheels, and four-piston Brembo brakes, the new model represented a significant improvement over the previous model, virtually unchanged since 1983. Unlike the K1, the K100RS featured rubber front engine mounts to minimize vibration, and compared to the previous K100RS, it had a wider handlebar for increased leverage.

→ New for 1990 in the United States was the K75RT, with a similar fairing to that of the K100RT. *Ian Falloon*

As the four-valve K100RS shared the excellent fairing of the earlier two-valve version, it functioned similarly, and with improved power, handling, brakes, and minimal driveshaft affect, the K100RS four-valve was just the sport touring motorcycle traditional BMW enthusiasts were looking for. The K100RS provided the heart of the radical K1 in a more familiar environment, and it proved considerably more popular than the K1.

As delayed production resulted in waiting lists for the K1 during 1989, this continued unchanged, as did the K100LT, now the only K series motorcycle retaining the two-valve four-cylinder engine. The K75 received the sporting K75S suspension, along with the 17-inch rear wheel and disc brake, and new for the United States and Spain only in 1990 was the K75RT, with a similar fairing to the K100RT. The K75S now came with three-spoke K1-style alloy wheels, and ABS was now an option on all K75 models.

1990 K100RS (4-VALVE)
(DIFFERING FROM THE 1989 K100RS AND THE K1)

Wheelbase	**1,564mm (61.6 inches)**
Wet weight	**235 kg (518 lbs.)**
Frame numbers	**6405001–6410000 (03/1989–07/1990)**
Numbers produced	**12,666 (1989–1992)**
Colors	**Silver, Green**

1990 K1 (DIFFERING FROM 1989)

Wheelbase	**1,565mm (61.6 inches)**
Frame numbers	**6373212–6376918 (09/1989–08/1990)** **6365003–6365516 USA (09/1989–09/1990)**

1990 K100LT (DIFFERING FROM 1989)

Frame numbers	**0177581–0190751 (09/1989–08/1990)** **0181120–0181407 USA (09/1989–05/1990)**

1990 K75S, K75, K75RT (DIFFERING FROM 1989)

Rear wheel and tire	**2.75x17 inches and 130/90H17 (K75 & K75RT)**
Rear brake	**Single disc 285mm (K75 & K75RT)**
Wet weight	**258 kg (569 lbs.), K75RT**
Frame numbers	**108503–0110000 (09/1989–07/1990), K75S** **0151949–0152464 USA (09/1989–06/1990), K75S** **6426494–6428882 (09/1989–08/1990), K75** **6018001–6020000 (01/1989–10/1990), K75RT** **6199001–6199662 USA (09/1989–10/1990), K75RT**
Numbers produced	**21,264 (1989–1996), K75RT**
Colors	**Blue, Black, Red (K75RT)**

1990 Boxers

R100RT, R100RS, R100GS, R100GS Paris-Dakar, R80GS, R80RT, and R80

Except for the introduction of the R100GS Paris-Dakar, the existing range of boxers continued unchanged. During 1989 a Paris-Dakar kit was produced for the R80GS and R100GS, and its success encouraged the release of the R100GS Paris-Dakar. Although the largest and most expensive dirt bike available, despite its intimidating size, the Paris-Dakar became an extremely successful niche model, particularly in Europe, because there was nothing else like it available and it suited larger-framed riders.

Continuing the theme of the earlier R80G/S Paris-Dakar, the R100GS Paris-Dakar was ostensibly a cosmetic rendition of the R100GS. This centered on a huge fiberglass 35-liter (9.3-gallon) fuel tank that incorporated a lockable 5-liter storage cavity. Connected to this fuel tank was a reinforced fiberglass fairing, with an external the tubular fairing support. Specific Paris-Dakar components included a small tachometer and matching quartz clock, a larger aluminum engine sump protector, and a solo seat with a longer luggage rack.

↑ Ostensibly a cosmetic rendering of the R100GS, the Paris-Dakar included a large fuel tank connected to fiberglass fairing with an external support. The seat was a solo type and an engine sump guard denoted the Paris-Dakar's suitability for off-road use. *BMW Group Press*

1990 R100GS, R100GS PD, R80GS
(DIFFERING FROM 1989)

Wet weight	236 kg (520 lbs.), R100GS PD
Frame numbers	6334435–6461527 (09/1989–08/1990), R100GS 6153379–6153468 USA (02/1990–03/1990), R100GS 6415001–6417557 (02/1989–07/1990), R100GS PD 6134001–0047160 USA (06/1989–09/1990), R100GS PD 0046001–0047018 (02/1990–07/1990), R80GS
Numbers produced	11,914 (1989–1994), R100GS PD
Colors	White/Red (R100GS PD)

1990 R100RS *(DIFFERING FROM THE 1989)*

Frame numbers	0163755–0164009 (09/1989–08/1990)
Numbers produced	337 (1990)
Color	Silver

1989 R100RT *(DIFFERING FROM 1989)*

Frame numbers	6167001–6168000 (09/1989–06/1990) 6293400–6293579 USA (02/1990–08/1990)
Numbers produced	901 (1990), 181 (USA 1990)

1989 R80RT *(DIFFERING FROM 1989)*

Frame numbers	6486352–6488024 (09/1989–08/1990)
Numbers produced	2,287 (1990)

1989 R80 *(DIFFERING FROM 1989)*

Frame numbers	6448815–6450000 (09/1989–06/1990)
Numbers produced	1,702 (1990)

↑ To try to stem flagging sales, the K1 was offered in more subdued black for 1991. The colors were less flamboyant, but the K1 was still unpopular. *BMW Group Press*

↓ After receiving more modern three-spoke wheels in 1990, the K75S was offered in violet for 1991. *BMW Group Press*

1991

K1, K100RS, K100LT, K75RT, K75S, K75, R100RT, R100RS, R100GS, R100GS Paris-Dakar, R100, R80GS, R80RT, and R80

With no new models this year, BMW concentrated on reducing emissions on the existing range. This included a catalytic converter for the K1, K100RS, K100LT, and K75RT, with SAS (Secondary Air Injection) as an option on all boxer models. Despite a slight decrease in torque, requiring lower final drive gearing, environmentally friendly BMW buyers accepted the catalytic converter with enthusiasm and soon 41 percent of all K1 and K100RS were so equipped.

After 10 years of production and sales of more than 50,000, the GS lineup was updated for 1991, with a subtle emphasis more toward road use. New was a Paris-Dakar-style frame-mounted fairing with external tubular frame, rectangular headlight, and tilting adjustable windshield, and an adjustable Bilstein rear shock absorber.

The final two-valve K series model was the K100LT Special Limited Edition, with an engine spoiler and sports suspension. For 1991 the regular R100 made a return, but only for the US market. This was essentially an R80 with the R100RS/RT engine and only lasted for one year. March 18, 1991, also marked the production of the one-millionth BMW motorcycle, a K75RT donated to the German Red Cross, Berlin, as a first aid accident vehicle. Production at Spandau increased to 150 motorcycles a day, with 33,980 produced during 1991.

1991 K1 *(DIFFERING FROM 1990)*

Wet weight	**259 kg (571 lbs.)**
Frame numbers	**6376919–6377817 (09/1990–08/1991)** **6365517–6365606 USA (02/1991–08/1991)**
Colors	**Red, Black**

1991 K100RS (4-VALVE) *(DIFFERING FROM 1990)*

Wet weight	**259 kg (571 lbs.)**
Frame numbers	**0200001–0205173 (07/1990–08/1991)** **6493001–6493941 USA (07/1990–08/1991)**
Colors	**Blue, Red, Black**

1991 K100RS (4-VALVE) *(DIFFERING FROM 1990)*

Rear tire	**140/80V17 (Limited Edition)**
Wet weight	**283 kg (624 lbs.)**
Frame numbers	**0190752–0193272 (09/1990–10/1991)** **0181408–0181628 USA (09/1990–03/1991)**
Color	**Green (Limited Edition)**

1991 K75S, K75, K75RT *(DIFFERING FROM 1990)*

Frame numbers	**0210001–0211627 (07/1990–08/1991), K75S** **0152465–0153252 USA (09/1990–08/1991), K75S** **6428883–6430000 (09/1990–03/1991), K75** **0133501–0133801 USA (07/1990–03/1991), K75** **0220001–0223856 (10/1990–08/1991), K75RT** **6199663–6199878 USA (11/1990–08/1991), K75RT**
Color	**Violet (K75, K75S)**

Wet weight	**220 kg (485 lbs.), R100GS; 215 kg (474 lbs.), R80GS**
Frame numbers	**6461528–6465420 (09/1990–08/1991), R100GS** **0230001–0230506 USA (11/1990–08/1991), R100GS** **0065001–0066836 (08/1990–08/1991), R100GS PD** **0047161–0047287 USA (04/1991–08/1991), R100GS PD** **0033501–0036161 (04/1990–08/1991), R80GS**
Colors	**Blue/Black, Red, Black/Yellow (R80/100GS),** **Red, Black/Green (R100GS PD)**

1991 R100RS *(DIFFERING FROM 1990)*

Frame numbers	**0164010–0164292 (09/1990–08/1991)**
Colors	**Red, Blue**
Numbers produced	**393 (1991)**

1991 R100RT *(DIFFERING FROM 1990)*

Frame numbers	**6337001–6337935 (06/1990–08/1991)** **6293580–6293729 USA (11/1990–08/1991)**
Colors	**Red, Blue**

1991 R80RT *(DIFFERING FROM 1990)*

Frame numbers	**6488025–6490000 (09/1990–04/1991)**
Colors	**Red, Blue**

1991 R80 *(DIFFERING FROM 1990)*

Frame numbers	**0121001–0122608 (06/1990–08/1991)**
Colors	**Red, Blue**

1992

K1100LT, K1, K100RS, K75RT, K75S, K75, R100R, R100RT, R100RS, R100GS, R100GS Paris-Dakar, R100R, R80GS, R80RT, and R80

With the release of the new generation oil-head R259 more than a year away, BMW introduced two new models for 1992: an enlarged K1100LT and classic R100R. Both proved exceptionally popular, particularly the retro R100R, this shaming the rest of the lineup with sales of 8,041, accounting for nearly 23 percent of production. Motorcycle production continued to increase, to 35,910 this year.

K1100LT, K1, K100RS, K75RT, K75S, and K75

Powered by BMW's largest capacity engine to date, the K1100LT set a new standard for luxury touring motorcycles. The larger bore four-valve engine included lighter pistons and 6mm longer connecting rods to reduce vibration, and although outright power was unchanged, with a Bosch Motronic MA 2.2 injection system, the torque was increased significantly. The chassis specifications were similar to the K1 and four-valve K100RS, with a Paralever swingarm, dual-front discs with four-piston calipers, and three-spoke wheels (still with an 18-inch front). The rear shock absorber was a Showa unit and the fairing included an electrically adjustable windshield. While the luggage capacity was increased, the K1100LT still vibrated annoyingly, and at more than 600 pounds it was no lightweight.

There were no changes to the K100RS for 1992 except the rear shock absorber was now Showa and gained infinite rebound damping adjustment. The K75 range also received a Showa front fork this year.

↓ The four-cylinder K engine grew to 1,100cc for 1992, initially installed in the luxury touring K1100LT.
BMW Group Press

1992 K1100LT *(DIFFERING FROM THE K100LT AND K100RS)*

Bore	**70.5mm**
Displacement	**1,092cc**
Power	**100 horsepower at 7,500 rpm**
Wheels	**2.50x18 and 3.00x17**
Tires	**110/80VR18 and 140/80VR17**
Wheelbase	**1,565mm (61.6 inches)**
Wet weight	**290 kg (639 lbs.)**
Numbers produced	**22,757 (1991–1998)**
Colors	**Black, Red, Blue, Green**

1992 K1 *(DIFFERING FROM 1991)*

Frame numbers	**6377818–6378094 (09/1991–08/1992)** **6365607–6365646 USA (12/1991–01/1992)**

1992 K100RS (4-VALVE) *(DIFFERING FROM 1991)*

Frame numbers	**0205174–0206575 (09/1991–06/1992)** **6493942–6494091 USA (09/1991–01/1992)**

1992 K75S, K75, K75RT *(DIFFERING FROM 1991)*

Frame numbers	**0211628–0212787 (09/1991–08/1992), K75S** **0153253–0153873 USA (09/1991–08/1992), K75S** **0250001–0253391 (03/1991–08/1992), K75** **0133802–0134404 USA (07/1991–08/1992), K75** **0223857–0227457 (09/1991–08/1992), K75RT** **6199879–6229384 USA (09/1991–08/1992), K75RT**

↓ Combining a modern Paralever swingarm with classic looks, the retro R100R proved extremely popular. *Ian Falloon*

R100R, R100RT, R100RS, R100GS, R100GS Paris-Dakar, R80GS, R80RT, and R80

Designed as a classic-look grassroots machine to maintain interest in the boxer lineage, BMW created the successful R100R Roadster out of the R100GS. Unfortunately, while the R100R Paralever chassis was functionally superior to earlier boxer street bikes, the styling and execution was questionable. A proliferation of gaudy and cheap components detracted from the quality, as did the parts bin nature of its execution.

Other than a new exhaust system and a return to the older-style (R68 through to /6) rocker covers, the R100R engine was identical to the R100GS. European versions featured 40mm Bing carburetors, while US models retained 32mm carburetors. The chrome-plated exhaust header pipes fed into the large pre-muffler and low-mounted stainless-steel K100 muffler, and the classic look extended to older-style spark plug caps. The silver-painted frame and Paralever swingarm was also shared with the R100GS, but with Japanese Showa suspension front and rear, including at the front a nonadjustable 41mm front fork. Further emphasizing the classic retro image were cross-spoked wheels with Akront aluminum rims.

Apart from a Marzocchi front fork (as on the GS models), the R100RS, R100RT, R80RT, and R80 were unchanged this year. As a final fling, nearly 1,000 R100RS were built during 1992, with 151 coming to the United States (these final series including 30 Rennsport in traditional blue and silver, each with a numbered plaque) and a black Classic Edition 200.

The 1980s were characterized by the success of the Gelände-Strasse and the near obsession with individuality with the idiosyncratic K series. Although selling around 140,000 examples in eight years, the K series still failed to strike a chord with many traditional buyers and wasn't appealing to the newer, affluent motorcyclist appearing by the 1990s. For these buyers, a motorcycle was a lifestyle accouterment, and characterful engines such as V-twins, triples, and boxer twins were enjoying rejuvenation. BMW finally succumbed, with a new boxer dominating its next phase, while shortly afterward the return of the entry-level single cylinder opened the door to a huge new market.

↑ One of the final R100RS models was the special Classic Edition 200 model of 1992. *BMW Group Archives*

1992 R100R *(DIFFERING FROM THE R100GS)*

Wheels	**2.50x18 MTH and 2.50x17 MTH**
Tires	**110/80V18 and 140/80V17**
Wet weight	**218 g (481 lbs.)**
Frame numbers	**0240001–0247618 (03/1991–08/1992)** **0280001–0280546 USA (09/1991–08/1992)**
Numbers produced	**20,589 (1991–1996)**
Colors	**Black, Amethyst, Turquoise Green**

1992 R100GS, R100GS PD, R80GS *(DIFFERING FROM 1991)*

Frame numbers	**6465421–6467033 (09/1991–08/1992), R100GS** **0230507–0231224 USA (09/1991–08/1992), R100GS** **0066837–0068313 (09/1991–08/1992), R100GS PD** **0047288–0047653 USA (09/1991–08/1992), R100GS PD** **0036162–0038083 (09/1991–08/1992), R80GS**

1992 R100RS *(DIFFERING FROM 1991)*

Frame numbers	**0164293–0165331 (09/1991–10/1992)**
Colors	**Black, Green, Blue/Silver (Rennsport)**
Numbers produced	**954 (1992)**

1992 R80RT *(DIFFERING FROM 1991)*

Frame numbers	**0270001–0271732 (04/1991–08/1992)**
Colors	**Black**

1992 R80 *(DIFFERING FROM 1991)*

Frame numbers	**0122609–0123260 (09/1991–08/1992)**
Colors	**Black**

1993–2000
RENAISSANCE:
BOXER REVOLUTION AND NEW SINGLES

Although still committed to the K series, during 1993 BMW headed down two new paths with the introduction of the R1100RS boxer followed by the F650 single. Work on the new boxer began nearly a decade earlier, when it was envisaged the K series would rescue motorcycle sales, with the new boxer a midrange supplement. Even in those early stages, the design parameters were clear. The traditional air-cooled longitudinal boxer twin layout would be maintained, the load-bearing crankcase would contribute to the frame structure, and four valves per cylinder were considered a necessity. And while BMW was often considered a conservative company, innovative frame and suspension design was endemic in its history. While other manufacturers maintained their allegiance to the conventional telescopic front fork, BMW's engineers were determined to overcome some of the inherent deficiencies in this design. A new solution combined a telescopic fork with a longitudinal arm linking the fork bridge to the frame, and the Telelever was born.

Looking for an entry-level machine to complement the R259, BMW decided to follow a different path that harkened back in 1978 with the R45 and R65. As the smaller twins were almost as expensive to build as their larger brothers, profitability was marginal, and in the interests of developing a motorcycle as quickly as possible, BMW embarked on a joint project with Aprilia. During 1990, Aprilia released its Pegaso 650, and a year later BMW began working on its version, soon signing a three-way joint-venture contract with Aprilia and Rotax. Aprilia would assemble the new model at its plant at Noale in Northern Italy, while Austrian engine manufacturer Rotax would supply engines similar to that used in the Pegaso. Development proceeded extremely quickly, with the first production versions rolling out of Noale in September 1993. While these new projects were coming to fruition, the K series continued to grow in capacity, and the range expanded to include a car and motorcycle synthesis: the C1.

The R259 of 1993 celebrated 70 years of boxer engines. Here are four generations: the new four-valve version on the left, the two-valve from 1969 to 1996, the 1951 to 1969 boxer, and the initial R32 on the far right. *BMW Group Press*

← After sales of more than 50,000, the dynamic K1100RS replaced the K100RS for 1993. No more powerful than its four-valve predecessor, the K1100RS was also considerably heavier, blunting performance. *Ian Falloon*

1993

K1100RS, K1100LT, K1, K75RT, K75S, K75, R1100RS, R100RT, R100GS, R100GS Paris-Dakar, R100R, R80GS, R80RT, R80R, & R80

A year after the release of the K1100RT, the larger K engine appeared in the K1100RS, marking the end of the road for the 1,000cc version and the controversial K1. The release of the new-generation R1100RS boxer also signaled the inevitable demise of the venerable air-cooled pushrod boxer twin. Motorcycle production continued to increase, reaching 36,990 during 1993, although toward the end of the year, this included F650s built by Aprilia.

K1100RS, K1100LT, K1, K75RT, K75S, & K75

Replacing the K100RS, the K1100RS was the most sporting K series yet and included a reinforced K100RS chassis, Marzocchi front fork and Showa shock absorber, and an updated fairing. With the trend toward full-coverage bodywork, this featured a new lower section and engine cowl, and it incorporated the distinctive BMW kidney grille, along with side air scoops similar to those on a Ferrari Testarossa car. Although it still had its foibles, particularly in regard to weight and vibration, as a high-speed long-distance tourer, the K1100RS was still most impressive.

The K75RT now had an optional electrically adjustable windshield, but all other K series models were unchanged for 1993. By the end of the year, the K1 was dead, marking the end of the era of brave adventurousness. In the future, BMW would concentrate on more conservative solutions, no longer pushing the envelope of daring originality.

↗ With its integral fairing, the R1100RS was a superb sports touring motorcycle. *BMW Group Press*

↓ The R1100RS reinstated the boxer as BMW's premier engine layout. *BMW Group Press*

1993 **K1100RS** *(DIFFERING FROM THE K1100LT)*

Wheels	**3.50x17 and 4.50x18**
Tires	**120/70VR17 and 160/60VR18**
Wet weight	**268 kg (591 lbs.)**
Numbers produced	**12,179 (1992–1996)**
Colors	**Black, Red, Blue**

1993 **K1** *(DIFFERING FROM 1992)*

Frame numbers	**6378095–6378246 (09/1992–09/1993)**
	6365647–6365676 USA (09/1992–11/1992)

1993 **K75S, K75, K75RT** *(DIFFERING FROM 1992)*

Frame numbers	**0212788–0213435 (09/1992–08/1993), K75S**
	0153874–0154322 USA (09/1992–08/1993), K75S
	0253392–0254553 (09/1992–08/1993), K75
	0134405–0134789 USA (09/1992–08/1993), K75
	0227458–0230000 (09/1992–10/1993), K75RT
	6229385–6229611 USA (09/1992–08/1993), K75RT

R1100RS

Codenamed the R259, the release of the new boxer coincided with the 70th anniversary of the R32. The air- and oil-cooled engine was the largest displacement and most powerful boxer yet, with a hybrid valve system. This system included an intermediate shaft beneath the crankshaft and two roller chains driving a single camshaft in each cylinder head. The camshafts were below the four valves, with the 36mm and 31mm valves actuated by rockers through short pushrods. With a new Bosch digital Motronic engine management 700-watt alternator and an optional catalytic converter, the R259 was the most advanced boxer yet.

Even more innovative than the engine design was the R259's Telelever front suspension. A longitudinal track control arm transited braking forces directly into the rigid engine block, effectively providing anti-dive, with a ball bearing connecting a telescopic fork with an A-shaped control arm. A second ball bearing connected the upper fork bridge to a central mounting point on the frame. The telescopic fork only served the purpose of guiding and steering the front wheel, with a single centrally mounted spring strut attached to the longitudinal arm responsible for suspension and damping. The result was improved stability,

with minimal additional unsprung weight and changes to camber. Highly distinctive, the Telelever would characterize BMW motorcycles for the next decade, while the success of the R259 and its derivatives reestablished the boxer as BMW's foremost engine layout. The R1100RS may not have been particularly light, or classically beautiful, but it was undoubtedly the most functionally superior sport-touring motorcycle available at the time. It also upheld the BMW RS tradition and proved a worthy successor to the earlier R100RS.

↑ BMW was known for innovative front suspension and the Telelever continued that tradition. The rear suspension was by the usual Paralever, the engine forming the central structure. *BMW Group Press*

↓ The new boxer engine had four-valves per cylinder driven by a pair of high camshafts. *BMW Group Press*

1993 R1100RS

Type	**Four-stroke, flat-twin, air/oil-cooled**
Bore x stroke	**99x70.5mm**
Displacement	**1,085cc**
Power	**90 horsepower at 7,250 rpm**
Compression ratio	**10.7:1**
Valve control	**Overhead-valve, high camshaft design**
Carburetion/ignition	**Bosch Motronic MA2.2**
Gears	**5-speed**
Frame	**Tubular space frame with the engine as a stressed member**
Front suspension	**Telelever**
Rear suspension	**Paralever swingarm**
Wheels	**3.50x17 and 4.50x18**
Tires	**120/70VR17 and 160/60VR18**
Brakes	**Dual front 305mm disc and 285mm rear disc**
Wheelbase	**1,473mm (58 inches)**
Wet weight	**239 kg (527 lbs.)**
Frame numbers	**0290001–0297127 (01/1992–08/1993)** **0310001–0311163 USA (06/1992–08/1993)**
Numbers produced	**26,403 (1992–2001)**
Colors	**Red, Green, Silver**

→ New for 1993 was the R80R. Setting this and the 1993 R100R apart were inconspicuous boxer emblems on the sides of the gas tank on the turquoise green examples. This retained the silver frame and rear rack, while the R100R, in black now, had a black frame and rack. *Ian Falloon*

R100RT, R100GS, R100GS Paris-Dakar, R100R, R80GS, R80RT, R80R, and R80

With the formula of the moderately powered, light, and simple twin firmly established, updates to the R100R for 1993 were cosmetic only. A similar R80R joined it this year, in 34- and 50-horsepower versions, but this wasn't sold in the United States and only lasted until 1994. All other boxers were unchanged this year.

1993 R100R *(DIFFERING FROM 1992)*

Frame numbers	0247619–0250000 (09/1992–02/1993) 0280547–0280773 USA (09/1992–01/1993)
Color	**Turkish Green**

1993 R80R *(DIFFERING FROM THE R100R AND R80)*

Wet weight	**217 kg (478 lbs.)**
Frame numbers	**0260001–0262830 (03/1991–08/1993)**

1993 R100GS, R100GS PD, R80GS *(DIFFERING FROM 1992)*

Frame numbers	6467034–6468086 (09/1992–08/1993), R100GS 0231225–0231420 USA (09/1992–08/1993), R100GS 0068314–0070000 (09/1992–06/1993), R100GS PD 0047654–0047967 USA (09/1992–08/1993), R100GS PD 0038084–0039373 (09/1992–08/1993), R80GS
Colors	**White/Green, White/Violet (R100GS PD)**

1993 R100RT *(DIFFERING FROM 1992)*

Frame numbers	6338476–6339226 (09/1992–08/1993) 6293882–6294013 USA (09/1992–08/1993)
Color	**Turkish Green**

1993 R80RT *(DIFFERING FROM 1992)*

Frame numbers	**02717331–0272533 (09/1992–08/1993)**

1993 R80 *(DIFFERING FROM 1992)*

Frame numbers	**0123261–0123495 (09/1992–08/1993)**

1994

K1100RS, K1100LT, K75RT, K75S, K75, R1100GS, R1100RS, R100RT, R100GS, R100GS Paris-Dakar, R100R, R100R Mystic, R80GS, R80RT, R80R, R80, and F650

As was becoming customary, BMW released two new models for 1994: the R1100GS, continuing the successful GS line, and the F650, re-creating the entry-level single. BMW's first single since the R27 nearly 30 years earlier, the F650 was also the first BMW motorcycle with chain final drive. The F650 contributed to massively increased sales this year, with total production up 20 percent, to 44,435.

F650

Targeted at younger riders and beginners, the F650 was based on the Aprilia Pegaso with a Rotax engine. Several updates were incorporated, including plain bearings instead of roller and a four-valve, rather than five-valve, cylinder head. A roller chain on the left drove the double-overhead camshafts while an engine-speed gear-driven balance shaft in front of the crankshaft quelled vibration. Carburetion was by two Mikuni CV carburetors, there were two spark plugs per cylinder, and lubrication was dry sump, with the oil tank in the upper part of the frame. In a departure from usual BMW practice, the gearbox was incorporated in the crankcases.

Unlike the Aprilia Pegaso, the single-loop sheet and square-section frame was steel instead of aluminum, with the engine as a semi-stressed member. The swingarm was a twin-sided deltabox type, with a rising-rate linkage, and the suspension included a 41mm Showa telescopic front fork and Showa shock absorber. With wire-spoked wheels and Brembo brakes, the F650 was marketed as a Funduro and soon set new standards for middleweight dual-purpose machines. Its off-road capability may have been marginal, but as in the tradition of the classic R80G/S, the F650 was one of the most competent handling tarmac motorcycles available. Not surprisingly, it was an immediate success, and by July 1994, 10,000 were produced. The F650 was also successful in competition, Jutta Kleinschmidt winning the women's trophy in the 1994 Paris-Dakar Rally.

↑ Aimed at the entry-level rider, the F650 was the result of a joint project with Aprilia and Rotax. *BMW Group Press*

↓ The single-cylinder Rotax engine was similar to the Aprilia Pegaso, but had a four-valve cylinder head. Carburetion was by a pair of Mikuni carburetors. *BMW Group Press*

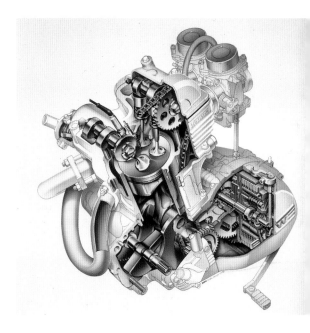

1994 **F650**	
Type	**Four-stroke, single-cylinder, liquid-cooled**
Bore x stroke	**100x83mm**
Displacement	**652cc**
Power	**48 horsepower at 6,500 rpm (34 horsepower at 5,700 rpm)**
Compression ratio	**9.7:1**
Valve control	**Double-overhead camshaft**
Carburetion	**2xMikuni 33mm CV**
Gears	**5-speed**
Frame	**Single-loop tubular-steel**
Front suspension	**Telescopic fork**
Rear suspension	**Rising rate swingarm**
Wheels	**2.50x19 and 3.00x17**
Tires	**100/90x19 and 130/80x17**
Brakes	**Single 300mm disc and 240mm rear disc**
Wheelbase	**1,480mm (58.3 inches)**
Wet weight	**191 kg (421 lbs.)**
Numbers produced	**50,990 (1993–2000)**
Colors	**Red, White**

↑ The F650 was the first BMW motorcycle with chain final drive. *BMW Group Press*

→ The R1100GS continued the established GS tradition of providing exceptional all-around performance, both on and off road. *BMW Group Press*

R1100GS and R1100RS

At a time when motorcycle sales were stagnating, the G/S steered BMW through a new, oblique path, creating its own successful niche market. And with the resurrection of the 1,000cc air-cooled boxer, the GS led the way. By 1993, and with more than 62,000 sales, Gelände Strasse was intrinsic to the BMW vocabulary, and the R1100GS appeared only a year after the release of the R1100RS. In the manner of previous GSs, the R1100GS proved exceptionally successful, immediately becoming the most popular large displacement enduro in Germany.

With the R80G/S, BMW initiated a tradition of features unique to the G/S series, and the R1100GS continued this. While sharing the engine with the R1100RS, this was detuned to provide improved enduro performance. Updates to the Telelever front suspension to make it more suitable for off-road use included increased shock absorber travel, with the handlebar separately mounted on the fork bridge and connected to the Telelever fixed tubes with two ball joints. The modified A-arm and front subframe provided an increased anti-dive ratio of 90 percent. ABS II was available as an option and could be manually deactivated so the rider could lock the wheels in loose gravel if required.

A large, 25-liter, plastic fuel tank ensured an adequate touring range, and the seat height of 860mm (33.8 inches) also guaranteed it was more suited to larger riders. Despite these impediments, beauty is always in the eye of the beholder, and the R1100GS met with astounding acclaim. And in the manner of earlier GSs, with its wide handlebar, unlimited ground clearance, and supple suspension, the R1100GS was arguably a more effective street bike than most repli-racers. Weird looks or not, the R1100GS was a hit from the outset and proved more popular than the R1100RS. Of the 80 1,100cc boxer engines produced every day at Spandau in early 1994, 60 were destined for the R1100GS.

1994 R1100GS *(DIFFERING FROM THE R1100RS)*

Power	**80 horsepower at 6,750 rpm (78 horsepower at 6,750 rpm)**
Compression ratio	**10.3:1**
Wheels	**2.50x19 and 4.00x17**
Tires	**110/80H19 and 150/70H17**
Rear brake	**276mm disc**
Wheelbase	**1,509mm (59.4 inches)**
Wet weight	**243kg (536 lbs.)**
Frame numbers	**0057001–0430361 (04/1993–08/1994)** **0380001–0381033 USA (02/1994–08/1994)**
Numbers produced	**39,842 (1993–1999)**
Colors	**Red, White, Black**

1993 R1100RS *(DIFFERING FROM 1993)*

Frame numbers	**0297128–0410771 (09/1993–08/1994)** **0311164–0311888 USA (09/1993–08/1994)**

R100 and R80 Series

For 1994 the R100R received dual-disc front brakes, all versions now had the SAS emission system standard, and a special Mystic version joined it. Designed to appeal to the connoisseur, the Mystic included special red metallic paint and a variety of chrome-plated fittings. The R100RT continued with few changes, US models including heated grips, a custom touring seat, and 22-liter rear trunk.

↑ With its distinctive metallic paint, chrome-plated components, sporting seat, and shorter license plate bracket, the R100R Mystic was a more successful rendition of the classic boxer theme. *BMW Group Press*

1994 **R100R, R80R** *(DIFFERING FROM 1993)*

Front brake	**2x285mm disc**
Frame numbers	**0165501–0167941 (02/1993–07/1994), R100R** **0280774–0280858 USA (04/1993–12/1993), R100R** **0169001–6435634 (12/1993–08/1994), Mystic** **0400001–0400145 USA (03/1994–08/1994), Mystic** **0262831–0263503 (09/1993–06/1994), R80R**
Color	**Red Mystic**

1994 **R100GS, R100GS PD, R80GS** *(DIFFERING FROM 1993)*

Frame numbers	**6468087–6468515 (09/1993–07/1994), R100GS** **0231421–0231715 USA (09/1993–09/1994), R100GS** **0340001–0340559 (06/1993–07/1994), R100GS PD** **0047968–0048136 USA (09/1993–08/1994), R100GS PD** **0039374–0039861 (09/1993–08/1994), R80GS**

1994 **R100RT** *(DIFFERING FROM 1993)*

Frame numbers	**6339227–6340000 (09/1993–11/1994)** **6294014–6294297 USA (09/1993–09/1994)**

1994 **R80RT** *(DIFFERING FROM 1993)*

Frame numbers	**0272534–0273599 (09/1993–11/1995)**

1994 **R80** *(DIFFERING FROM 1993)*

Frame numbers	**0123496–0123695 (09/1993–01/1995)**

K Series

Updates to both the K1100RS and K1100LT included several features from the new R259 boxer, notably the 700-watt alternator, Motronic MA 2.2 electronic injection and ignition system, and the option of second-generation ABS II. This year there was a 10-year K series anniversary K1100LT Special Edition with special gray paint and a numbered script. K75s also received the larger capacity alternator but were otherwise unchanged.

1994 **K75S, K75, K75RT** *(DIFFERING FROM 1993)*	
Frame numbers	0213436–0213847 (09/1993–08/1994), K75S
	0154323–0154600 USA (09/1993–09/1994), K75S
	0254554–0255511 (09/1993–08/1994), K75
	0134790–0135457 USA (09/1993–08/1994), K75
	0370001–0372028 (10/1993–08/1994), K75RT
	6229612–6229847 USA (09/1993–08/1994), K75RT

1995

K1100RS, K1100LT, K75RT, K75S, K75, R1100RS, R1100GS, R1100R, R850R, R100RT, R100GS Paris-Dakar, R100R, R100R Mystic, R80R Mystic, and F650

BMW concentrated on boxers for 1995, retiring the older air-head boxer with four farewell models and introducing two new versions with the four-valve boxer engine. After 18 months, the R259 boxer was proving outstandingly successful, and the demand for a new generation of naked bikes, such as Ducati's Monster and BMW's own R100R, prompted the release of the naked R1100R and smaller displacement R850R for 1995. The classic farewell models were only slightly cosmetically updated over their predecessors and billed as future collectors' items, while the K series included K100LT and R1100RS Special Editions. The concentration on singles and twins was proving a highly successful formula, with production of 52,653 exceeding 50,000 for the first time.

R1100R, R850R, R1100GS, and R1100RS

Continuing a long BMW tradition of mix and match, the R1100R took the milder tuned, higher torque engine of the R1100GS and placed it in the more sporting R1100RS chassis, with R1100GS front and rear subframes. Without a fairing, this was termed a "grassroots" motorcycle, and again BMW created a winner.

Either cast-alloy or wire-spoked wheels were available, and the only real disadvantage of the R was its considerable weight. This disadvantaged the lower-powered R850R even more so, and it proved so unpopular in some export markets that it was soon discontinued. Its rather hefty weight aside, the R1100R was an impressive motorcycle. If the R1100RS and R1100GS hadn't managed to convert the diehard traditionalist to the benefits of the modern boxer, the R1100R certainly did. The styling was still unusual, but the R1100R set a new standard for naked motorcycles.

Otherwise unchanged, the R1100GS received a lower and further forward front fender for 1995, and the R1100RS included the previously Germany-only ergonomics package as standard worldwide.

↑ An amalgam of R1100RS and R1100GS components, the naked R1100R was extremely popular. *BMW Group Press*

1995 **R1100R, R850R** *(DIFFERING FROM THE R1100GS)*

Bore	**87.8mm (R850R)**
Displacement	**848cc (R850R)**
Power	**70 horsepower at 7,000 rpm (R850R)**
Wheels	**3.50x17 and 4.50x18**
Tires	**120/70VR17 and 160/60VR18**
Wheelbase	**1,487mm (58.5 inches)**
Wet weight	**235 kg (518 lbs.)**
Frame numbers	***Data unavailable after 1995*** **0360001–0363665 (09/1993–03/1995)** **6378501–6379160 USA (09/1994–03/1995)**
Numbers produced	**26,073 (1993–2001), R1100R;** **11,212 (1994–1997), R850R**
Colors	**Red, Gray**

1995 **R1100RS, R1100GS** *(DIFFERING FROM 1994)*

Frame numbers	***Data unavailable after 1995*** **0410772–0412292 (09/1994–03/1995), R1100RS** **0311889–0312325 USA (09/1994–02/1995), R1100RS** **0430362–0432750 (09/1994–03/1995), R1100GS** **0381034–0381376 USA (09/1994–03/1995), R1100GS**
Colors	**Black, Blue (R1100RS)**

→ Four "Farewell Model" R100s were available for 1995. From the left are the R100RT Classic, R100R Classic, R100R Mystic, and R100GS PD Classic. *BMW Group Press*

R100 "Farewell Models"

As the new boxer lineup expanded, it was inevitable the aging two-valve R80 and R100 series would be discontinued. The four "farewell models" were the R100R Mystic, R100R Classic, R100GS PD Classic, and R100RT Classic. While the R100R Mystic was unchanged from 1994, the R100R Classic was finished in black, with black detailing. The R100GS PD Classic was also finished in black, with nostalgic features such as the earlier rounder valve covers, while the R100RT Classic was in gray and graphite.

1995 **R100R, R80R MYSTIC** *(DIFFERING FROM 1994)*	
Frame numbers	***Data unavailable after 1995*** 0167942–0169000 (09/1994–03/1995), R100R 0280859–0280889 USA (12/1994–01/1995), R100R 6435635–6437226 (09/1994–12/1995), Mystic 0400146–0400255 USA (09/1994–09/1995), Mystic 0390001–0390090 (03/1994–03/1995), R80R Mystic

1995 **R100GS** *(DIFFERING FROM 1994)*	
Frame numbers	***Data unavailable after 1995*** 0340560–0341218 (09/1994–03/1995), R100GS PD 0048137–0048251 USA (09/1994–01/1995), R100GS PD

K and F Series

After surpassing sales expectations, apart from a standard catalytic converter, the F650 continued unchanged. Now nearing the end of its production life, the three-cylinder K75 range was also as before. The K1100LT Special Edition continued, in violet with a Muscat seat this year, and a new red K1100RS Special Edition also was available.

↑ As it was nearing the end of its production cycle, this Marrakesh Red K100RS Special Edition was available for 1995 and 1996. *BMW Group Press*

1995 **K1100RS, K1100LT** *(DIFFERING FROM 1994)*	
Colors	**Graphite, Green, Violet, Red**

1995 **K75S, K75, K75RT** *(DIFFERING FROM 1994)*	
Frame numbers	***Data unavailable after 1995*** 0213848–0214049 (09/1994–05/1995), K75S 0255512–0256066 (09/1994–11/1995), K75 0135458–0135901 USA (09/1994–09/1995), K75 0372029–0374860 (09/1994–11/1995), K75RT 6229848–6229909 USA (09/1994–01/1995), K75RT
Colors	**Graphite, Silver (K75 and K75S), Graphite, Green (K75RT)**

1995 **F650** *(DIFFERING FROM 1994)*	
Color	**Green**

1996

K1100RS, K1100LT, K75RT, K75, R1100RT, R1100RS, R1100GS, R1100R, R850R, R100RT, R100GS Paris-Dakar, R100R, R100R Mystic, R80GS Basic, and F650

With the K75 triple's imminent demise and the expansion of the new boxer range to include the R1100RT, BMW's emphasis clearly shifted away from the K series and toward the four-valve boxer and F650 single in 1996. Although no longer in production, the "farewell model" R100 Classics were still available while stocks lasted, and the air-cooled boxer finally came to an end with the R80GS Basic. The K1100RS and LT soldiered on while there was still a market, but it was the continued success of the R1100s and F650s that ensured the healthy production of 48,950 motorcycles.

R1100RT, R1100R, R850R, R1100GS, and R1100RS

With more than 40,000 examples sold up until July 1995, the R1100 series grew to include the touring R1100RT for 1996. The RT lineage was well established, and while the R100RT fairing was aerodynamically efficient and provided supreme rider protection, the twin-cylinder RT was always underpowered. This was especially noticeable with the R80RT and post-1987 R100RTs, and by 1995, the RT was crying out for a more powerful engine. Of course, there was always the option of the K1100LT, but this gargantuan four-cylinder tourer wasn't for the boxer enthusiast.

↓ Continuing an RT tradition of supreme touring motorcycles, the R1100RT also completed the R1100 lineup.
BMW Group Press

↑ The R1100RS was always available with a full fairing, the lower part finished in white aluminum for 1996. An R1100RT-style front fender was also new this year. *BMW Group Press*

↓ In keeping with the R1100RT's touring nature, 33-liter panniers were standard. Options included a cassette radio, heated handlebar grips, and a 30-liter top box. *BMW Group Press*

Unlike with the earlier RTs that were identical to the parent RS underneath the bodywork, BMW provided the R1100RT an individual identity. While the engine and drivetrain were identical to those of the R1100RS, the R1100RT chassis was unique, with a R1100GS front subframe, R1100R front shock absorber, and R1100RS Telelever A-arm with separately mounted R1100GS handlebar. Standard on the R1100RT was the second-generation ABS. The distinctive large thermoplastic fairing and bodywork was highly efficient, and although still a large and heavy touring motorcycle, the R1100RT was the right machine at the right time. Whereas the four-cylinder K1100LT was moderately successful, with the R1100RT, BMW had an immediate winner. Although not functionally superior, the R1100RT was seen as more modern, and the boxer engine appealed to traditionalists. Already successful, with 9,000 sales, this year saw no change to the R1100R and R850R, the R1100GS also continuing as before. Minor updates to the R1100RS included a new front fender and the optional full fairing finished partly in white aluminum.

1996 R1100RT (DIFFERING FROM THE R1100RS)

Rear brake	276mm disc
Wheelbase	1,485mm (58.5 inches)
Wet weight	282 kg (622 lbs.)
Numbers produced	53,092 (1995–2001)
Colors	Red, Green, Silver

1996 R1100GS, R1100R, R850R (DIFFERING FROM 1995)

Colors	Yellow (R1100GS), Green (R1100R, R850R)

K and F Series

The K75 series bowed out this year, 1996, with two special Ultima editions: the K75 Ultima and K75RT Ultima. These included the three-spoke K75S wheels and a few additional features, but after 11 years the K75 departed with barely a whimper. Production had numbered nearly 68,000, and of all the K series machines, the K75 was perhaps the most unappreciated. Another K1100RS Special Edition was available this year, in black and silver, with a polished front fork, while the K1100LT received ABS II as standard equipment. The F650 was unchanged.

↑ The final air-head boxer twin was the R80GS Basic. Primarily for the German market, this was basically an earlier R80GS with a small fuel tank, headlight cowl, and round rocker covers.
BMW Group Press

1996 F650 *(DIFFERING FROM 1995)*

Color	Black

R100s and R80GS Basic

BMW announced at the end of 1994 that production of the range of traditional air-cooled boxers would cease at the end of 1995, and as production lasted only a few months into the 1996 model year, the four "farewell models" were unchanged. Although the street R models finished in December 1995, production of the GS Basic continued for a little longer and an R80GS Basic was the final air-cooled boxer, the last leaving the Spandau production line on December 19, 1996.

The end finally came for one of BMW's most classic engine designs, in production for 27 years and remarkably similar throughout its life. Considering the Type 246 was originally perceived as an interim engine design, it was astonishing it lasted so long, but the air-cooled boxer twin endured because it was reliable and charismatic. Ultimately, noise and emission regulations killed it, but for the many thousands who bought and rode air-cooled boxers, they were inimitable.

1996 R80GS BASIC *(DIFFERING FROM 1995)*

Colors	White/Blue

1997

K1200RS, K1100LT, R1100RT, R1100RS, R1100GS, R1100R, R850R, F650, and F650ST

After concentrating on the boxer range for several years, this year saw the third-generation K series, the K1200RS, and an addition to the F650 single lineup, the F650ST Strada. Although the K1100LT was unchanged, a Highline special version joined it, and while the range was smaller than in 1996, sales increased to 56,295 in 1997.

K1200RS and K1100LT

As development resources were fully engaged on the R259 boxer during the early 1990s, it wasn't until 1993 that the much overdue development of the K series could begin. Rather than continue along the path initiated by the K1, BMW decided on a change in direction. Although financial constraints and development time still tied the design to the longitudinal horizontal four-cylinder layout, the new K series would provide real Superbike performance in a state-of-the-art chassis.

There was no way the heavy engine and transmission layout was ever going to power a lithe Superbike, so the design parameters aimed toward a powerful sport-tourer in the best BMW tradition. The first task was to cure the vibration that had plagued the K series since its inception, and BMW turned to the Italian frame specialist Bimota to provide a monocoque aluminum backbone-style frame with rubber engine mounts.

↓ Designed by Bimota and built by Verlicchi in Italy, the aluminum K1200RS frame provided excellent handling, successfully isolated engine vibration, and was easy to manufacture. The only disadvantage was the 60-pound bare weight. *BMW Group Press*

← The K1200S was the third evolution of the K series, with the largest and most powerful BMW engine yet. *Ian Falloon*

1997 **K1200RS**

Type	Four-stroke, horizontal inline four-cylinder, liquid-cooled
Bore x stroke	70.5x75mm
Displacement	1,171cc
Power	130 horsepower at 8,750 rpm
Compression ratio	11.5:1
Valve control	Double-overhead camshaft
Carburetion	Bosch Motronic MA 2.4
Gears	6-speed
Frame	Cast-aluminum
Front suspension	Telelever
Rear suspension	Paralever swingarm
Wheels	3.50x17 and 5.00x17
Tires	120/70ZR17 and 170/60ZR17
Brakes	Dual front 305mm discs and single 285mm rear disc
Wheelbase	1,555mm (61.2 inches)
Wet weight	285 kg (628 lbs.)
Numbers produced	37,992 (1997–2005)
Colors	Red, Blue, Yellow

1997 **K1100LT** *(DIFFERING FROM 1996)*

Colors	Red, Gray/Red (Highline)

With the vibration problem solved, the engine could now be developed to produce more power. As the voluntary 100-horsepower limit was now irrelevant, more displacement and higher compression pistons created the most powerful BMW motorcycle engine to date. Drive was by a new six-speed Getrag gearbox, and complementing the more powerful engine was Telelever front suspension and a single shock absorber mounted to provide a rising rate action.

New enveloping bodywork included a large, rounded plastic fuel tank and cover that seemed excessively wide, but despite the considerable weight, the K1200RS was possibly the first BMW motorcycle without any idiosyncratic quirks. With surprisingly light steering, exceptional stability, no vibration, and a tight driveline, the K1200RS could be ridden incredibly fast with ease. The K1100LT was offered in two versions for 1997, a basic version without panniers and an elaborately finished Highline model.

↑ The F650 received a mild facelift for 1998, the turn signals now on short stalks and the radiator and cylinder cover in one unit. *Ian Falloon*

R and F Series

The newly released R1100RT continued without any changes, as did the R1100GS, R1100R, and R850R, while the R1100RS received an adjustable front shock absorber and hydraulic preload adjustment for the rear shock. With more than 30,000 units sold until mid-1996, the F650 was the best-selling BMW motorcycle and received a mild facelift for 1997. This included a redesigned fairing and narrower radiator, higher windscreen, and lower seat. A more street-oriented F650ST Strada also joined the F650 Funduro this year, with stiffer suspension, a smaller front wheel, and road tires. This year also saw Dave Morris win the first of three successive single-cylinder TTs at the Isle of Man on a Harris-framed F650.

1997 **R1100RS, R1100R, R850R** *(DIFFERING FROM 1996)*

Colors	Yellow (R1100RS), Blue, Silver (R1100R, R850R)

1997 **F650F, F650ST** *(DIFFERING FROM 1996)*

Front wheel	2.50x18 (F650ST)
Front tire	100/90x18 (F650ST)
Wheelbase	1,465mm (57.7 inches), F650ST
Colors	Yellow (F650); Orange, Blue, White (F650ST)

1998

K1200RS, K1100LT, R1200C, R1100RT, R1100RS, R1100GS, R1100R, R850R, F650, and F650ST

The motorcycle market changed dramatically during the late 1980s and early 1990s, with cruisers the new growth segment. As cruiser sales were doubling annually in America, the introduction of a BMW cruiser wasn't totally unexpected. The year 1998 was also the 75th anniversary of BMW motorcycle production, and several special anniversary edition models were offered. Motorcycle production also increased to 60,308, a new record.

BMW Grafik Design VT-T

R1200C

The traditional American cruiser was the Harley-Davidson large capacity V-twin, assiduously copied by the Japanese manufacturers, but it was neither feasible, nor part of the BMW psychology, to pursue this approach. BMW already had a suitable engine in the R259 boxer, and this was easily adapted for the particular requirements of a cruiser. There was no need for the engine to rev hard, but it required an extremely fat torque curve. So the engine capacity was increased and the power reduced, with smaller valves, lower lift camshafts, and narrower intakes.

The demands of the cruiser also called for a distinctive chassis. While BMW was committed to the Telelever, the front aluminum subframe couldn't be easily disguised so it was designed to be integral with the styling and image. The cruiser also saw a return of the Monolever, with the drive

↑ The cruiser chassis included a long Monolever swingarm and Telelever front fork. *BMW Group Press*

1998 R1200C	
Type	**Four-stroke, flat-twin, air/oil-cooled**
Bore x stroke	**101x73mm**
Displacement	**1,170cc**
Power	**61 horsepower at 5,000 rpm**
Compression ratio	**10:1**
Valve control	**Overhead-valve, high camshaft design**
Carburetion/ignition	**Bosch Motronic MA 2.4**
Gears	**5-speed**
Frame	**Tubular space frame with the engine as a stressed member**
Front suspension	**Telelever**
Rear suspension	**Monolever swingarm**
Wheels	**2.50x19 and 3.00x17**
Tires	**100/90ZR18 and 170/80ZR15**
Brakes	**Dual front 305mm disc and 285mm rear disc**
Wheelbase	**1,650mm (65 inches)**
Wet weight	**256 kg (564 lbs.)**
Numbers produced	**29,788 (1997–2003), including R850C**
Colors	**Black, Red, Ivory**

↑ The R1200C represented a radical departure for BMW and was initially very successful. *BMW Group Press*

shaft and two universal joints running inside the long hollow swingarm, this mounted on the tubular-steel subframe and not the transmission housing. Apart from allowing twin silencers, the most obvious by-product of the long swingarm was the long wheelbase. Although not considered ideal in more sporting machines, the long wheelbase provided the cruiser with exceptional stability, with a lot of rider room.

Soon after its release, the R1200C made a spectacular appearance with James Bond in the 007 thriller, *Tomorrow Never Dies*, and during 1998, it was the best-selling BMW motorcycle.

K1200RS, K1100LT, R1100RT, R1100RS, R1100GS, R1100R, R850R, F650, and F650ST

Apart from a facelift to the naked R1100R and R850R, all other models were unchanged for 1998. The two R model boxers had already received mild updates during 1997, including a new headlight and cockpit with a standard clock and tachometer, and further updates for 1998 centered on a number of cosmetic details. All the R1100s were also available this year in 75th Anniversary Special Editions, and the K1200RS was available with a wider (5.50-inch) rear wheel with 180/55ZR17 tire.

1998 **K1100LT** *(DIFFERING FROM 1997)*

Colors	Graphite, Green (Highline)

1998 **R1100RS, R1100RT** *(DIFFERING FROM 1997)*

Colors	Dolphin Blue (R1100RS), Gray (R1100RT)

1998 **F650F, F650ST** *(DIFFERING FROM 1997)*

Color	Red (F650ST)

1999

K1200LT, K1200RS, R1200C, R850C, R1100S, R1100RT, R1100RS, R1100GS, R850GS, R1100R, R850R, F650, and F650ST

While the R1200C cruiser took the boxer in a radical new direction, the following year saw the reintroduction of the sporting boxer. This continued a tradition initiated in 1952 with the R68, which lapsed following the demise of the R100CS in 1984. These two models at the extreme ends of the motorcycling spectrum expanded the boxer twin lineup, boosting its appeal. Also this year the K1200LT luxury tourer replaced the K1100LT, further rejuvenating the K series range, and the R850GS joined the R1100GS. Production increased to 69,157 during 1999.

R1100S

As the "S" designation was significant within the boxer's historical context, it was no surprise to see the R259 develop into the R1100S. In the style of the earlier R69S and R90S, the R1100S was still a sport-touring motorcycle, with the emphasis on sport rather than touring. Also with more power and less weight than the R1100RS, the R1100S was the most sporting and best handling boxer yet.

↓ **The R1100R received a mild facelift for 1998 and was also available in this 75th Anniversary Special Edition.**
BMW Group Press

→ **With most powerful boxer engine yet, BMW resurrected the sporting "S" with the R1100S.** *BMW Group Press*

Although the engine was ostensibly that of the R1100RS, modifications were made to improve the power output without sacrificing the torque curve. New pistons provided an increase in the compression ratio, and a plate-type air filter, instead of circular, ensured improved breathing. Stronger, forged con rods allowed the safe engine speed to rise to 8,400 rpm, and visibly distinguishing the R1100S engine were lighter magnesium cylinder head covers. Around 70 percent of the extra power was attributed to the new stainless-steel exhaust system, the twin mufflers positioned directly beneath the tailpiece.

To provide improved handling and stability, the chassis was completely updated, the Telelever with machined fork sliders, with a unique four-piece frame. The engine and gearbox were still load bearing, but with an additional welded aluminum central frame section, with a die-cast aluminum front section. The wide-cast aluminum 17-inch wheels were a new style, and with its wind tunnel–developed four-piece sporting fairing, the R1100S maintained an individual sporting look initiated with the earlier R90S.

Although it endeavored to emulate the character of the magnificent earlier S series, by 1999, motorcycles were more specialized, and the categories more polarized. Sporting motorcycles were harder edged, much lighter, and more powerful than their predecessors. In the 1960s and 1970s, the gap between pure sporting and touring motorcycles wasn't so large, but by the time the R1100S was released, a huge chasm separated the two types. The R1100S found itself in the middle ground, unable to compete with the current crop of race replicas and unable create its own niche identity.

1999 R1100S *(DIFFERING FROM THE R1100RS)*

Power	**98 horsepower at 7,500 rpm**
Compression ratio	**11.3:1**
Carburetion/ignition	**Bosch Motronic MA 2.4**
Gears	**6-speed**
Frame	**Cast-aluminum frame, tubular space frame with the engine as a stressed member**
Wheels	**3.50x17 and 5.00x17**
Tires	**120/70ZR17 and 170/60ZR17**
Rear brake	**276mm disc**
Wheelbase	**1,478mm (58.2 inches)**
Wet weight	**229kg (505 lbs.)**
Numbers produced	**33,741 (1998–2005)**
Colors	**Black, Red, Mandarin**

← Representing a significant departure for BMW, the K1200LT provided luxury and supremely comfortable motorcycle touring. *BMW Group Press*

K1200LT

Largely undeveloped since its inception back in 1991, by 1998 the K1100LT was the only remaining Compact Drive System K series motorcycle. Arguably outclassed by the six-cylinder Honda Gold Wing even when it was released, the K1100LT had largely insignificant sales in the full-dress luxury touring market when compared with its competition. Even as the Gold Wing aged, it remained the standard by which large touring motorcycles were judged, until the advent of the remarkable K1200LT.

Following on from the K1200RS and R1200C Cruiser, both motorcycles with distinctive new personalities and aimed at a specific rider demographic, the K1200LT was intentionally designed to sit at the extreme end of the touring motorcycle spectrum. Offered an alternative to the R1100RT, the K1200LT emulated BMW's luxury 7 series sedan by providing exceptional comfort and storage space.

Although the basic architecture was closely related to the K1200RS, unlike the earlier LT that was essentially a K100 or K1100RS with extra equipment, the new LT design was unique. The engine was tuned for more consistent off-idle running and a flatter torque curve, and the gearbox was only a five-speed, with an electric reversing assister, operated by the electric start motor.

The chassis was also a development of the K1200RS with a cast-aluminum frame, rubber-mounted engine, Telelever front suspension, and a longer Paralever swingarm. The rear brake was upgraded with a four-piston caliper. Intended to convey an aura of luxury, comfort, and convenience, the integrated bodywork was quite unlike that of earlier BMW motorcycles and was a new concept in motorcycle design. The fairing, fuel tank, seats, side luggage, top box, and even the exhaust system were integral parts of the complete motorcycle body. The cockpit was almost automotive-like; the wide fairing offered unparalleled wind and weather protection, with built-in, nonremovable luggage. BMW set out to build a better motorcycle than the GL1500 Gold Wing, and the company succeeded. The K1200RS was available in three equipment levels: Standard, Icon, and Custom. In the United States, it was the best-selling BMW motorcycle during 1999.

1999 K1200LT *(DIFFERING FROM THE K1200RS)*

Power	**98 horsepower at 6,750 rpm**
Compression ratio	**10.8:1**
Carburetion/ignition	**Bosch Motronic MA 2.4**
Gears	**5-speed**
Rear tire	**160/70ZR17**
Brakes	**Dual front 305mm discs and single 285mm rear disc (4-piston caliper)**
Wheelbase	**1,633mm (64.3 inches)**
Wet weight	**378 kg (833 lbs.)**
Numbers produced	**37,872 (1998–2005)**
Colors	**Gray, Red, Silver**

→ Richard Sainct rode the F650RR to victory in the 1999 Granada-Dakar rally, BMW's first win in this major off-road event since 1985.
BMW Group Press

↓ HPN prepared this R1100GSRR for Oscar Gallardo in the 1999 Tunisia Rally. GS-based, the RR had a lightweight frame, White Power suspension, and a pair of Bing carburetors instead of fuel injection. Producing 85 horsepower, the RR weighed a substantial 419 pounds.
BMW Group Press

K1200RS, R1200C, R850C, R1100RT, R1100RS, R1100GS, R850GS, R1100R, R850R, F650, and F650ST

Production of the F650 and F650ST by Aprilia at Noale concluded at the end of 1999 following the termination of the assembly contract, and a new assembly plant was built at Berlin-Spandau. The existing boxer range was also unchanged, although an R850C cruiser and R850GS were added, while the K1200RS was available with an optional higher handlebar and more comfortable seat.

After a tentative and unsuccessful return to the 1998 Dakar Rally, Gottfried Michels and team manager Richard Schalber prepared four F650RR rally machines for the 1999 Granada-Dakar rally. With twin Mikuni flat-slide carburetors, the power of the 700cc single was boosted to a claimed 75 horsepower and handling improved with a perimeter-style chrome-molybdenum frame. Richard Sainct, a 28-year French rider, switched from KTM, and narrowly won (by five minutes) with Andrea Mayer taking out the women's trophy. Sainct also won the Tunisia Rally in April, this event noted for the entry of Oscar Gallardo on an HPN-prepared R1100GS. Gallardo only managed 34th, but it was an encouraging return for the BMW boxer twin in off-road events.

1999 K1200RS *(DIFFERING FROM 1998)*

Colors	Graphite, Silver

1999 R850C, R850GS
(DIFFERING FROM THE R1200C AND R1100GS)

Bore x stroke	87.5x70.5mm
Displacement	848cc
Power	50 horsepower at 5,250 rpm (R850C), 70 horsepower at 7,500 rpm (R850GS)

1999 R1100R, R850R, R1100RT *(DIFFERING FROM 1998)*

Colors	Black, Graphite (R1100R, R850R); Graphite (R1100RT)

1999 F650F, F650ST *(DIFFERING FROM 1998)*

Colors	Orange, Blue (F650); Gray (F650ST)

← Celebrating 20 years of the GS, the new R1150GS was large, heavy, and relatively intimidating, but was still the finest adventure motorcycle available in 2000. *BMW Group Press*

2000

K1200LT K1200RS, R1150GS, R850GS, R1200CE, R1200C, R850C, R1100RT, R1100RS, R1100R, R850R, F650, F650ST, F650GS, and F650GS Dakar

The R1100GS received what was termed "mid-life freshening" during 1999. Despite a tarnished durability image, sales of the four-valve GS models over their six-year lifespan numbered more than 45,000 and it made sense to incorporate some of the updates of both the R1200C and R1100S on the replacement. Evolution saw the engine enlarged, a six-speed gearbox, and a new face. Joining the R1150GS was a more subdued Avantgarde cruiser, as an alternative to the classic chrome style. Apart from a new F650GS, introduced early in 2000, all the existing models continued as before, and production continued to climb, to 74,397.

R1150GS and R850GS

Released to coincide with the 20-year anniversary of the Gelände Strasse, and to celebrate the production of nearly 115,000 examples of the GS genre, the 1150GS expanded and improved the concept of the large adventure and long-distance enduro motorcycle. Updates were designed to increase power and midrange torque, with the chassis and styling also receiving attention. The R1150GS utilized many components from newer models in the R259 Boxer family, including R1200C cylinders, and R1100S crankshaft, cylinder heads, magnesium valve covers, six-speed gearbox, and lighter Telelever. A new face included two asymmetrical ellipsoidal headlights. While not really a serious off-road machine, when fitted with some of the optional touring equipment (panniers and top box), the R1150GS presented a viable alternative to pure street and touring motorcycles. On the move, the disadvantage of weight and size was cleverly disguised, and in the manner of all GSs, the R1150GS was a surprisingly good street motorcycle. There was no disguising the R1150GS was large, but it continued to reign as the king of dual-purpose bikes. The previous R850GS continued unchanged.

2000 R1150GS *(DIFFERING FROM THE R1100GS AND 1999)*

Bore	101mm
Displacement	1,130cc
Power	85 horsepower at 6,750 rpm
Carburetion/ignition	Bosch Motronic MA 2.4
Gears	6-speed
Wet weight	249 kg (549 lbs.)
Numbers produced	58,023 (1999–2003)
Colors	Black, Silver, Mandarin (R1150GS), Yellow (R850GS)

K1200LT K1200RS, R1200CE, R1200C, R850C, R1100RT, R1100RS, R1100R, R850R, F650, and F650ST

Featuring a black enamel engine and drivetrain finish, and graphitane (graphite and magnesium) for many of the previously chromed components, the Avantgarde cruiser (R1200CE in the United States) supplemented the classic cruiser for 2000. The intention was to create a darker and more modern-looking alternative to chrome. A special F650ST was also available this year, this with heated handlebars, higher windscreen, a rear top box, and a catalytic converter. These were the remaining stock of Aprilia-built BMW singles.

2000 **R1100RS, R1100S, R1100RT, R1200C, R850C** *(DIFFERING FROM 1999)*	
Colors	Silver (R1100RS, R1100S); Black (R1100RT); Blue, Green, Peach (R1200C, R850C)

↓ Now fuel injected and built in Berlin, the F650GS was the most popular BMW motorcycle in 2000. *BMW Group Press*

2000 **F650, F650ST** *(DIFFERING FROM 1999)*	
Colors	Silver (F650); Red, Green (F650ST)

F650GS and F650GS Dakar

BMW's success in the Dakar rally coincided with the decision to move production of the F650 to Berlin-Spandau, and early in 2000, a revised F650GS, along with a special Dakar version, were released. As before, Bombardier-Rotax in Austria provided the engines. Along with the digital engine management arrangement, the F650GS was the first single-cylinder motorcycle to feature a standard catalytic converter.

The suspension, wheels, and brakes were carried over from the F650, but the rectangular steel bridge-type frame with a bolted-on steel lower section was new. The F650GS Dakar came with a 21-inch front wheel, increased suspension travel, a higher seat, and an F650RR windshield. The F650GS's styling was strongly influenced by the new R1150GS and F650RR, but underneath the restyled plastic dummy tank hid the large airbox, with the fuel tank located under the seat. Fuel filling was through the aircraft-type filler on the right. The F650GS was immediately popular, with production exceeding 30,000 units by the summer of 2001, and was the best-selling BMW motorcycle worldwide.

↑ With its 21-inch wheel, the F650GS Dakar was more off-road oriented than the standard F650GS. *BMW Group Press*

2000 **F650GS AND F650GS DAKAR** *(DIFFERING FROM THE F650)*	
Power	50 horsepower at 6,500 rpm
Compression ratio	11.5:1
Carburetion	Digital BMS
Frame	Tubular-steel bridge
Front wheel	1.60x21 (F650GS Dakar)
Front tire	90/90x21 (F650GS Dakar)
Wheelbase	1,479mm (58.3 inches), F650GS; 1,489mm (58.6 inches), F650GS Dakar
Wet weight	193 kg (425 lbs.), F650GS; 192 kg (423lbs.), F650GS Dakar
Numbers produced	85,194 (2000–2008), F650GS; 21,499, (F650GS Dakar)
Colors	Blue, Red, Yellow (F650GS); White (F650GS Dakar)

2000 Paris-Dakar-Cairo Rally

Richard Sainct was back on a BMW F650RR for the 2000 Paris-Dakar-Cairo rally, and this year the BMWs totally dominated. BMW again fielded four F650RRs, plus a pair of HPN-prepared R900GSRRs for John Deacon and Jimmy Lewis. Not only did Sainct win, by a massive margin of 32 minutes, but F650-mounted Spaniard Oscar Gallardo finished second, Lewis was third, and Frenchman Jean Brucy fourth, also on an F650. This completed a BMW whitewash in this prestigious and grueling event.

2001–2009
PERFORMANCE FIRST:
NEW SINGLES, TWINS, AND FOURS

In 2001 BMW concentrated on expanding its model lineup, building on the existing range and creating new niche markets. While the C1 scooter wasn't proving as popular as expected, technological advances such as integrated ABS ensured BMW maintained its reputation for innovation. And this decade would see both the K and R series evolve into high-performance Superbikes that would finally eradicate BMW's staid image.

2001

R1150R, R1150RT, R1200C Independent, K1200RS, K1200LT, R1200CE, R1200C, R1150GS, R1100RS, R1100S, F650GS, and F650GS Dakar

BMW had previously pursued a policy of introducing two new motorcycle models each year, but this changed during 2001 with the release of four models. Along with three new boxers—the R1150R, R1150RT, and R1200C Independent—was a K1200RS; the existing R1100RS, R1100S, F650GS, and F650GS Dakar continued unchanged. Although the R1150GS was also unchanged this year, it was available in special commemorative Dakar-inspired colors. Excluding the C1, 74,614 motorcycles were built this year, with the F650GS the most popular (17,445) and the R1150GS the strongest seller 750cc with 14,558 built. Integrated ABS was also introduced for 2001. With an electrohydraulic brake servo, this was partially integrated on sporting models, with the handbrake acting on the front and rear brakes and the footbrake operating the rear brake. The fully integrated system acted on front and rear brakes simultaneously. While adapting to varying loads and riding conditions, the new ABS wasn't universally accepted, but it did indicate BMW's continued commitment to innovation and originality.

R1150R

The first new release for 2001 was the naked R1150R. In response to the backlash against repli-racers, nicknamed "yoghurt-cups" in Germany because of their extreme multi-coloured plastic bodywork, BMW restyled the naked R1150R to emphasize its elemental nature. In the process the company created one of the finest renditions by any manufacturer of the naked bike concept. Continuing the R1100R theme, the R1150R's higher torque engine was from the R1150GS, with the cylinder heads and crankshaft of the sporting R1100S.

The updated oil cooling system had the twin oil coolers contained in aerodynamic ducts in the sides of the fuel tank, these now looking integrated and no longer an afterthought. The six-speed gearbox was also shared with the R1150GS, while the wheels were the R1100S's lighter double-spoke type. New this year was an EVO front brake with updated Brembo-Tokico four-piston calipers with the new generation Integral ABS as an option. The R1150R's purposeful and elegant styling was one of the most successful renditions of the new boxer.

To use up the stock of R1100R and R850R components after the introduction of the new R1150R, a R1100R/R850R classic Special Model was also offered. While the R1100R Special Model ended during 2001, the R850R version continued for 2002.

← Replacing the R1100R for 2001, the R1150R was much more attractive than its predecessor. *BMW Group Press*

↓ Alongside the new R1150R for 2001 was a special edition R1100R Sondermodell retro-style example with wire-spoked wheels and chrome-plated cylinder head covers. *BMW Group Press*

2001 R1150R *(DIFFERING FROM THE R1100R)*

Bore	**101mm**
Displacement	**1,130cc**
Power	**85 horsepower at 6,750 rpm**
Compression ratio	**11.5:1**
Fuel supply	**Bosch Motronic MA2.4**
Gears	**6-speed**
Rear wheel	**5.00x17 inches**
Tires	**120/70ZR17 and 170/60ZR17**
Front brakes	**Dual 320mm disc**
Wet weight	**238 kg (525 lbs.)**
Numbers produced	**43,026 (2001–2006)**
Colors	**Blue, Red, Black**

R1200C Independent (R1200CA Phoenix)

A third cruiser version, the Independent (Phoenix in the United States), became available for 2001. This had a solo seat, oval mirrors, new wheels, additional small fog lamps, and a small speedster-type handlebar fairing. The alternator cover, new oil cooler intakes, levers, and fluid reservoirs were chrome-plated. The aluminum wheels were two-piece, with three-spoke inner hubs connected by titanium bolts replacing the usual cross-spoke wheels. In addition to the existing R1200C and CE (or Avantgarde), the United States received the R1200CM (Montana) with touring equipment that included a windshield, heated handgrips, engine guards, and saddlebags. The other R1200C cruisers continued unchanged for 2001.

2001 R1200C *(DIFFERING FROM 2000)*

Colors	**Ivory/Peach, Mandarin/Graphitane (Independent); Silver, Graphite (Avantgarde)**

→ With more chrome, cast-alloy wheels, a solo seat, oval mirrors, an additional headlight, and a speedster windshield, the R1200C Independent (or Phoenix) offered cruiser customers more style and individuality. *BMW Group Press*

With Sainct returning to archrival KTM, BMW provided HPN-prepared twins to Jimmy Lewis, John Deacon, Juan "Nani" Roma, and Cyril Despres for the 2001 Dakar Rally. Andrea Mayer rode the only official BMW F650RR. In the UAE Desert Challenge, or the Dubai rally, a lead-up to the 2001 Dakar, Deacon rode an R1100RR, but Lewis won on the lighter and smaller R900RR. While the dry weight of the 900 was now down to 190 kilograms, developments saw a new fuel tank layout in order to centralize the huge mass, with rear pannier and under seat tanks. After Lewis' 2000 Dakar failure, a new torque arm extended from the rear hub to the main frame, but the most significant improvement was a wind tunnel–designed fairing that incorporated the front fender, contributing to improved high-speed behavior.

This year the Dakar course was slower and more technical than the previous year, favoring the lighter singles. An electrical fault delayed Deacon, Roma crashed out while holding third, and Lewis broke a collarbone on the run in to Dakar. Deacon managed sixth, while Lewis remounted and limped home to seventh. Capable of around 125 miles per hour, the R900RR was a formidable desert weapon, but it wasn't destined to repeat the victory of its illustrious predecessors.

BMW Motorrad BoxerCup's success continued during 2001 and 2002, now becoming more international with more than 30 riders from all over Europe competing in seven races on the MotoGP and FIM Endurance calendar. Guest riders included BoxerCup ambassador and ex–Grand Prix star Randy Mamola and former World Superbike racer Stéphane Mertens, who won the 2001 and 2002 series.

→ Former Grand Prix racer Randy Mamola made some BoxerCup guest appearances on the R1100S during 2001. *BMW Group Press*

↓ Finishing sixth overall, British rider John Deacon was the highest finishing BMW entry in the 2001 Paris-Dakar Rally. Deacon died a few months later during the Masters Rally in Syria after his R900RR flipped and he sustained head injuries. This tragedy prompted BMW's withdrawal from off-road rallies. *BMW Group Press*

R1150RT

In the spring of 2001, BMW released the R1150RT with the larger displacement engine, six-speed gearbox, and significant chassis and styling updates. Although the chassis and suspension were similar to the R1100RT, as the six-speed gearbox required a larger housing, the swingarm was shorter. The lighter, double five-spoke 17-inch aluminum wheels were shared with the R1100S, while the braking system included larger discs, EVO calipers, and fully integrated Integral ABS. After the R1100RT's rather plump styling, the R1150RT received a facelift with more attractive tandem headlights, integrated with twin fog lamps.

2001 **R1150RT** (DIFFERING FROM THE R1100RT AND R1150R)	
Power	**95 horsepower at 7,250 rpm**
Wet weight	**279 kg (615 lbs.)**
Numbers produced	**57,137 (2001–2005)**
Colors	**Aquamint, Silver, Blue, Red**

K1200RS

After more than 21,000 examples, the K1200RS received a facelift, customer demand requiring improved comfort and weather protection, and a less aggressive sporting riding position. For 2001, wind tunnel development resulted in a more slender upper fairing and a wider and taller windshield. As on other recent models, the two water radiators were now integrated in a BMW kidney grille in the fairing, with the air scoop feeding air into the intake system, and while rider comfort was improved, the biggest development was the incorporation of the new-generation partially integrated ABS. Although undeniably fast and competent, the K1200RS was still an extremely large and heavy motorcycle and its focus was even more biased toward sports touring.

↑ Not only did the new styling provide the R1150RS a more attractive face than its predecessor, the engine produced more power and torque. *Ian Falloon*

→ The K1200RS was restyled slightly for 2001, the fairing providing more weather protection. Also new was the EVO braking system, with partially integrated ABS. *BMW Group Press*

2001 **K1200RS** (DIFFERING FROM 2000)	
Rear wheel and tire	**5.50x17 with 180/55ZR17 (optional)**
Front brakes	**Dual 320mm disc**
Colors	**Blue, Black, Frost Blue/Red**

← The R1150RS replaced the R1100RS for 2002, but the style was still very similar. *BMW Group Press*

2002

R1150RS, F650CS, R1150GS Adventure, K1200RS, K1200LT, R1200C Independent, R1200C Avantgarde, R1200C, R1150RT, R1150GS, R1150R, R1100S, F650GS, and F650GS Dakar

After releasing four new examples for 2001, BMW reverted to its usual program of two new models for 2002: the R1150RS sports tourer and an updated single, the F650CS. Also available later during the model year was a special R1150GS Adventure. The entire motorcycle lineup was now relatively new, the most senior the R1200C cruiser launched four years earlier, and motorcycle production increased to 92,559 this year.

R1150RS

For 2002, the R1150RS replaced the long-serving R1100RS. Almost the forgotten model in the lineup, the R1100RS was the firstborn and least loved, but it always maintained a loyal following from those interested in carving miles and apexes. Less bulky than the RT, but not as extreme as the S, the RS still filled a niche so it was inevitable that it would eventually share the updates of the other boxers. The engine and gearbox were shared with the R1150RT, but the chassis and steering geometry were unchanged from the R1100RS. New were the 17-inch five-spoke wheels and the front EVO brakes, but unlike the R1150RT, the Integral ABS was an option, and it was the more sporting-oriented partial setup.

Other than a higher and wider windshield, visually the R1150RS was similar to the R1100RS. The previously optional full fairing, continuing underneath the cylinders and enclosing the engine, was now standard. Also carried over from the R1100RS were the imprecise rubber-mounted handlebars. Considering that all the other new boxers had separately mounted handlebars, this seemed incongruous and detracted from the R1150RS's ultimate sporting ability. Undoubtedly an interim design, the R1100RS was the subject of rumors about receiving a new motor and a further restyle even before its release.

2002 **R1150RS** *(DIFFERING FROM THE R1100RS AND R1150RT)*

Brakes	**Dual front 320mm disc and 285mm rear disc**
Wheelbase	**1,469mm (57.8 inches)**
Wet weight	**248 kg (547 lbs.)**
Numbers produced	**7,309 (2001–2005)**
Colors	**Dark Blue, Silver, Pacific Blue**

↑ Designed primarily for city use, with its belt final drive, the F650CS represented another new departure for BMW. *BMW Group Press*

F650CS

Replacing the mundane F650ST for 2002, and continuing a tradition to redefine existing concepts, BMW released the astounding F650CS (City Sport) or Scarver, as it was known in Europe. Unlike the F650ST that was very similar to the F650 Funduro, the F650CS was individual and distinctive, intended primarily for city use, and incorporated unique storage solutions. The BMW-developed Rotax engine and five-speed gearbox were shared with the F650GS, but the rectangular steel frame included the engine oil reservoir as on the first F650. An integrated storage compartment was located in the central fairing and dummy tank above the airbox, with the fuel tank under the seat, as on the F650GS.

Also new was the aluminum single-sided swingarm with toothed-belt final drive. The toothed-belt drive required no lubrication and provided superior durability. Also included were new 17-inch three-spoke cast-aluminum wheels with a curved design from the hub to the rim to accommodate the brake and toothed-belt sprocket.

Although low and narrow, making it a perfect city motorcycle, out of the city environment the F650CS was limited by its weight and moderate power. The riding position, accentuated by a low seat and wide handlebars, emulated that of a dirt bike in that the rider sat "in" the bike rather than "on" it. But in the city, where it was intended, the F650CS provided scooter maneuverability with motorcycle performance.

2002 **F650CS** *(DIFFERING FROM THE F650GS)*

Frame	**Single-loop tubular-steel**
Wheels	**3.00x17 front, 4.50x17 rear**
Tires	**110/70 ZR 17 and 160/60 ZR 17**
Wheelbase	**1,473mm (58 inches)**
Wet weight	**189 kg (417 lbs.)**
Numbers produced	**20,845 (2001–2005)**
Colors	**Orange, Blue**

← BMW upped the ante for adventure touring with the high-spec R1150GS Adventure. *BMW Group Press*

R1150GS Adventure

Expanding the GS lineup was the R1150GS Adventure for mid-2002. Designed as the ultimate go-anywhere motorcycle, this was either the perfect desert motorcycle or one for the ultimate Walter Mitty outback dreamer. Whatever the intended use, with its optional huge 30-liter fuel tank and 105-liter aluminum baggage system, the Adventure raised the ante for the size of off-road motorcycles. If the R1150GS seemed intimidating to smaller riders, the huge Adventure was even more so.

The engine was shared with the R1150GS, but as the Adventure was designed for use in any part of the world, an alterative ignition map allowed the engine to run on regular 91-octane fuel and the sixth gear ratio was shortened. An optional lower first gear to improve maneuverability in difficult terrain also was available. Chassis updates included longer travel suspension (the rear unit a White Power), a special seat (designed for hours in the saddle), a larger windshield, a longer and wider front fender, handlebar protectors, and a huge aluminum bash plate under the engine.

2002 R1150GS ADVENTURE *(DIFFERING FROM THE R1150GS)*

Wet weight	**274 kg (605 lbs.)**
Numbers produced	**17,828 (2002–2005)**
Colors	**Gray/Red, Yellow/Black**

All other models continued for 2002 unchanged or with minor updates. The R850GS and R850C were discontinued, and the F650GS Dakar was now available with optional ABS.

2002 F650GS, F650GS DAKAR *(DIFFERING FROM 2001)*

Colors	**Yellow (F650GS); Blue/White (F650GS Dakar)**

2002 R1150R, R1150GS, R1100S *(DIFFERING FROM 2001)*

Colors	**Red (R1150R); Graphitane (R1150GS); Gray, Blue (R1100S)**

2002 R1200C *(DIFFERING FROM 2001)*

Colors	**Flashstone, Green**

2002 K1200LT *(DIFFERING FROM 2001)*

Front brakes	**Dual 320mm disc**
Colors	**Mauve, Green**

↑ Introduced for 2003, the K1200GT bridged a chasm in the K series range between the sporting K1200RS and luxury touring K1200LT.
BMW Group Press

2003

K1200GT, R1200CL, R1100S BoxerCup Replica, R850R, R1150R Rockster, K1200RS, K1200LT, R1200C Independent, R1200C Avantgarde, R1200C, R1150RT, R1150RS, R1150GS, R1150GS Adventure, R1150R, R1100S, F650CS, F650GS, and F650GS Dakar

The introduction of four new variations on existing themes saw the range expand to 19 models. After nearly 20 years in production, the straight four K series evolved into the K1200GT Gran Turismo, and although it appeared that every sector of the touring market was well covered, 2003 saw the release of a further variant, the R1200CL, or Cruiser Luxury. Based on the R1200C cruiser, this was intended as an American-style cruiser that could also swallow up miles in comfort, steering a different path to its touring brethren. Celebrating the success of the International Boxer Cup series was the R1100S Boxer Cup Replica, and a smaller R850R was available for most European markets as an alternative to the R1150R. In March 2003 a concept roadster boxer, the Rockster, also went into limited production. All boxers except the R1200C received an updated Getrag-built six-speed gearbox this year, lighter, quieter, and with an improved gearshift. Despite the largest ever lineup, motorcycle production declined slightly, to 89,745.

K1200GT

Supplementing the full touring K1200LT, but providing a more touring emphasis than the K1200RS, was the K1200GT. Another example of the new BMW design philosophy of focusing on specific categories, the K1200GT was intended to plug the wide gap between the luxurious LT and sporting RS. This was the motorcycle for fans of high-horsepower four-cylinder engines requiring touring comfort. In many ways the K1200GT continued where the K100RT left off in 1988. While the subsequent K100LT, K1100LT, and K1200LT were more luxurious, becoming increasingly opulent in the process, all this equipment sacrificed ultimate performance. The K1200GT still offered the essential touring equipment, but it wasn't excessively heavy for this type of motorcycle.

The engine and drivetrain of the K1200GT was identical to the K1200RS, but new for the K1200GT was the fairing, electrically adjustable taller windshield, higher handlebars, and a new two-way height adjustable seat. Standard equipment on the GT included partially integrated ABS and matching luggage rack and cases. As on the K1200GT, the K1200RS also had the previously optional wider rear wheel and tire, with the option of a stiffer sports suspension package, further tightening the handling.

R1200CL

The cruiser lineup expanded beyond traditional boundaries with the release of the R1200CL luxury cruiser. The idea of the CL was to incorporate touring features into the cruiser, creating a unique machine that incorporated the distinctive characteristics of both parent types. Based on the R1200C, but with the new six-speed gearbox, the most distinctive feature of the CL was the new face. The handlebar-mounted touring fairing included four headlights. Standard touring features included integral hard cases and a removable top box, while the chassis included a flatter Telelever, wider front tire, reinforced swingarm, and rear-axle housing to accommodate a K1200LT rear brake. Aimed at the American market, the R1200CL emphasized luxury and comfort, but style was also paramount. Also available in the United States was the R1200CLC, with heated seats and a CD player in the right saddlebag. Other R1200s continued unchanged, while the R1200C was now available with the Independent's cast-alloy wheels as an option this year.

↑ Expanding the luxury touring range for 2003 was the R1200CL. Although based on the R1200C, most components were new, including the wider front fork to accommodate the fat tire.
BMW Group Press

2003 R1200CL *(DIFFERING FROM THE R1200C)*
R1200C *(DIFFERING FROM 2002)*

Gears	**6-speed**
Frame	**Composite, front aluminum section**
Front wheel	**3.50x16**
Front tire	**150/80-16**
Wheelbase	**1,641mm (64.4 inches)**
Wet weight	**308 kg (679 lbs.)**
Numbers produced	**5,160 (2002–2004)**
Colors	**Silver, Blue, Brown (R1200CL); Blue, Brown (R1200C)**

R1100S BoxerCup Replica

After three successful seasons, the International Boxer Cup grew to nine rounds for 2003, the first at the Daytona 200. Robert Panichi won at Daytona, Mugello, and Sachsenring, with other victories shared by Thomas Hinterreiter, Andy Hoffman, and Sébastien Legrelle. The Boxer Cup was notable in that the machines were all very similar, with only minimal modifications to the exhaust and engine management system permitted, along with a sport package to provide increased ground clearance and a wider rear tire. A production BoxerCup Replica became available during 2003, this a standard R1100S with the sport package, carbon-fiber-reinforced cylinder head covers, engine spoiler, and rear seat cover. Specific decals, including a Randy Mamola signature, set the BoxerCup Replica apart, and a BoxerCup without the special decals, spoiler, seat cowl, and carbon-fiber valve covers was available for some markets.

↓ The BoxerCup Replica had longer spring struts for improved ground clearance, but on a racetrack the carbon-fiber cylinder head covers were still vulnerable. *BMW Group Press*

2003 R1100S BOXERCUP REPLICA
(DIFFERING FROM THE R1100S)

Rear wheel	**5.50x17 inches**
Rear tire	**180/55ZR17**
Colors	**Blue/White**

← Due to the positive response received to the concept displayed at the end of 2002, the R1150R Rockster made it into production early in 2003.
BMW Group Press

R1150R Rockster and R850R

After its presentation as a concept Roadster boxer at the Munich Intermot show toward the end of 2002, the R1150R Rockster went into production in March 2003. With aggressive Streetfighter styling, the Rockster was aimed at a younger, more extrovert rider. One of the Rockster's technological innovations was new dual spark cylinder heads. Providing more efficient combustion and lower emissions, these eventually were phased in across the boxer range during 2003. Most Rockster components were shared with the R1150R, but the headlights came from the R1150GS and the Telelever and wider rear wheel from the R1100S. For the 2003 model year, the R850R also made a return, now with a six-speed transmission and R1150R styling.

2003 R1150R ROCKSTER AND R850R
(DIFFERING FROM THE R1150R) R1150R *(DIFFERING FROM 2002)*

Bore	**87.5mm (R850R)**
Displacement	**848cc (R850R)**
Power	**70 horsepower at 7,000 rpm (34 at 5,000 rpm) (R850R)**
Rear wheel	**5.50x17 (Rockster)**
Rear tire	**180/55ZR17 (Rockster)**
Wet weight	**239 kg (527 lbs.) (Rockster)**
Numbers produced	**15,013 (2002–2007) (R850R)**
Colors	**Citrus/Black, orange/Black (Rockster); Silver, Bronze, Yellow (R1150R & R850R)**

The R1150RT, RS, GS, and F650s continued with minor updates. All 1150 boxers received the new six-speed transmission, and this year the R1150GS's optional ABS was the new Partial Integral system. In the United States, a more basic R1150GS Sport without ABS was available.

2003 F650CS, F650GS *(DIFFERING FROM 2002)*

Colors	**Silver, Graphite (F650CS); Silver, Silver/Yellow (F650GS)**

2003 R1150RT, R1150RS *(DIFFERING FROM 2002)*

Colors	**Gray (R1150RT); Gray/Ivory (R1150RS)**

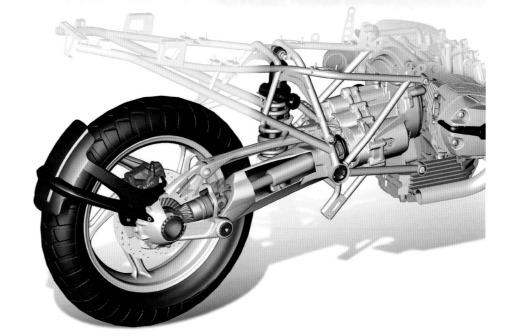

→ The R1200GS Paralever and single White Power shock absorber. *BMW Group Press*

↓ The new engine had a pair of balance weights 180 degrees apart, running in the opposite direction to the crankshaft. *BMW Group Press*

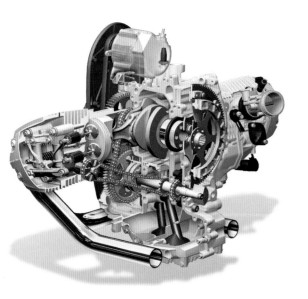

2004

R1200GS, R1200C Montauk, K1200RS, K1200GT, K1200LT, R1200CL, R1200C Independent, R1200C, R1150RT, R1150RS, R1150GS Adventure, R1150R, R1150R Rockster, R850R, R1100S, R1100S BoxerCup Replica, F650CS, F650GS, and F650GS Dakar

Although only two new models were released for 2004, this year was significant as it saw the introduction of a new 1,200cc R1200GS boxer and the phasing out of the entire R1150 series, R1200C cruisers, and the K1200RS. The F650 series and K1200LT received midcycle updates, and motorcycle production increased to 93,836, with 13,316 sales in the United States.

R1200GS

As in the past, BMW introduced the next-generation boxer engine in the popular GS, the development team's main aim to enhance the power-to-weight ratio, at the same time improving the handling. Weighing 13 kilograms less than its predecessor, the new longer stroke engine included a pair of gear-driven balancers, larger (36mm and 31mm) valves, and a new BMS-K engine management system. With the engine still employed as a principal load-bearing component, the revised Telelever bolted at two points, with the rear tubular-steel subframe located at four. As the previous lower torque rod was prone to damage off road, the new Paralever included the rod above the swingarm, braking was by EVO brakes with Partial Integral ABS, and the lightweight wheels were either cross-spoke wire or alloy. Lighter and more maneuverable than the R1150GS, the R1200GS was a landmark model and a true all-rounder. Voted *Cycle World*'s Best Open-Class Streetbike and *Motorcyclist*'s Motorcycle of the Year, the R1200GS was arguably BMW's most significant release since the R259.

2004 **R1200GS** *(DIFFERING FROM THE R1150GS)*	
Stroke	**73mm**
Displacement	**1,170cc**
Power	**98 horsepower at 7,000 rpm**
Compression ratio	**11:1**
Fuel supply	**BMS-K**
Wheelbase	**1,519mm (59.8 inches)**
Wet weight	**225 kg (496 lbs.)**
Numbers produced	**90,142 (2004–2007)**
Colors	**Blue, Red, Yellow**

F650CS, GS, and GS Dakar

Updates to the single-cylinder F650s included a dual-ignition engine, with a new BMS-CII engine management system. Power and torque were unchanged, but fuel economy improved. F650GS styling updates included a new front fender, fairing, headlight, windshield, and instruments.

↑ Lighter and more powerful than before, the new R1200GS was almost the perfect all-around motorcycle. *BMW Group Press*

2004 **FC650CS** *(DIFFERING FROM 2003)*

Colors	Yellow, Graphite (F650CS)

K1200LT

After five years, one of the more successful models in the lineup, the K1200LT, received a number of important updates for 2004. The highlight was a much-acclaimed electrohydraulic centerstand, automatically raising the motorcycle with a button, while larger (36mm) throttles contributed to a 15 percent power increase. An extended spring strut improved stability and a new lower seat helped shorter riders. Styling updates included a split headlight, a larger front fender, and a variety of chrome-plated items.

2004 **K1200LT** *(DIFFERING FROM 2003)*

Power	116 horsepower at 8,000 rpm
Compression ratio	11.5:1
Wheelbase	1,627mm (64 inches)
Wet weight	387 kg (853lbs.)
Colors	Blue, Graphite, Yellow

↑ Only available for one year, the R1200C Montauk was characterized by a vertical double headlight and windshield. The R1200CL's wider Telelever allowed for a fat front tire on a 16-inch wheel. *BMW Group Press*

↓ The R1100S BoxerCup continued for 2004, now with a new color scheme. *BMW Group Press*

Boxers

Now comprising 13 models in addition to the R1200GS, all boxers (except the 850s) had dual-ignition cylinder heads. A special black R850R Comfort was produced for the Italian market, while the BoxerCup Replica received a new tricolor paint scheme and white-faced instruments. Although the cruiser was in its final year, another version of the R1200C was available for 2004, the R1200C Montauk. Based on the R1200CL, with a wide front tire and cast-aluminum composite frame, but a five-speed gearbox, this semi-naked version slotted in between the luxury R1200CL and basic R1200C. This year also saw the R1150GS Adventure take center stage, in Ewan McGregor and Charley Boorman's epic *Long Way Round* circumnavigation of the world.

2004 R1200C MONTAUK *(DIFFERING FROM THE R1200CS)* R1200CL, R1200C, INDEPENDENT *(DIFFERING FROM 2003)*

Gears	5-speed
Wet weight	265 kg (584 lbs.)
Numbers produced	3,276 (2003–2004)
Colors	Black; Champagne; Blue (Montauk); Black (R1200CL); Aluminum (R1200C); Red, Blue (Independent)

2004 R1150R, R1100S, R1100S BOXERCUP *(DIFFERING FROM 2003)*

Colors	Blue (R1150R); Blue, Silver, Red (R1100S); Blue/White/Red (BoxerCup)

2005

K1200S, K1200R, R1200RT, R1200ST, K1200GT, K1200LT, R1200C Montauk, R1200GS, R1150GS Adventure, R1150R, R1150R Rockster, R850R, R1100S, R1100S BoxerCup Replica, F650CS, F650GS, and F650GS Dakar

While the R1200GS continued a predictable evolutionary path, BMW was concurrently developing a new performance four-cylinder range in secret design studios. As a result, BMW briefly overreached itself with the premature release of the radical new K1200S, originally scheduled for 2004. The K1200S finally made it for 2005, joined soon after by the world's most powerful naked bike, the K1200R, with two new 1200 boxer twins replacing the R1150RT and R1150RS. Motorcycle production decreased slightly this year to 92,012, but with 25,705 sales, the R1200GS was the most popular model and was now the most successful BMW motorcycle ever.

K1200S and K1200R

After 20 years, the limitations of the old K series layout in terms of ultimate performance necessitated a change in direction, and while the K1200S was conventional in some respects, as it was a BMW, it was also unique in others. The transverse four-cylinder engine followed Japanese practice, but with the cylinders canted 55 degrees to lower the center of gravity, the drive was by BMW's usual shaft and Paralever. The engine included two balance shafts and the four valves per cylinder were set at a narrow included angle of 21 degrees. Lubrication was dry sump, the oil reservoir in a frame triangle behind the engine, with a multiplate wet clutch and cassette-type gearbox.

↑ Fast and extremely effective, the K1200S was an impressive sport tourer. *BMW Group Press*

↓ With its radical Duolever front suspension, the K1200S continued BMW's tradition of innovation but was initially underdeveloped. The canted forward engine provided a very low center of gravity. *BMW Group Press*

→ Derived from the K1200S, the K1200R was the most powerful unfaired bike available in 2005. *BMW Group Press*

↓ At 56, Andy Sills set a new world speed record in 2005 on a stock K1200S. *BMW Group Press*

The front suspension was an entirely new arrangement, a double wishbone Duolever invented by Englishman Norman Hossack in the 1980s, providing a smoother ride than the Telelever but with a similar anti-dive effect. A first for a production motorcycle was ESA (Electronic Suspension Adjustment). As the most powerful BMW motorcycle yet, the K1200S promised much, but was initially insufficiently developed, with erratic fuel delivery and dubious high-speed stability.

Soon the K1200S established itself as a highly effective and very fast sports tourer, and it was joined soon afterward by the naked brutal-looking K1200R. At the time this was the most powerful naked bike available, and this year BMW sponsored a K1200R Power Cup racing series instead of the BoxerCup, the 2005 series won by the Italian Roberto Panichi. *Motorcyclclist* magazine also named the K1200R its "Motorcycle of the Year."

A K1200S also set a new world land speed record for naturally aspirated 1,000-1,350cc stock motorcycles at Bonneville in 2005, with Andy Sills of San Francisco averaging 173.57 miles per hour on a stock K1200S. Sills had amassed more than 300,000 miles on four BMW motorcycles within the previous seven years and nearly matched Henne's 1937 outright world speed record.

2005 K1200S, K1200R

Type	Four-stroke, transverse four-cylinder, liquid-cooled
Bore x stroke	79x59mm
Displacement	1,157cc
Power	167 horsepower at 10,250 rpm (163-horsepower K1200R)
Compression ratio	13:1
Valve control	Double-overhead camshaft, four valves per cylinder
Fuel supply	BMSK
Gears	6-speed
Frame	Composite aluminum
Front suspension	Duolever
Rear suspension	Paralever swingarm
Wheels	3.50x17 and 6.00x17
Tires	120/70ZR17 and 190/50ZR17
Brakes	Dual-front 320mm disc and 265mm rear disc
Wheelbase	1,571mm (61.9 inches)
Wet weight	248 kg (547 lbs.), K1200S; 237 kg (522 lbs.), K1200R
Numbers produced	29,788 (1997–2003), including R850C
Colors	Gray, Blue, Yellow/White, Blue/White (K1200S); Graphite, White, Yellow (K1200R)

← Considerably lighter than its predecessor, the R1200RT was an impressive tourer. *BMW Group Press*

↓ Replacing the R1150RS for 2005, the R1200ST had styling that was marred by the unusual vertical twin headlight arrangement. *BMW Group Press*

R1200RT and R1200ST

Although the R1150RT was extremely successful, a lighter and more powerful evolutionary R1200RT replaced it for 2005. The 1,200cc boxer engine was a more powerful version of the new R1200GS powerplant, while the frame design was also similar. The R1200RT also boasted optional electronic suspension adjustment and an on-board computer. As it was lighter by 44 pounds, it provided considerably sharper handling than its predecessor.

Also released for 2005 was the R1150RS replacement, the R1200ST. Aimed at more sporting touring riders, the R1200ST shared the R1200RT engine and basic frame with a welded-steel front section, and while the two vertically stacked headlights provided a distinctive look, the styling polarized opinion and wasn't universally accepted. As a result the R1200ST would only last two years.

2005 **R1200RT, R1200ST**
(DIFFERING FROM THE R1200GS, R1150RT, AND R1150RS)

Power	**110 horsepower at 7,500 rpm**
Compression ratio	**12:1**
Rear brake	**265mm disc**
Wheelbase	**1,485mm (58.5 inches), R1200RT;** **1,502mm (59.1 inches), R1200ST**
Wet weight	**259 kg (571 lbs.), R1200RT; 205kg (452 lbs.), R1200ST**
Colors	**Blue, Red, Gray**

F, R and K Series

With many examples replaced and deleted this year, some overlap occurred. The only cruiser was now a R1200C Montauk Special Edition, in red/silver, now the end of the cruiser line. New colors were also only limited to a few models this year, all others continuing unchanged.

2005 **K1200GT, R1150R, R850R, R1100S**
(DIFFERING FROM 2004)

Colors	**Silver (K1200GT); Gray, Blue (R1150R, R850R);** **Silver (R1100S)**

↑ Jimmy Lewis at speed on an HP2 in the Erzberg off-road race in Austria in June 2005. *BMW Group Press*

2006

HP2 Enduro, R1200S, R1200GS Adventure, K1200GT, F800S, F800ST, K1200S, K1200R, R1200RT, R1200ST, K1200LT, R1200GS, R1150R, R850R, F650GS, and F650GS Dakar

As an early release 2006 model, in 2005 BMW introduced the HP2 (high-performance two-cylinder) Enduro. An uncompromising, light, sporting road-legal off-road motorcycle, the HP2 was the first model in a new category of performance motorcycles built in comparatively small numbers. Five other new models were released this year: the fourth new R1200 boxer, the R1200S, two 800cc parallel twins, and a new-generation K1200GT. The best-selling R1200GS evolved into the R1200GS Adventure, and motorcycle production increased to 103,759 during 2006, with sales of 100,064. By far the most popular model was the R1200GS (31,138) and the United States was the third largest market (after Germany and Italy), with 12,825 sales.

HP2 Enduro

With considerable attention to weight saving, the HP2 Enduro was BMW's first serious production sporting off-road motorcycle, and as a testament to its faith in the design, BMW supported privately entered HP2s in the Erzberg race in Austria and German Cross Country Championship (GCC) with current champion, the Finnish rider Simo Kirssi, and the Baja 500 and 1,000 races with Jimmy Lewis. The boxer engine was a more powerful version of the

R1200GS, while the tubular-steel space frame was similar to that of the 1999–2001 Paris-Dakar R900RR racing machines. As the Telelever couldn't provide sufficient travel, the front suspension was by an upside-down fork with a 30mm longer Paralever swingarm. In a world first, the rear spring/damper unit ran exclusively on air. Lightweight engineering resulted in a sub-200-kilogram wet weight, with a dry weight of 175 kilograms (386 pounds). As a high-quality limited-production performance model, the HP2's detailing was exceptional, including tapered aluminum handlebars and stainless-steel footrests, and the HP2 was a supreme testament to how effective the boxer could be as a serious performance motorcycle.

2006 HP2 ENDURO (DIFFERING FROM THE R1200GS)

Power	**105 horsepower at 7,000 rpm**
Frame	**Steel-tubular space frame, nonload-bearing engine**
Front suspension	**45mm upside-down fork**
Wheels	**1.85x21 and 2.50x17**
Tires	**90/90x21 and 140/80x17**
Front brakes	**Single front 305mm disc**
Wheelbase	**1,610mm (63.4 inches)**
Wet weight	**196.5 kg (433 lbs.)**
Numbers produced	**2,910 (2005–2006)**
Colors	**Blue/Gray**

↑ Although based on the R1200GS, with its conventional upside-down front fork, the HP2 was a much more serious off-road motorcycle. *BMW Group Press*

↓ The HP2's tubular-steel space frame was based on the Paris-Dakar R900RR and the rear suspension was an air shock absorber. *BMW Group Press*

R1200S

After six years, never growing to 1,150cc and remaining largely unchanged throughout its life, the R1100S was replaced by a new R1200S for 2006. Lighter, agile, and the most powerful boxer yet, the R1200S shared little with its predecessor. The boxer engine included BMS-K engine management with larger, 52mm throttle bodies, higher compression pistons, stronger con rods, and higher lift camshafts running in three, rather than two, bearings, with reinforced rockers allowing more than 8,000 rpm. The three-piece frame was made of steel and aluminum tubing, while the Telelever front suspension included beefy 41mm tubes. Slender and more dynamic than the R1100S, R1200S had an asymmetric dual headlight that dominated the front end styling, while the wheels were the K series lightweight 17-inch, with a 6.0-inch rear rim an option. Neither a real superbike nor all-rounder, the R1200S was still considered eccentric compared to other Superbikes and would only last two years.

2006 **R1200S** *(DIFFERING FROM THE R1200ST AND R1100S)*	
Power	**122 horsepower at 8,250 rpm**
Compression ratio	**12.5:1**
Rear brake	**265mm disc**
Wheelbase	**1,487mm (58.5 inches)**
Wet weight	**213 kg (470 lbs.)**
Colors	**Black, White, Yellow, Red/Silver**

R1200GS Adventure

Replacing the successful R1150GS for 2006 was the R1200GS Adventure. Now based on the newer generation boxer R1200GS, this included a huge 33-liter gas tank, new windshield, and height adjustable seat. New digital instrumentation and an onboard network with CAN bus technology represented a significant technological advancement over the R1150GS Adventure. Factory-fitted features included partially integrated ABS, off-road tires, and additional headlights, with options extending to aluminum cases and navigation. A 25th Anniversary Special Edition in white was also available and *Motorcyclist* magazine named the R1200GS Adventure the "Best Adventure Motorcycle" for 2006.

2006 **R1200GS** *(DIFFERING FROM THE R1200GS)*	
Power	**100 horsepower at 7,000 rpm**
Wheelbase	**1,571mm (61.9 inches)**
Wet weight	**223 kg (492 lbs.)**
Numbers produced	**18,320 (2006–2007)**
Colors	**White, Aluminum**

K1200GT

Following the introduction of the two new K series models, the K1200S and K1200R, it was inevitable a new K1200GT would replace the older-style K model, completing a trio of new K series bikes spanning sport, long-distance sport touring, and high-performance naked. Sharing the K1200S's chassis with Duolever front suspension, Paralever, and aluminum frame, the K1200GT was 17 percent more powerful than its predecessor and 6 percent lighter. Standard equipment included an aerodynamic fairing with electrically adjustable windshield, with Electronic Suspension Adjustment (ESA) optional, and the K1200GT was good enough to win *Cycle World* magazine's "Best Sport-Touring Motorcycle" award.

2006 **K1200GT** *(DIFFERING FROM THE K1200S)*	
Power	**152 horsepower at 9,500 rpm**
Rear wheel	**5.50x17**
Rear tire	**180/55ZR17**
Rear brake	**294mm disc**
Wheelbase	**1,571mm (61.9 inches)**
Wet weight	**249 kg (549 lbs.)**
Colors	**Gray, Blue, Graphite**

⇓ The new K1200GT completed a three-model lineup for the new K series. *BMW Group Press*

→ The F800ST had a larger fairing, higher windshield and handlebars, and R1200ST-style wheels.
BMW Group Press

↓ The F800's unique engine balancing system included an additional center con rod attached to a horizontal lever underneath the crankshaft.
BMW Group Press

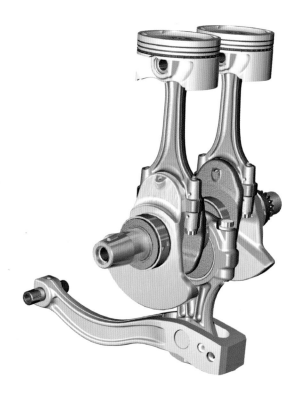

F800S and F800ST

With little in between 650cc and 1,200cc, for 2006 BMW released a pair of 800cc parallel twins to bridge this gap. Built in cooperation with Bombardier-Rotax, the new liquid-cooled engine was unusual in that it featured a 360-degree crankshaft (with both pistons rising and falling together), with an additional con rod in the middle of the crankshaft attached to a horizontal balance arm, almost completely eliminating primary and secondary imbalance. The cylinders were inclined 30 degrees, and the four-valve cylinder head design was similar to that of the K series. Final drive was by a F650CS-type toothed rubber belt, and the 800cc engine was installed in a twin spar aluminum frame, with the engine as a load-bearing component, along with a single-sided aluminum swingarm and 43mm conventional telescopic fork. Innovative features extended to the fuel tank located underneath the seat, lowering the center of gravity, and both F800s were available with optional Bosch two-channel ABS. Balancing power and weight with BMW individuality, the F800s were immediately successful and would spawn more models over the next few years.

2006 F800S, F800ST

Type	**Four-stroke, twin-cylinder, liquid-cooled**
Bore x stroke	**82x75.6mm**
Displacement	**798cc**
Power	**85 horsepower at 8,000 rpm (34 horsepower at 7,000 rpm)**
Compression ratio	**12:1**
Valve control	**Double-overhead camshaft**
Fuel supply	**BMS-K 46mm throttles**
Gears	**6-speed**
Frame	**Aluminum load-bearing bridge**
Front suspension	**Telescopic fork**
Rear suspension	**Monoshock single-sided swingarm**
Wheels	**3.50x17 and 5.50x17**
Tires	**120/70ZR17 and 180/55ZR17**
Brakes	**Twin 320mm front discs and 265mm rear disc**
Wheelbase	**1,466mm (57.7 inches)**
Wet weight	**204 kg (450 lbs.), F800S; 209 kg (461 lbs.), F800ST**
Colors	**Yellow, Red (F800S); Blue, Graphitane (F800ST)**

F, R, and K Series

With several models discontinued and replaced, the F, R and K series continued with minimal updates, and color changes restricted to the R1200GS.

2006 R1200GS (DIFFERING FROM 2005)	
Colors	Gray (R1200GS)

↓ With wheels similar in style to the K1200S, the F800S was the more sporting of the two new 800cc twins. Both 800s shared the toothed-rubber belt final drive. *BMW Group Press*

↑ German rider Markus Barth on the factory-prepared prototype R1200S at the 2007 Le Mans 24-hour race. Finishing 16th overall, he and the team won the Open Class. *BMW Group Press*

2007

HP2 Megamoto, R1200R, G650X, K1200R Sport, K1200S, K1200GT, K1200R, K1200LT, R1200RT, R1200ST, R1200S, R1200GS, R1200GS Adventure, HP2 Enduro, F800S, F800ST, F650GS, and F650GS Dakar

With an off-road racing tradition going back more than 80 years, the introduction of the HP2 signaled a serious return to off-road competition. During 2007, BMW expanded this off-road involvement to include the German Cross Country and World Enduro Championships with 450cc four-stroke prototypes. Other official motorsport entries included an entry in the Le Mans 24-hour race on a modified R1200S, with Markus Barth, Thomas Hinterreiter, and Rico Penzkofer winning their class and finishing 16th.

The production range also expanded this year to include the G650X, "G" signifying a new generation of sporting motorcycles. These were in three different versions, joined by the HP2 Megamoto, the faired K1200R Sport, and the final new R1200 series, the R1200R. This year signaled the end of the R1150, with the K1200LT the only remaining version of the earlier K series. Production increased slightly, to 104,396, with sales of 102,461. During 2007, Ewan McGregor and Charley Boorman undertook their second adventure, *A Long Way Down*, riding R1200GS Adventures from John O'Groats, Scotland, to Cape Agulhas, South Africa.

HP2 Megamoto

A second HP2, the road-oriented HP2 Megamoto, appeared for 2007. Based on the HP2 Enduro, the Megamoto engine was more highly tuned, with a rear Öhlins shock absorber replacing the Enduro's air shock and the front brakes upgraded to larger twin discs. At the 85th running of the Pikes Peak International Hill Climb, Gary Trachy on an HP2 Megamoto set a record for bikes up to 1,200cc in 11 minutes and 46 seconds. Light, lithe, and skeletal and only built in limited numbers, the minimalist and highly effective HP2 Megamoto was the perfect platform for carving twisty roads.

2007 **HP2 MEGAMOTO** (DIFFERING FROM THE HP2 ENDURO)	
Power	110 horsepower at 7,500 rpm
Wheels	3.50x17 and 5.50x17
Tires	120/70ZR17and 180/55ZR17
Front brakes	Dual front 320mm discs
Wheelbase	1,615mm (63.6 inches)
Wet weight	199 kg (439 lbs.)
Colors	Blue, White, Gray

↑ Combining a more powerful engine in a lightweight chassis, the HP2 Megamoto emphasized function over form. *BMW Group Press*

↓ BMW entered a team of five HP2 Megamotos in the 2007 Pikes Peak Hill Climb, Gary Trachy setting a new record. *BMW Group Press*

R1200R

Continuing the process of gradually replacing the R1150 series with the more powerful and lighter R1200 series, the R1200R was introduced for 2007. The final model in this boxer evolution, the R1200R continued the R1150R's naked style, but with 28 percent more power and less weight, and for the first time the new generation of Integral ABS included optional ASC anti-spin control and tire pressure monitoring.

The six-speed gearbox with helical gears was shared with the R1200RT, as was the front half of the two-piece frame. New for the R1200R was a lighter rear tubular space frame. As on the other new R1200s, the introduction of the Single-Wire-System simplified the structure and configuration of the on-board electrics, reducing the number of cables and connections. The updated styling provided a slightly more modern look and the R1200R continued to provide excellent handling and performance.

↓ With more power and less weight, the slightly more conservatively styled R1200R continued a successful naked formula. *BMW Group Press*

2007 **R1200R** *(DIFFERING FROM THE R1150R AND R1200GS)*

Power	**109 horsepower at 7,500 rpm**
Compression ratio	**12:1**
Rear wheel	**5.50x17**
Rear tire	**180/55ZR17**
Rear brake	**265mm disc**
Wheelbase	**1,495mm (58.9 inches)**
Wet weight	**223 kg (492 lbs.)**
Colors	**Black, Crystal Gray, Granite Gray**

G650Xchallenge, G650Xmoto, and G650Xcountry

In an endeavor to broaden its range and fill new niches in the market, BMW released three G650X variations for 2007: the G650Xchallenge Enduro, G650Xmoto Street Moto, and the G650Xcountry Scrambler. Sharing the same technical structure, each version presented a distinct characteristic. They were not intended as entry-level models, but designed to attract new riders to BMW, and with minimal weight and moderate power, all three G650X versions offered excellent sporting performance. Powered by a more powerful version of the F650GS engine, now built in China to keep costs down, they shared chain final drive, a bridge-type tubular-steel frame with cast-aluminum side sections, an aluminum subframe, and an aluminum swingarm. While the suspension, including a 45mm upside-down front fork, was also shared between models, each was provided with an individual setup—the Xchallenge with air damping and the Xcountry with an adjustable spring strut. The wheels were also tailored for a specific purpose, the Xmoto with 17-inch alloys, the Xcountry with 19- and 17-inch spoked wheels, and the Xchallenge with 21- and 18-inch spoke wheels. Braking also varied between models, the street-oriented Xmoto with a larger diameter front disc and four-piston caliper. The G650Xchallenge soon proved a worthy addition to the stable as Japanese rider Yoshio Ikemachi won the 10-day 3,600-kilometer Ulaanbaatar to Uvs international cross-country rally on a G650Xchallenge.

2007 G650XCHALLENGE, G650XCOUNTRY, G650XMOTO *(DIFFERING FROM THE F650GS)*

Power	**53 horsepower at 7,000 rpm**
Frame	**Steel bridge tubular frame with bolted cast-aluminum components**
Front suspension	**45mm upside-down fork**
Wheels	**1.60x21 and 2.50x18 (G650Xchallenge)** **2.50x19 and 3.00x17 (G650Xcountry)** **3.50x17 and 4.50x17 (G650Xmoto)**
Tires	**90/90x21 and 140/80x18 (G650Xchallenge)** **100/90x19 and 130/80x17 (G650Xcountry)** **120/70x17 and 160/60x17 (G650Xmoto)**
Front brakes	**Single front 300mm disc (320mm G650Xmoto)**
Wheelbase	**1,500mm (G650Xchallenge, G650Xmoto);** **1,498mm (G650Xcountry)**
Wet weight	**156 kg (G650Xchallenge); 160 kg (G650Xcountry); 159 kg (G650Xmoto)**
Colors	**White, Blue (G650Xchallenge); Black, White (G650Xcountry); Graphitane, Red (G650Xmoto)**

← The G650Xchallenge was tailored for more serious off-road use and featured longer travel suspension, with an air rear shock absorber like the HP2 Enduro's. The 21- and 18-inch wheels were shod with specific off-road tires. *BMW Group Press*

↓ The Street Moto G650Xmoto had smaller 17-inch wheels, more powerful brakes, shorter travel suspension, and an aluminum handlebar fastened with short mounting clamps. *BMW Group Press*

↑ As an adventure-style bike, the G650Xcountry was the all-rounder of the then three G650Xs, with the shortest suspension travel and a gas-strut rear shock absorber with adjustable ride height. *BMW Group Press*

→ Essentially a half-faired version of the naked K1200R, the K1200R Sport was an extremely capable all-rounder. *BMW Group Press*

K1200R Sport

Ostensibly a half-faired version of the naked K1200R, with its high handlebars, comfortable riding position, and wind tunnel–developed fairing, the K1200R Sport provided the best of both worlds and was a brilliant combination. A capable and functional superbike with intoxicating power, the K1200R Sport was a welcome addition to the 2007 lineup.

2007 **K1200R SPORT** *(DIFFERING FROM THE K1200R)*	
Wet weight	**241 kg (547 lbs.)**
Colors	**White, Blue**

F800S and F800ST

Both the F800S and F800ST were available with an optional suspension lowering kit, the seat height reduced by 60mm (2.4 inches).

2007 **F800S** *(DIFFERING FROM 2006)*	
Color	**Lahar Gray**

2008

HP2 Sport, F800GS, F650GS, G450X, R1200GS, R1200GS Adventure, K1200S, K1200GT, K1200R, K1200R Sport, K1200LT, R1200RT, R1200R, HP2 Megamoto, HP2 Enduro, F800S, F800ST, and G650X

With 17 new models released since 2004, BMW had virtually renewed its entire range within three years, and model expansion for 2008 concentrated on replacement for the F650 single, adding a third motorcycle in the HP2 series, updates to the popular R1200GS, and a competition enduro G450X. Some of the less popular models (R1200ST and R1200S) were discontinued, and although the K1200 series was soon to be replaced, *Cycle World* magazine named the K1200GT the best sport-tourer of 2008. Motorcycle sales dropped slightly, to 101,685, and BMW announced it would be developing a new 1,000cc inline four-cylinder Superbike in partnership with Alpha Technik, with the intention of entering the 2009 World Superbike Championship.

HP2 Sport

Intended for the road or track, the third model in the high-performance range, the HP2 Sport, was the fastest, sportiest, and lightest boxer-engined sport bike yet. Ostensibly a street-legal replica of the 2007 factory endurance racer, the HP2 Sport was powered by a 1,200cc boxer engine with all-new double-overhead camshaft cylinder heads. The more compact, flatter combustion chamber saw the inlet and exhaust valves disposed radially, operated by chain-driven conically ground camshafts. Only a single spark plug was required, additional modifications including new forged pistons and connecting rods allowing the boxer twin to rev to 9,500 rpm. Firsts for a production BMW included a racing power shift for the close-ratio six-speed gearbox, forged alloy wheels, and a MotoGP-inspired dashboard.

The chassis was based on that of the now-discontinued R1200S, but included a carbon-fiber rear subframe, fully adjustable Öhlins racing shock absorbers, and Brembo four-piston radial mount front brake calipers. This was the lightest and most sporting powerful boxer, yet only around 1,000 examples of the HP2 Sport were available in 2008 at a premium price of $25,375. Richard Cooper and Brian Parriott placed fifth and sixth in the Daytona 200, vindicating the HP2 Sport's performance.

2008 **HP2 SPORT** *(DIFFERING FROM THE R1200S)*	
Power	**128 horsepower at 8,750 rpm**
Rear wheel	**6.0x17 inches**
Rear tire	**190/55ZR17**
Wet weight	**199 kg (439 lbs.)**
Colors	**White/Black**

↑ Powering the HP2 Sport was a boxer engine with the first double-overhead camshaft cylinder heads since the RS54 racing model. The valves were radially located and the combustion chamber very flat. *BMW Group Press*

↓ Expensive and only available in limited numbers, the HP2 Sport was lightest and most powerful sporting boxer yet. *BMW Group Press*

→ The F800GS (foreground) was intended to complement the R1200GS while the F650GS (rear) continued the style of the previous F650GS single. An 800cc parallel twin engine powered both. *BMW Group Press*

F800GS and F650GS

Two new enduro models powered by the F800S and ST twin-cylinder engine replaced the single-cylinder F650GS for 2008. Engine updates saw the cylinders canted forward 8.3 degrees instead of the 30 degrees of the F800S/ST, the F650GS with milder camshafts and a power-reducing valve. The two enduros were distinctly individual, the F800GS more dual-purpose, combining road and off-road capability, while the F650GS was less adventure oriented, with shorter suspension travel and a lower seat. Although both models shared the 800cc parallel twin engine, the F800GS was envisaged as a smaller brother to the R1200GS. The F650GS was seen as a successor to the F650 single-cylinder series.

Although the engine came from the existing F800, both enduros featured chain final drive, a new tubular steel frame, suspension, and double-sided aluminum swingarm. The F800GS was generally higher specification, with a 45mm upside-down fork and dual floating front disc brakes, and adventure-style wire spoke wheels. The more basic F650GS made do with a conventional 43mm fork, single front disc brake, and cast-alloy wheels.

While the F650GS was an improvement over its predecessor, the F800GS provided a near impeccable balance between road and moderate off-road use. Its minimal weight and exceptional agility made it a perfect bike for many real world situations.

2008 **F800GS, F650GS** *(DIFFERING FROM THE F800S/ST)*	
Power	**85 horsepower at 7,500 rpm (F800GS);** **71 horsepower at 7,000 rpm (F650GS)**
Fuel supply	**BMS-KP**
Frame	**Tubular steel**
Front suspension	**Upside-down fork (F800GS), Telescopic fork (F650GS)**
Rear suspension	**Monoshock double-sided swingarm**
Wheels	**2.15x21 and 4.25x17 (F800GS),** **2.50x19 and 3.50x17 (F650GS)**
Tires	**90/90x21 and 150/70R17 (F800GS),** **110/80R19 and 140/80R17 (F650GS)**
Brakes	**Twin 300mm front discs and 265mm rear disc** **(single 300mm front disc F650GS)**
Wheelbase	**1,578mm (62.1 inches), F800GS;** **1,575mm (62 inches), F650GS**
Wet weight	**207 kg (456 lbs.), F800GS; 199 kg (439 lbs.), F650GS**
Colors	**Yellow/Black, Magnesium (F800GS);** **Blue, Red, Silver (F650GS)**

R1200GS and R1200GS Adventure

Although only four years old, as the best-selling model (with more than 75,000 sold), the R1200GS and R1200GS Adventure were mildly updated for 2008. A more powerful engine and redesigned six-speed gearbox were introduced, along with optional enduro ESA, the first time on an off-road motorcycle. This comprehensive system provided a choice of six damping settings, further cementing the R1200GS's status as the foremost large-capacity dual-purpose motorcycle.

2008 R1200GS AND R1200GS ADVENTURE
DIFFERING FROM 2007)

Power	**105 horsepower at 7,500 rpm**
Compression ratio	**12:1**
Fuel supply	**BMS-KP**
Wheelbase	**1,507mm (59.3 inches), R1200GS; 1,511mm (59.5 inches), R1200GS Adventure**
Wet weight	**229 kg (505 lbs.), R1200GS; 256 kg (564 lbs.), R1200GS Adventure**
Colors	**Blue, Orange, Silver, Slate (R1200GS); Magnesium, Red (R1200GS Adventure)**

↑ The R1200GS was updated for 2008 with more power, the optional Electronic Suspension Adjustment allowed for more efficient suspension operation in a variety of terrain. *BMW Group Press*

↓ Although large and heavy, the R1200GS Adventure was even more competent in the dirt with the 2008 updates. *BMW Group Press*

↑ The G450X was BMW's first really serious competition production off-road motorcycle and was very successful in European Enduro events. *BMW Group Press*

→ Several innovative features set the G450X apart, including the swingarm pivot coaxial with the countershaft sprocket and a canted cylinder to allow a downdraft intake.

G450X

After a year of development in the World Enduro Championship, BMW introduced its first production competition enduro motorcycle, the G450X. Race bred, battle hardened, and designed for serious competition, the G450X was delivered ready to race and included a number of technologically advanced features. Continuing BMW's obsession with a low center of gravity, the long swingarm featured a coaxial mount with the countershaft sprocket to maintain constant chain tension, while the engine was placed further backward, allowing the cylinder to be canted 30 degrees. With a similar cylinder head design to the K1200S, the engine included crankshaft and con rod roller bearings, a two-ring forged piston, and balance shaft to reduce vibration. An unusual feature was the engine speed wet clutch mounted on the end of the crankshaft, with an intermediate shaft between the crankshaft and gearbox. The G450X frame design was also innovative, built of thin-walled stainless-steel tubing, with an aluminum swingarm and Öhlins shock absorber. This was a serious enduro motorcycle, evidenced by Finnish rider Juha Salminen finishing runner-up in the Enduro World Championship E2 class.

2008 G450X

Type	**Four-stroke, single-cylinder, liquid-cooled**
Bore x stroke	**98x59.6mm**
Displacement	**449.5cc**
Power	**52 horsepower at 9,000 rpm (41 horsepower at 7,000 rpm)**
Compression ratio	**12:1**
Valve control	**Double-overhead camshaft**
Fuel supply	**Keihin digital**
Gears	**5-speed**
Frame	**Bridge-type stainless-steel**
Front suspension	**Upside-down fork 45mm**
Rear suspension	**Monoshock swingarm**
Wheels	**1.60x21 and 2.15x18**
Tires	**90/90x21 and 140/80x18**
Brakes	**Single 260mm disc and 220mm rear disc**
Wheelbase	**1,475mm (58 inches)**
Wet weight	**121 kg (267 lbs.)**
Color	**White**

↓ BMW engaged in serious testing before releasing the G450X. Simo Kirssi rides in an XCC Enduro at Mernes in 2007. *BMW Group Press*

2009

K1300S, K1300GT, K1300R, F800R, G650GS, K1200LT, R1200RT, R1200R, R1200GS, R1200GS Adventure, HP2 Sport, HP2 Megamoto, F800S, F800ST, F800GS, F650GS, G650X, and G450X

With BMW concentrating on developing the S1000RR for Superbike racing and Europe gripped by recession, the only new models this year were the new K1300 series, the F800R, and, primarily for the United States, the G650GS. Production dropped dramatically, to 93,243 motorcycles, and in June 2009 BMW celebrated 40 years of motorcycle production in Berlin with 1,882,400 motorcycles leaving the Spandau factory over that period. This year also saw the establishment of the company's second motorcycle production facility, with motorcycles assembled from completely knocked down (CKD) sets in Manaus, Brazil, in cooperation with local motorcycle producer DAFRA Motos.

Although Simo Kirssi won the European Cross Country Championship on the G450X, the big news this year was BMW's foray into the highly competitive class of World Superbike racing. After displaying the future production S1000RR in April, seasoned campaigners Troy Corser and Ruben Xaus provided the BMW Motorrad Motorsport Team Alpha Racing S1000RRs some promising results in their initial season. Corser set the fastest lap in the first race at Phillip Island, ultimately finishing the season 13th overall, with Xaus 17th.

↑ All new for 2009, the S1000RR World Superbike racer included many conventional components, notably an inline four-cylinder engine, Öhlins suspension, Brembo brakes, a stacked gearbox, and a twin spar aluminum frame. *BMW Group Press*

↓ In its initial shakedown season, Troy Corser proved the new S1000RR was competitive but not yet a race winner. *BMW Group Press*

K1300S, K1300R, and K1300GT

Marking 25 years of the K series, the K1300 replaced the K1200, the three guises similar to before. The new K1300s scored a number of updates over the outgoing K1200s. Not only was the engine capacity increased, but changes to timing, intake, combustion chamber shape, engine management, and the muffler—plus an electronically controlled exhaust valve—boosted power. The drivetrain also received a work over, with undercut gears and an optional factory-fitted quick shift, while the chassis scored an aluminum Duolever lower arm, revisions to the rack and trail, and a revised swingarm to suit ESA II.

The K1300S was the most powerful BMW motorcycle yet, with the K1300R and K1300GT not far behind in the power stakes. Each possessed their own identity and came with the usual vast array of standard equipment and factory options. Still amongst the lightest in their respective classes, the new K1300s were considerably improved over their predecessors with the host of small updates; the low center of gravity belied the weight.

↖ The K1300R may have lost the title of the world's most powerful naked bike, but with 173 horsepower and more torque, it was still a fiercely brutal and aggressive machine. *BMW Group Press*

↑ Although an evolution of the K1200S, the K1300S updates resulted in significant improvements. *BMW Group Press*

↓ Tuned for more midrange torque than before, the K1300 four-cylinder engine still featured inclined cylinders to lower the center of gravity, with the intake camshaft driven by a gear from the exhaust camshaft. *BMW Group Press*

2009 K1300S, K1300R, K1300GT *(DIFFERING FROM THE K1200S, K1200R, K1200GT)*	
Bore x stroke	80x64.3mm
Displacement	1,293cc
Power	175 horsepower at 9,250 rpm (K1300S); 173 horsepower (K1300R), 160 horsepower (K1300GT)
Wheelbase	1,585mm (62.4 inches), K1300S, K1300R; 1,572 mm (61.9 inches), K1300GT
Wet weight	254 kg (560 lbs.), K1300S; 243 kg (536 lbs.), K1300R; 288 kg (635 lbs.), K1300GT
Colors	Gray, Orange, Gray/Red (K1300S); White, Orange, Gray (K1200R); Red, Blue, Beige (K1300GT)

↗ A new fairing graced the K1300GT and with an adjustable windshield, handlebar, and seat, it could be tailored to suit any rider. *BMW Group Press*

↘ Inspired by champion stunt rider Christian Pfeiffer's F800R, a production version became available in 2009. *BMW Group Press*

F800R

In the wake of Christian Pfeiffer winning the European Stunt Riding Championship three years in succession on a special F800R, BMW released a production version for 2009. Based on the F800S, this third in the Roadster series continued the minimalist naked concept of light weight and outstanding dynamics. The parallel twin engine and twin spar aluminum frame came from the F800S, but with a double-sided swingarm and chain final drive, with the K1300R's aggressive styling cues.

2009 **F800R** (DIFFERING FROM THE F800S)	
Power	**87 horsepower at 8,000 rpm**
Fuel supply	**BMS-KP**
Rear suspension	**Monoshock double-sided swingarm**
Wheelbase	**1,520mm (59.8 inches)**
Wet weight	**199 kg (439 lbs.)**
Colors	**Aluminum, Orange, White/Black**

G650GS

For the United States and a few other markets, BMW reintroduced the budget 650GS single, ostensibly the F650GS last seen in 2007, but now titled the G650GS to differentiate it from the twin-cylinder F650GS. Offered alongside the similar G650Xcountry, this was rereleased due to American demand for an affordable BMW with a low seat height. Other than sharing the slightly more powerful China-built engine with the G650X, the equipment was as on the earlier F650GS, but with switchable ABS and heated grips standard, all for the budget $7,670 asking price.

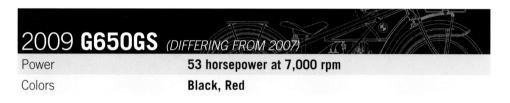

2009 **G650GS** *(DIFFERING FROM 2007)*

Power	**53 horsepower at 7,000 rpm**
Colors	**Black, Red**

G, F, R, and K Series

Marking 15 years of the GS with the four-valve engine, an R1200GS Special Model was offered, in white with black wire-spoked wheels, while the 500,000th GS came off the production line on May 12. Several less popular models were discontinued, and apart from some new colors, the existing range was unchanged.

By the end of the 2000s, all motorcycle manufacturers were suffering, but as Europe's premier motorcycle producer, BMW was optimistically planning for the future, one centering on the new S1000RR. Targeting a younger clientele than the traditional BMW buyer, this hopefully spearheaded an ambitious entry into the highly competitive sports bike sector. With even more emphasis on competition, the next decade would see some of BMW's most impressive new models yet.

2009 **G650XCOUNTRY, F650GS, F800S, F800ST, R1200R, R1200GS SPECIAL MODEL** *(DIFFERING FROM 2008)*

Colors	**Yellow (G650Xcountry, F650GS); White, Gray (F800S); Beige (F800ST); Blue, White (R1200R); White (R1200GS Special Model)**

2010–2015
HYPER PERFORMANCE, HYPER TOURING:
WORLD-BEATING FOURS AND SIXES

BMW's motorcycle sales had gradually grown since the 2004 launch of the groundbreaking R1200GS, but while known for excellence, quality, and innovation, BMWs were still generally considered idiosyncratic and individual. Only BMW made boxer twins and Telelever, Duolever, and Paralever suspension, and its take on the traditional parallel twin and single was also unique. All this changed with the new S1000R Superbike, an uncompromising performance model embracing a purely conventional format, and BMW didn't finish there, presenting a six-cylinder concept at the end of 2009. Over the next few years, BMW would also redefine its traditional touring category.

↑ Unlike previous BMW motorcycles, the S1000RR followed a tried and tested conventional Superbike formula and was immediately successful. Less successful was the green color, this only lasting one year. *BMW Group Press*

← As a class-leading Superbike, the S1000RR completely eradicated BMW's staid image. *BMW Group Press*

2010

S1000RR, R1200RT, R1200GS, R1200GS Adventure, R1200R Touring Special, F800R Pfeiffer Replica, G450X, K1300S, K1300GT, K1300R, K1200LT, R1200R, HP2 Sport, HP2 Megamoto, F800S, F800ST, F800R, F800GS, F650GS, & G650GS

Alongside the breathtaking S1000RR, BMW released updated R1200RT and GSs with the HP2 Sport double-overhead camshaft cylinder heads, a Chris Pfeiffer F800R, and a slightly revised G450X. With replacement imminent, a K1300GT Exclusive Edition was offered, while the range was streamlined with the G650Xs disappearing. Motorcycle production numbered 112,271 during 2010, and while BMW had moderate success in the World Superbike Championship, in production-based national championships, the S1000RR's results were outstanding.

S1000RR

BMW's first real Superbike since the R90S, the S1000RR made history when it was released in 2010. With unparalleled technical innovation and eye-watering performance, the S1000RR immediately became the class-setting Superbike, forcing all other manufacturers back to the drawing board. Although a succession of new high-performance models had gradually eroded BMW's staid image over the past few years, the S1000RR completely obliterated it. With a class-leading power-to-weight ratio, a superb balance of overall dynamics, and groundbreaking ABS and traction control, the S1000RR immediately became the new Superbike king.

↑ **Another conventional feature was the aluminum bridge frame.** *BMW Group Press*

Unlike previous BMW designs, the S1000RR layout was surprisingly conventional. The water-cooled inline four-cylinder in an aluminum bridge frame was already proven and established as the most efficient for a Superbike, as was an upside-down front fork and linkage rear suspension. BMW then added its interpretation within this traditional framework.

The primary objective was to create an extremely powerful narrow engine in a compact package. Derived from BMW's Formula One program, the engine was tilted forward 32 degrees, lowering the center of gravity. A short stroke and light titanium valves were operated by a small, single cam, allowing for higher revs. The included valve angle was 24.5 degrees, the camshafts arranged directly above the valves and driven by a toothed chain running on a secondary gear shaft just above the crankshaft. Lubrication was by wet sump, and the BMS-KP engine management included fully sequential fuel injection, with variable length intake manifolds to improve the torque curve.

Weighing only 12 kilograms (26 pounds), the aluminum bridge frame was constructed of four castings and included the engine as a load-bearing element. The conventional suspension was a 46mm Sachs upside-down fork and rising-rate single shock absorber, while the 17-inch alloy wheels and radial Brembo front brakes were the usual Superbike fare. Where the S1000RR excelled was in the sophisticated four-mode electronic ABS and DTC, conveniently accessible on the right side switch block. With its distinctive asymmetrical headlight arrangement, the S1000RR broke with aesthetic convention but delivered in performance and function. The S1000RR also took the International Bike of the Year 2010 award, and *Cycle World* magazine named it "the Best Superbike" and *Motorcyclist* voted it "Motorcycle of the Year."

← The modern large-bore, short-stroke four-cylinder engine was extremely compact and powerful. The cam followers were finger style.
BMW Group Press

↓ Whereas other large-displacement BMW motorcycles had Telelever or Duolever front suspension, the S1000RR followed other Superbikes with an upside-down fork with the obligatory radial brake calipers.
BMW Group Press

2010 **S1000RR**

Type	**Four-stroke, transverse four-cylinder, liquid-cooled**
Bore x stroke	**80x49.7mm**
Displacement	**999cc**
Power	**193 horsepower at 13,000 rpm**
Compression ratio	**13:1**
Valve control	**Double-overhead camshaft, four valves per cylinder**
Fuel supply	**BMS-KP**
Gears	**6-speed**
Frame	**Bridge aluminum**
Front suspension	**Upside-down fork**
Rear suspension	**Monoshock swingarm**
Wheels	**3.50x17 and 6.00x17**
Tires	**120/70ZR17 and 190/55ZR17**
Brakes	**Dual front 320mm disc and 220mm rear disc**
Wheelbase	**1,432mm (56.4 inches)**
Wet weight	**204 kg (449 lbs.), 206.5 kg (455 lbs.) with Race ABS**
Colors	**Green, Gray, Silver/Blue**

↑ Another conventional feature was the aluminum bridge frame.
BMW Group Press

↓ Although the style was largely unchanged, the new R1200RT engine was more powerful than before.
BMW Group Press

R1200RT, R1200GS, and R1200GS Adventure

The popular R1200RT and R1200GS received updated double-overhead camshaft cylinder heads for 2010, increasing power and torque, and raising the rev ceiling 500 rpm, with a resulting improvement in acceleration. The HP2 Sport's radial valve arrangement continued, but unlike the HP2 Sport, the R1200RT and GS featured dual spark plug ignition. The cylinder head included larger (39mm and 33mm) valves, the throttle butterflies were increased to 50mm (from the HP2 Sport's 47mm), and also included was an electronically controlled exhaust flap. The Telelever/Paralever chassis was as before, but with optional ESA II Electronic Suspension Adjustment with damping, spring base, and now spring-rate adjustable with the touch of a button. The R1200RT received a slightly redesigned fairing, was lighter and more dynamic in appearance, and had a new front fender.

2010 R1200RT, R1200GS, R1200GS ADVENTURE
(DIFFERING FROM 2009)

Power	110 horsepower at 7,750 rpm
Fuel supply	BMS-K+
Colors	Gray (R1200RT); Gray, Black, White, Red (R1200GS); Gray, Yellow (R1200GS Adventure)

→ The double-overhead camshaft layout was similar to the HP2 Sport's.
BMW Group Press

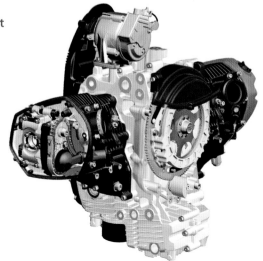

After a promising introduction during 2009, BMW worked hard at creating a competitive S1000RR racer for the 2010 season. Under the direction of Davide Tardozzi, and with Troy Corser and Ruben Xaus again riding, the engine was developed with Dell'Orto fuel injection, 48mm throttle bodies, a 14:1 compression ratio, and a ride-by-wire BMW RsM5 EFI system to produce 215 horsepower at 14,000 rpm. With Öhlins suspension and Nissin (Corser) or Brembo (Xaus) brakes, the S1000RR weighed right on the 162-kilogram weight limit. As the basic credentials were sound, after much experimentation with swingarm geometry, race results improved, Corser finishing on the podium at Monza and Misano, and 11th overall in the championship.

↑ The factory S1000RR had a huge radiator and a unique swingarm with the top and bottom halves glued together. *BMW Group Press*

← Troy Corser's 2010 World Superbike S1000RR had an Öhlins TTX20 front fork with Nissin brake calipers and race ABS. *BMW Group Press*

↙ Corser provided the S1000RR two podium finishes during the 2010 World Superbike season. *BMW Group Press*

While it was an uphill struggle in World Superbike, in the Superstock 1000 FIM Cup Italian rider Ayrton Badovini rode a production-spec S1000RR to 9 wins from 10 races, and a comfortable title victory. Success in production-based national championships continued throughout Europe, with victories to Gregory Fastre (Belgium), Javier Fores Querol (Spain), Jon Kirkham (British Superstock Championship), Steve Brogan (British Superbike EVO Championship), Sami Penna (Finland), Martin Choi (Bulgaria), Maxim Averkin (Russia), and Erwan Nigon (France). In Germany, the S1000RR dominated several series, winning the DMV Road Racing Championship, Endurance Cup, and DMSB Endurance Championship.

R1200R Touring Special

In order to maintain interest in the older boxer engine prior to its incorporation in the R1200R, a R1200R Touring Special became available during 2010. Special features included a new comfort seat, onboard computer, chrome exhaust, sports windshield, and locking saddlebags.

↑ **In an endeavor to maintain interest in the earlier boxer, a R1200R Touring Special was available for 2010.** *BMW Group Press*

↓ **Champion stunt rider Chris Pfeiffer demonstrating the abilities of the F800R Pfeiffer special edition.** *BMW Group Press*

2010 **R1200R TOURING SPECIAL** *(DIFFERING FROM 2009)*	
Color	White

F800R Chris Pfeiffer

With four-time World and European Stunt-Riding Champion Chris Pfeiffer convincingly demonstrating the F800R's abilities, a special Pfeiffer replica was available for 2010. Resembling the competition version, the standard production model was only separated from the race version by its paint scheme and Akrapovič muffler. The bespoke color scheme included a black drivetrain and swingarm, with a Chris Pfeiffer signature and sponsor decals further differentiating it.

2010 **R800R CHRIS PFEIFFER** *(DIFFERING FROM THE F800R)*	
Colors	White/Blue/Red

G450X

After several seasons of moderate competition success, notably Juha Salminen's second-place finish in the 2009 World Endurance Championship, the G450X received a number of updates for 2010. These included a modified ECU, a slip-on racing muffler, a new upside-down front fork, and a recalibrated rear shock absorber.

G, F, R, and K Series

As usual, except for new colors, BMW continued its policy of continuing with most existing models unchanged in 2010. As a final version, a K1300GT Exclusive Edition was produced with heated grips and seat, an onboard computer, ESA II, and ASC (automatic stability control). In addition to the standard panniers, it also received a 49-liter top case. Also new this year were F650GS, F800GS, and R1200GS Adventures commemorative editions in original R80G/S colors, celebrating 30 years of the GS.

<table>
<tr><td colspan="2">2010 K1300GT EXCLUSIVE EDITION, F650GS, F800GS, R1200R, 30TH ANNIVERSARY GS (DIFFERING FROM 2009)</td></tr>
<tr><td>Colors</td><td>Gray (K1300GT Exclusive); White, Orange (F650GS); White, Orange/Black (F800GS); Gray (R1200R); White (30th GS)</td></tr>
</table>

↖ For 2010, the G450X received a few updates to make it more competitive. *BMW Group Press*

↓ The final K1300GT was the 2010 Exclusive Edition with a host of electronic aids, plus a top case included as standard equipment. *BMW Group Press*

← This F800GS was one of three commemorative 30 Years GS editions. *BMW Group Press*

↑ Packed with technical innovation, the K1600GT was supremely smooth and comfortable. *BMW Group Press*

↓ The compact six-cylinder K1600 engine featured chain-driven double-overhead camshafts with bucket-type tappets. *BMW Group Press*

2011

K1600GTL, K1600GT, R1200R, R1200R Classic, K1300S, K1300R, R1200RT, R1200GS, R1200GS Adventure, HP2 Sport, S1000RR, F800ST, F800R, F800GS, F650GS, G650GS, and G450X

After doing the unthinkable, and creating a Superbike that annihilated the competition first time out, one year later BMW turned toward its traditional touring segment with a pair of six-cylinder luxury tourers. In a difficult retail environment, BMW was continuing to expand, selling 104,286 motorcycles, and on May 6, 2011, the company celebrated the two millionth motorcycle emanating from the Berlin factory.

K1600GTL and K1600GT

Although BMW already had several extremely competent touring motorcycles in its range, the release of the K1600GT and GTL grand tourers set a new benchmark for sophisticated mile crunching. Six-cylinder inline engines had been a significant layout for BMW cars over the years, but six-cylinder motorcycle engines had always been either very long or very wide, compromising chassis geometry and weight distribution. For the K1600, BMW's engineers concentrated on a light and compact inline six-cylinder, an undersquare bore/stroke ratio, and 5mm between cylinder sleeves contributing to engine width of only 555mm. Based on the K1300 four-cylinder, the cylinders were canted 55 degrees, but the usual 120-degree crank spacing negated the need for any balance shaft. The included valve angle was 25 degrees, the lubrication dry sump, and the alternator and starter motor moved behind the crankshaft to free space above the gearbox. Tuned for a broad spread of power, the motorcycle had more than 70 percent of its maximum torque available from 1,500 rpm. Also included on the K1600 was BMW's newest engine management system, BMS-X, this providing three different riding modes (Rain, Road, Dynamic).

The chassis was based on the current four-cylinder K series, including an aluminum bridge-type frame, Duolever and Paralever, and similar wheels and brakes. The instrument panel also included a 5.7-inch TFT color information display and options extended to electronic suspension adjustment II (ESA II), and an adaptive headlight that compensated for pitch and banking through corners. The K1600 exceeded all the design and engineering team's expectations and would be a game changer in the touring market. Smooth, fast, and bristling with technology, although the weight was considerable, the K1600GT was a surprisingly adept handler and arguably the ultimate fast tourer. It was no surprise that the K1600GT followed the S1000RR by winning the International Bike of the Year 2011 award, as well as voted "Best Touring Motorcycle" by *Motorcyclist* and *Cycle World* magazines.

2011 **K1600GT, K1600GTL** *(DIFFERING FROM THE K1300GT)*

Type	Four-stroke, transverse six-cylinder, liquid-cooled
Bore x stroke	72x67.5mm
Displacement	1,649cc
Power	160.5 horsepower at 7,750 rpm
Compression ratio	12.2:1
Fuel supply	BMS-X
Rear tire	190/55ZR17
Rear brake	320mm disc
Wheelbase	1,618mm (63.7 inches)
Wet weight	319 kg (703 lbs.), K1600GT; 348 kg (767 lbs.), K1600GTL
Colors	Gray, Red (K1600GT); Silver, Blue (K1600GTL)

↑ A host of luxury fittings differentiated the GTL, including a top box, chrome trim, fog lights, and a taller screen. The rider's pegs were also set lower and further forward, with a lower seat. *BMW Group Press*

← The K1600 chassis was similar to the K1300's, the main spar running over the top of the low-lying engine, allowing the rider to sit lower. Usual K series features included the Duolever and Paralever, but the rear disc was now a huge 320mm, the same as the front. *BMW Group Press*

→ Although the style was similar, the new R1200R now had stouter fork tubes and the double-overhead camshaft engine had two-bolt valve covers. *BMW Group Press*

↓ In black with a white stripe, the R1200R Classic had wire-spoked wheels and a chrome-plated muffler. *BMW Group Press*

↑ Light, economical, and affordable, the reintroduced G650GS may have been an entry-level dual-purpose model but was surprisingly capable. Redesigned bodywork included a new windshield and asymmetrical headlamp. *BMW Group Press*

R1200R and R1200R Classic

The final R1200s to receive the new HP2 Sport-derived double-overhead camshaft cylinder heads were the R1200R and R1200R Classic. The updated engine provided these do-anything Roadsters with more torque and top end performance, with the R1200R Classic's wire-spoked wheels and chrome-plated muffler introducing a nostalgic theme. In addition to the updated engine, the R1200R's Telelever tubes were enlarged to 41mm (from 35mm), with partially integral ABS, ESA, and ASC (automatic stability control) optional. Both models also featured a standard centerstand this year.

2011 R1200R, R1200R CLASSIC (DIFFERING FROM 2010)

Power	110 horsepower at 7,750 rpm
Fuel supply	BMS-K+
Colors	Gray, Red (R1200R); Black (R1200R Classic)

G650GS

Although the G650GS was already available in the United States as an entry-level model, for 2011 it made a return to the general lineup. Slightly detuned for impending EU regulations, the G650GS received new cast-aluminum wheels, the rear slightly wider than before, for most markets. US versions retained wire-spoked wheels, though. Remarkably similar to the updated F650GS of 2004, and even the original 2000 version, the venerable five-speed G650GS proved there was still a market for a sensible, lightweight, low-cost passport to adventure, especially with a wide array of options available.

2011 G650GS (DIFFERING FROM 2010)

Power	48 horsepower at 6,500 rpm
Fuel supply	BMS-CII
Rear wheel	3.50x17 inches
Tires	110/80R19 and 140/80R17
Wheelbase	1,477mm (58.2 inches)
Wet weight	192 kg (423 lbs.)
Colors	White, Orange/Red

G, F, R, K, and S Series

By 2011, the HP2 Sport was the only remaining HP2, with the F800S and long-lived K1200LT discontinued, seeing the end of the horizontal four-cylinder K series that began in 1984. Also introduced this year was an R1200GS Triple Black, with black fork, wheels, and engine.

2011 S1000RR, K1300S, K1200R, F800R, AND R1200GS TRIPLE BLACK *(DIFFERING FROM 2010)*	
Colors	Gray, Yellow (S1000RR); Red, Blue (K1300S); Yellow, Black (K1300R); Yellow (F800R); Black, Gray (F800ST); Black (R1200GS Triple Black)

↑ A Special Edition R1200GS for 2011 was the Triple Black. *BMW Group Press*

SUPERBIKE RACING 2011

After dominating sportbike sales and Superstock racing during 2010, there was reason to expect this would translate into World Superbike success during 2011. Second the previous season, Leon Haslam lined up alongside Troy Corser, the short-stroke S1000RR engine now producing around 220 horsepower at 14,000 rpm. With the latest Öhlins TRSP25 front fork and RSP40 rear shock absorber and lightweight OZ forged wheels, the S1000RR weighed right on the class minimum, 165 kilograms, but weight distribution was a problem. A stock road bike swingarm replaced last year's trick item, but results were elusive. Haslam managed only three podium finishes and was beaten nine times by Ayrton Badovini on the BMW Italia privateer S1000RR. Haslam finished the season in 5th overall, with Corser 15th.

Although World Superbike results were disappointing during 2011, Sébastien Gimbert won the French Superbike title, Glenn Allerton took out the Australian Superbike Championship, and Team Motorrad France 99 came a close second in the FIM World Endurance Championship.

↗ Leon Haslam's factory S1000RR had a stock swingarm for 2011. All the front brakes were Brembo this year. *BMW Group Press*

→ After finishing second in the 2010 World Superbike Championship, Haslam struggled with the S1000RR during 2011. *BMW Group Press*

→ Often referred to as "America's Queen of Speed," seven-time land speed record holder Valerie Thompson poses with her S1000RR. *BMW Group Press*

↓ After only two years, the S1000RR received a significant update. The style was similar but underneath was a completely new frame. The fairing had small winglets on each side to improve aerodynamics. *BMW Group Press*

2012

S1000RR, F800R, G650GS Sertão, K1600GTL, K1600GT, K1300S, K1300R, R1200RT, R1200GS, R1200GS Adventure, R1200R, R1200R Classic, F800ST, F800GS, F650GS, and G650GS

With significant new model releases in 2010 and 2011, 2012 was a year of updates. While the S1000RR was still setting the Superbike standard, this received a significant update to keep it ahead of the pack, the R800R was visually updated, a more serious G650GS Sertão was added, and BMW released special versions of the R1200GS, K1300S, and K1300R. Also new this year were a pair of maxi scooters, the C600 Sport and C650GT (not covered here), while BMW became the first motorcycle manufacturer in the United States to offer ABS as standard on all models. Sales increased to 106,358, with Germany (20,516) the predominant market followed by the United States (12,057), and the most popular model worldwide was the R1200GS, about to be superseded.

S1000RR

Responding to racing and customer feedback, the already impressive S1000RR received more than the customary minor facelift, with updates to the chassis geometry, suspension, and engine tweaks to provide improved low and midrange torque. Frame modifications included an enlarged cross section for the air intake, while the steering head angle, offset swingarm pivot, and spring strut length were all altered. Also included this year was a mechanical steering damper and a new dash with more functions. The engine was now provided with three performance curves (as opposed to the previous two), Rain (163 horsepower), Sport, and Race/Slick. While the power and weight remained unchanged, the updated S1000RR steered with more precision and felt more nimble. And 35-year-old Valerie Thompson, a daring woman from Scottsdale, Arizona, vindicated the S1000RR's performance in June with a measured top speed of 209.5 miles per hour at the Mojave Air and Space Port airfield in California. Apart from gearing and approved racing fuel, Thompson's S1000RR was stock. Over the next few years Thompson continued to set more records, achieving 217.7 miles per hour in the Texas Mile Speed Festival in October 2014.

2012 **R1000RR** *(DIFFERING FROM 2011)*	
Wheelbase	**1,422.7mm (56 inches)**
Colors	**Red, Blue, Black, Motorsport**

F800R

For a midcycle update, the F800R was slightly more aggressively styled, with the front and side trim serving as radiator covers, a new front fender, red rear spring strut, and a sport windshield in body color.

2012 **F800R** *(DIFFERING FROM 2011)*	
Wheelbase	**1,514mm (59.6 inches)**
Colors	**White, Red, Silver**

G650GS Sertão

After being sidelined since 2007, the previous F650GS Dakar made a comeback as the G650GS Sertão. With the current trend of adventure bikes becoming more street oriented, the Sertão was designed for the genuine off-roader. Sharing the basic engine and chassis with the standard G650GS, the Sertão included longer travel suspension, wire-spoked wheels, and an aluminum engine guard. Underpowered for pure street use, when the going got tough, the well-balanced Sertão could more than hold its own.

↑ The F800R received a more aggressive look for 2012 but was unchanged technically. *BMW Group Press*

↓ Remarkably similar to the earlier F650GS Dakar, the G650GS Sertão was more off-road oriented than others in the GS lineup. *BMW Group Press*

2012 **G650GS SERTÃO** *(DIFFERING FROM THE G650GS)*	
Wheels	**1.60x21 and 3.00x17**
Tires	**90/90R21 and 130/80R17**
Wheelbase	**1,484mm (58.4 inches)**
Colors	**White/Blue**

↑ The R1200GS Rallye included contrasting white bodywork with a black engine and forks tubes and gray swingarm and cylinder head covers, with a red frame. *BMW Group Press*

↓ Bristling with carbon fiber and technical innovation, the K1300S HP was the sportiest K series yet. *BMW Group Press*

↑ The K1300R special edition also featured a dynamics package, plus a distinctive engine spoiler. *BMW Group Press*

2012

R1200GS Rallye, K1300S HP, and K1300R

Ostensibly a special version of the R1200GS Adventure, the R1200GS Rallye included special colors, a chrome exhaust system, and onboard computer, while the HP package for the K1300S created the sportiest K series yet. Technical updates included a numbered badge, numerous HP carbon parts, an Akrapovič muffler, ESA II, ASC stability control, a speed gearshift, and paddock stand. The K1300R included special paint, a carbon engine spoiler, and the ESA II and an ASC dynamics package.

2012 R1200GS RALLYE, K1300S HP, K1300R SPECIAL MODELS

Colors	White (R1200GS Rallye), White/Blue/Black (K1300S HP), Gray/Black (K1300R)

G, F, R, and K Series

As BMW reoriented its range, the G450X and HP2 Sport were discontinued, with other existing models unchanged.

2012 F650GS, F800GS, F800ST, R1200GS, R1200GS ADVENTURE, K1300S *(DIFFERING FROM 2011)*

Colors	Black/Yellow (F650GS); Gray, Blue/White, Black (F800GS); Blue (F800ST, R1200GS); Red, White, Black (R1200GS Adventure); Silver (K1300S)

SUPERBIKE RACING 2012

After three years of investment and development, the S1000RR finally tasted World Superbike success in 2012 with six race wins. Following Corser's retirement, Marco Melandri joined Leon Haslam on the factory S1000RR, now based on the new production version. Updates included the revised engine and swingarm mounts, an aerodynamically and ergonomically improved fuel tank and seat, and improved electronics to smooth the power delivery. The engine included a lighter crankshaft, with the power increased to 225 horsepower at 14,500 rpm. An underslung swingarm superseded the stock item, the brakes Brembo, and new wheels were Marchesini. Melandri briefly led the series midseason, but some poor results toward the end saw him finish third overall. In other championships, Sylvain Barrier won the Superstock 1000 FIM Cup, Sébastian Gimbert the French Superbike Championship, and Erwan Nigon the German IDM Superbike championship. In the IDM series, S1000RRs filled the top four positions. Again the BMW Motorrad France Team Thevant finished second in the FIM Endurance World Championship. The team of Nigon, Gimbert, Damian Cudlin, and Hugo Marchand won the Doha 8-hour race in Qatar, also finishing on the podium in the prestigious Le Mans 24-hour race.

This year also saw BMW's return to the Sidecar World Championship, with Jörg Steinhausen (son of 1975 and 1976 world champion Rolf Steinhausen) teaming with Grégory Cluze on an HP-supported LCR outfit. Powered by an S1000RR engine, Steinhausen and Cluze finished runner-up in the championship, with two race wins; it was BMW's first world championship three-wheeler race victory in 38 years.

↑ The BMW Motorrad Motorsport 2012 World Superbike team. The riders are Leon Haslam (left) and Marco Melandri (right). Director Bernhard Gobmeier and head of race operations Andrea Dosoli are in the center. *BMW Group Press*

↖ Melandri demonstrating the style that took him to third overall in the 2012 World Superbike Championship. *BMW Group Press*

← Jörg Steinhausen and Gregory Cluze on their way to victory in the Hungarian round of the 2012 Sidecar World Championship, BMW's first sidecar victory in 38 years. *BMW Group Press*

↓ Marco Melandri's considerably updated 2012 model S1000RR provided six World Superbike race wins. *BMW Group Press*

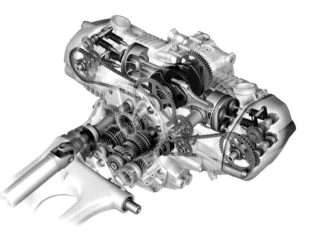

2013

R1200GS, HP4, F800GS, F700GS, F800GT, S1000RR, K1600GTL, K1600GT, K1300S, K1300R, R1200RT, R1200GS Adventure, R1200R, R1200R Classic, F800R, G650GS, and G650GS Sertão

↑ In addition to the water-cooling, the six-speed gearbox was incorporated in the engine casting. The clutch was also a wet multiplate type.
BMW Group Press

↓ BMW's first water-cooled boxer, the 2013 R1200GS, was new from the ground up. The swingarm was now on the left and Brembo front brakes were radially mounted. *BMW Group Press*

As it continued to be the pivotal model in BMW's lineup, making up a quarter of all sales, the R1200GS received its fourth significant update in less than a decade, the boxer engine now with water-cooled cylinder heads. BMW also expanded its HP range with the HP4, the lightest 1,000cc Superbike ever, while the twin-cylinder F series was significantly updated. This year BMW celebrated 90 years of the boxer motorcycle, and in addition to three special 90-year editions, a concept memorial air-cooled boxer was displayed. Sales continued to increase, with an all-time high of 115,215 motorcycles supplied, an 8.3 percent increase over 2012. In the United States, 14,100 motorcycles were sold, the second highest on record, fueled by sales of more than 2,000 of the new water-cooled R1200GS. BMW Motorrad was also the outright winner of a 2013 customer satisfaction survey carried out by the Motorcycle Industry Council in the USA. During the year, BMW also announced a partnership with India's fourth largest motorcycle manufacturer, TVS, to develop and build a range of entry-level bikes under 500cc.

R1200GS

BMW's most impressive success story in recent years was undoubtedly the R1200GS, but after selling more than 170,000 examples, it received a ground-up redesign for 2013. Central to the new GS was the addition of 35 percent water-cooling in combination with 65 percent air-cooling to target areas of high thermal stress. The new cylinders had vertical through flow, with the intake on the top and exhaust underneath, while the valves were larger (40mm and 34mm), with a narrow 18-degree included angle. The cylinders were integrated with the vertically split crankcases, and with two inconspicuous small radiators, the result was an engine that still looked very traditional while providing more power and being able to meet stricter noise and environmental regulations. Other new features included the six-speed gearbox incorporated in the engine casting, a wet clutch with a slipper function, and the shaft drive now on the left. Electronic updates included a ride-by-wire throttle and five selectable riding modes (Rain, Road, Dynamic, Enduro, and Enduro Pro).

The chassis included a new tubular-steel bridge frame, with a separate bolted-on rear subframe, longer swingarm, wider wheels with larger tires, updated radially mounted Brembo Monobloc front brake calipers, and a larger rear disc. Both the Telelever and Paralever were reworked, a new adjustable windshield offered improved protection, and the seat was adjustable for height and tilt angle. As the R1200GS was already set, the class standard BMW was presented with a difficult task to create an improvement, but somehow they managed it. Although slightly heavier than before, the new bike was more agile than its predecessor, and the sophisticated electronics added to the safety and overall competence.

2013 R1200GS *(DIFFERING FROM 2012)*

Power	**125 horsepower at 7,700 rpm**
Compression ratio	**12.5:1**
Fuel supply	**BMS-X**
Wheels	**3.00x19 and 4.50x17**
Tires	**120/70R19 and 170/60R17**
Rear brake	**276mm disc**
Wet weight	**238 kg (525 lbs.)**
Colors	**White, Red, Blue, Gray**

SUPERBIKE RACING 2013

BMW Motorrad ceased direct involvement in the World Superbike Championship for 2013, instead supplying engines and electronics to Andrea Buzzoni's BMW Motorrad Italia, which was responsible for the racing team, along with testing and chassis development. Andrea Dosoli continued as technical director, and with Serafino Foti as team manger, the riders this were Marco Melandri and Chaz Davies. The power was around 230 horsepower at 14,500 rpm, and both riders struggled to find the optimum setup, the team experimenting with many different chassis and Öhlins suspension options. Davies took three race wins and Melandri two, Davies finishing fifth and Melandri fourth overall. After five seasons, BMW still hadn't won the World Superbike Championship and wouldn't field a team in 2014. There was, however, some consolation, with 19-year-old Markus Reiterberger winning the German IDM Championship and BMW taking the manufacturers' title for the third successive year.

↑ Chaz Davies struggled with setup during the 2013 World Superbike season but still managed three race wins. *BMW Group Press*

↓ Sylvain Barrier repeated his 2011 success by winning the 2012 FIM 1000 Superstock Cup. *BMW Group Press*

HP4

With the S1000RR already at the pinnacle of Superbike performance, BMW released the HP version, raising the bar yet another notch. Ostensibly a tarted-up S1000RR, updates included a numbered top triple clamp, special paint, semi-active suspension, titanium Akrapovič exhaust, new ABS and traction control, Brembo Monobloc brake calipers, forged alloy wheels, and a quickshifter. An HP4 Competition package was also available, with carbon panels, blue wheels, and various HP components. As a homologation model for Superstock and World Superbike racing, the HP4 was the lightest inline four-cylinder Superbike available, and Sylvain Barrier rode the HP4 to victory in the FIM 10000 Superstock Cup. Andy Sills, on an S1000RR, continued to set world speed records at Bonneville, this year managing 224.190 miles per hour, the fastest speed ever for a BMW motorcycle.

2013 **HP4** *(DIFFERING FROM THE S1000RR)*	
Rear tire	200/55ZR17
Wet weight	199 kg (439 lbs.)
Colors	Blue/White

→ Included on the HP4 was a 10-pound-lighter titanium Akrapovič exhaust system, Brembo Monobloc brake calipers, and lightweight-forged aluminum wheels. *BMW Group Press*

F700GS and F800GS

Continuing the F series GS success story, both the F650GS and F800GS were updated for 2013. As before, the F800GS was a more serious dual-purpose model, with the F700GS replacing the F650GS but continuing as an entry-level version geared more toward street use. Still powered by the 800cc parallel twin, the F700GS was more powerful than before and now included a dual-disc front brake. Styling updates featured new side panels, while electronic suspension adjustment (ESA) and automatic stability control (ASC) were optional. The F800GS was available with lowered suspension, but most updates were to the F700GS, this continuing as a highly impressive urban warrior, both models vindicating BMW's approach of evolution rather than revolution as the way forward.

↑ Replacing the F650GS for 2013 was the F700GS. With new styling, more power, and dual-front discs, it was still very street oriented. *BMW Group Press*

↓ With its larger front wheel, the new F800GS was more suited to off-road riding and was a very effective dual-purpose machine. *BMW Group Press*

2013 F800GS, F700GS *(DIFFERING FROM 2011 AND THE F650GS)*

Power	**75 horsepower at 7,300 rpm (F700GS)**
Front brake	**Twin 300mm front discs (F700GS)**
Wheelbase	**1,562mm (61.5 inches), F700GS**
Wet weight	**214 kg (472 lbs.), F800GS; 209 kg (461 lbs.), F650GS**
Colors	**Kalamata, Blue, White (F800GS); Gray, Red, Silver (F700GS)**

F800GT

A successor to the F800ST, the F800GT included more power, a new full fairing with improved weather protection, and dedicated luggage. Continuing with belt final drive, options included ASC and ESA and a titanium Akrapovič sports silencer, saving 3.7 pounds. Rear spring preload was now remotely adjustable, new design wheels lighter, and the aluminum handlebars higher. To improve stability, the swingarm was lengthened 2 inches with less spring travel, allowing a reduction in seat height from 33.1 inches to 31.5 inches. A stronger rear subframe allowed for a 24-pound increased load capacity, to 456 pounds. The resulting F800GT was a versatile all-rounder providing surprisingly nimble handling and enough power for most riders.

↗ Replacing the F800ST for 2013, the F800GT included a near full fairing for improved weather protection, along with higher handlebars and taller screen. Luggage was optional. *BMW Group Press*

↓ Three 90-year anniversary R1200 boxers were released for 2013. This is the R1200RT 90th, in Sapphire Black, with a black engine and gray swingarm. *BMW Group Press*

2013 **F800GT** *(DIFFERING FROM THE F800ST)*	
Power	**90 horsepower at 8,000 rpm**
Wheelbase	**1,514mm (59.6 inches)**
Wet weight	**213 kg (470 lbs.)**
Colors	**Orange, Graphite, White**

2013 Special Editions and Facelift

Special editions this year included a K1300S 30-Year K model, and three R1200 90-year versions. Marking the 30th anniversary of the K series, the K1300S 30-Year featured special colors, ESA II, and the RDC and ADC safety pack. Also included was an HP shift assistant and Akrapovič sports silencer. Marking the 90th anniversary of BMW motorcycles, three 90 Jahre BMW Motorrad ("90 years of BMW Motorrad") models were offered: the R1200GS Adventure, R1200R, and R1200RT. These all continued with the earlier air-cooled engine and were ostensibly standard models with a black and gray finish, and a nickel-plated and polished brass plate on the upper fork bridge. Facelift color updates occurred this year for the F800R, G650GS, R1200R, S1000RR, K1300S, K1300R, K1600GT, and K1600GTL. The F800R was also offered with a dynamics package (including an engine spoiler and seat cover) and a touring package (heated grips, onboard computer, and luggage rack). The K1300R previously optional sports wheels were now standard.

↑ Celebrating 30 years of the K series, this K1300S special edition came with a host of electronic aids plus an Akrapovič muffler. *BMW Group Press*

2013 **K1300S 30TH, R1200RT 90TH, R1200R 90TH, R1200GS ADVENTURE 90TH, F800R, G650GS, R1200R, S1000RR, K1300S, K1300R, K1600GT, K1600GTL** *(DIFFERING FROM 2012)*	
Colors	**White/Black/Red (K1300S 30th); Black (R1200 90th); Blue/White, Black (F800R); Yellow (G650GS); Blue, Beige (R1200R); Gray (S1000RR); Black/Graphite (K1300S); Red/Black, Black (K1300R); Graphite, Blue (K1600GT); Graphite, Red (K1600GTL)**

2014

R nineT, K1600GTL Exclusive, S1000R, R1200RT, R1200GS Adventure, F800GS Adventure, HP4, S1000RR, K1600GTL, K1600GT, K1300S, K1300R, R1200GS, R1200R, R1200R Classic, F800R, F800GT, F800GS, F700GS, G650GS, and G650GS Sertão

Headed by the 90th year commemorative boxer, the magnificent R nineT, this was a big year for model releases, with six new models, including the early release F800GS Adventure, the naked S1000R, a replacement for the successful R1200RT, and the R1200GS Adventure. While BMW no longer provided full factory support for racing, this year the S1000RR achieved its most significant success yet, Michael Dunlop winning three TTs at the Isle of Man. Production continued to increase, to a new record of 123,495 motorcycles (and Maxi-Scooters) delivered during 2014, a 7.2 percent increase, while the United States followed Germany as the second largest market, with 15,301 in sales. The R1200GS and GS Adventure continued as the most successful models (40,622 sold), and in March the 500,000th GS series, an R1200GS, rolled off the Berlin production line. BMW motorcycles continued to win awards, clinching 16 Best Bike Awards from *Cycle Word*, *Motorcyclist*, and *Motorcycle.com*.

R nineT

Heading the 2014 lineup was the R nineT, marketed as the world's first production motorcycle designed as a basis for a custom: either Roadster, Café Racer, or Bobber. Continuing from the 2013 Concept Ninety custom created in partnership with Roland Sands design, the R nineT blended the boxer's iconic character and classic design of a bygone era with modern technology. It also provided a modular concept, offering a wide range of opportunity for individual customization. Replacing the usual Telelever front fork was a 46mm upside-down fork from the S1000RR, with the rear suspension the usual Paralever swingarm and single shock absorber that allowed for an optional 6-inch rear rim. Classic features included wire-spoked wheels with black anodized alloy rims and black hubs, contrasting with modern radial four-piston monoblock brake calipers and floating brake discs. With the R nineT's hand-built feel, the attention to detail was staggering, from the embossed nineT aluminum plate above the air intake duct to the BMW emblem in the center of the headlight.

Synthesizing modern technical features with classic components, the R nineT was no retro bike but one that provided old-world emotion with a modern sporting twist. Embodying the brand's values of 90 years, the R nineT uniquely summed up the company's illustrious past, exuding style and cleverly allowing individual expressiveness. Individualization was becoming a growing phenomenon in motorcycling, one the R nineT looked set to capitalize on. This was soon evident with a long waiting list for an R nineT, even the factory workers in Berlin having to wait 18 months before delivery.

↓ The R nineT combined classic features in a modern framework and provided different platforms for customization. This is the café racer version with an aluminum seat hump.
BMW Group Press

↑ With the rear subframe removed, the R nineT could be converted into a more radical bobber. The front suspension was a 46mm upside down, BMW eschewing its usual Telelever.
BMW Group Press

2014 **R NINET** *(DIFFERING FROM THE R1200R)*	
Frame	**Tubular-steel bridge load-bearing engine**
Front suspension	**Upside-down telescopic fork**
Wheelbase	**1,476mm (58.1 inches)**
Wet weight	**222 kg (489 lbs.)**
Color	**Black Storm Metallic**

S1000R

Endeavoring to attract a younger customer, the impressive S1000RR Superbike evolved into naked S1000R for 2014. Combining Superbike dynamics and power with emotive roadster styling, the S1000R targeted a new group, one that Triumph had successfully managed to achieve with its Speed Triple, and replaced the powerful, but much heaver, K1300R (in those markets where it was still available).

As on the S1000RR, fuel injection was fully sequential, with two injectors per cylinder, the new BMS-X engine management system supporting a throttle-by-wire system. Based on the S1000RR, the chassis included the proven aluminum alloy perimeter frame, with the engine load-bearing, an adjustable 46mm upside-down fork, and a dual swingarm with adjustable Monoshock. The steering geometry was slightly revised, but the radial front braking system was unchanged. With less top end power and more low and midrange, moderate weight, and a comprehensive electronics package (including Race ABS, ASC, and a choice of two riding modes as standard), the S1000R was a dynamic sports roadster.

↑ Expanding the S series for 2014 was the naked S1000R, one of the most impressive naked sportbikes available. *BMW Group Press*

↓ Although the R1200RT's styling was new, it continued the unmistakable BMW RT theme. *BMW Group Press*

2014 S1000R *(DIFFERING FROM THE S1000RR)*

Power	**160 horsepower at 11,000 rpm**
Compression ratio	**12:1**
Fuel supply	**BMS-X**
Wheelbase	**1,439mm (56.7 inches)**
Wet weight	**207 kg (456 lbs.)**
Colors	**Red, Dark Blue, White**

R1200RT

The second R series to receive the water-cooled boxer engine and updated drivetrain was the popular R1200RT. Along with the updated engine with wet clutch and new frame with Paralever on the left were new electronic aids, notably Rain and Road riding modes, automatic stability control (ASC), and optional Riding Mode Pro with hill start control. A new instrument cluster featured a 5.7-inch TFT color display with standard onboard computer with factory-installed options, including an audio system with multi-controller operation. The more powerful engine and chassis were ostensibly that of the R1200GS, the stiffer structure resulting in improved directional stability. New styling and larger brakes completed the package. Although the weight increased, improved weight distribution resulted in a much sportier and more rigid feel than its predecessor had.

2014 R1200RT *(DIFFERING FROM THE R1200GS AND 2013 R1200RT)*

Power	**125 horsepower at 7,750 rpm**
Rear wheel	**5.50x17**
Brakes	**Dual front 320mm disc and 276mm rear disc**
Wheelbase	**1,485mm (58.6 inches)**
Wet weight	**274 kg (604 lbs.)**
Colors	**Blue, Gray, Ebony**

R1200GS Adventure

Now based on the water-cooled R1200GS, the new R1200GS Adventure continued the tradition as the quintessential long-distance and off-road all-around touring motorcycle. Apart from a 2.1-pound heavier crankshaft, the engine and tubular-steel space frame were shared with the R1200GS, while the R1200GS Adventure included a larger, 7.9-gallon, aluminum gas tank, and a chassis setup providing additional 0.8 inches of spring travel, increased ground clearance, and a trailing arm with modified geometry for improved handling. A larger windshield, additional air flaps, and hand guards increased weather protection, while enduro footrests, reinforced adjustable foot levers, and restyled bodywork completed the R1200GS Adventure's specification. Already provided with ABS, automatic stability control (ASC), and two riding modes, Rain and Road, three additional riding modes were available with the optional Ride Modes Pro feature, Dynamic, Enduro and Enduro Pro, accompanied by the Enduro settings for ABS and ASC for off-road riding. The R1200GS Adventure may have been the heaviest and largest adventure bike, but when it came to all-around ability, the comfort, weather protection, and electronic wizardry simply placed it in a class of its own. It was no coincidence the R1200GS Adventure continued as the world's most popular large-capacity adventure bike.

↑ While it was heavier and larger than before, more power and sophisticated electronic aids improved the R1200GS Adventure's capability. *BMW Group Press*

2014 R1200GS ADVENTURE *(DIFFERING FROM THE 2013 R1200GS)*

Power	**125 horsepower at 7,750 rpm**
Compression ratio	**12:1**
Wheelbase	**1,510mm (59.4 inches)**
Wet weight	**260 kg (573 lbs.)**
Colors	**Olive, White, Blue**

↑ Offering the Adventure experience in a smaller and lighter package, the F800GS Adventure was arguably the perfect all-around motorcycle. *BMW Group Press*

↓ From the passenger's armrests to keyless starting, no luxury feature was left wanting on the opulent K1600GTL Exclusive. *BMW Group Press*

F800GS Adventure

Released midway through 2013 as an early release 2014 model, BMW added the Adventure to the already capable F800GS. As riders demanded bikes that looked like they could travel the world, adventure bikes were one of the growing markets, the F800GS version offering a lighter and more agile alternative to the sometimes-intimidating R1200GS. Just as it did in 1980, BMW sensed an opportunity for a midrange adventure bike, agile enough for novices but with enough power to satisfy experienced riders. Updates over the F800GS included a reinforced rear subframe to accommodate the larger, 6.3-gallon tank; a larger windshield; enduro footpegs; engine protection bar; and pannier rack. Offering excellent performance on a variety of road surfaces, the F800GS Adventure was almost the perfect all-rounder, a large dirtbike or touring streetbike—two bikes in one.

2014 F800GS ADVENTURE *(DIFFERING FROM THE F800GS)*

Wet weight	229 kg (505 lbs.)
Colors	Sandrover, Red

K1600GTL Exclusive

Taking the Luxury Touring concept to a new level for 2014 was the opulent K1600GTL Exclusive. Based on the K1600GTL, standard equipment for the Exclusive included central locking with anti-theft alarm system, ESA II, DTC, hill start control, and the obligatory ABS. A radio antenna was embedded in the top case lid while a new seat, a heated backrest, and armrests improved pillion comfort. Also standard were LED auxiliary headlights, an adaptive xenon headlight, tire pressure monitor, floor lighting, and, for the first time on a BMW motorcycle, keyless ride. From the gas tank's aluminum molding and fully chromed exhaust system to the new-look instrumentation, the Exclusive took luxury motorcycle touring to a new level.

2014 K1600GTL EXLUSIVE *(DIFFERING FROM THE K1600GTL)*

Wet weight	360 kg (794 lbs.)
Colors	Mineral White

SUPERBIKE RACING 2014

For 2014, BMW realigned the racing program, increasing the level of support offered to around 150 customer teams worldwide and launching an innovative customer racing project, the BMW Motorrad Race Trophy. This was very successful, highlighted by Michael Dunlop's historic triple victory at the Isle of Man in June. Celebrating the 75th anniversary of Meier's Senior TT victory on the Type 255 Kompressor, BMW Motorrad UK joined forces with Hawk Racing with the factory supplying Superbike engines for Dunlop's S1000RR. After winning the Superstock and Superbike races at the North West 200 in May, 25-year-old Dunlop won three TTs (Superbike, Superstock, and Senior) on the S1000RR, taking his total to 11 TT victories. Dunlop's average speed for the six-lap Senior TT was 128.680 miles per hour, with a new Senior TT lap record of an astonishing 131.668 miles per hour.

Other notable victories this year included the BMW Motorrad Italia SBK Team celebrating seven victories in the EVO class of the Superbike World Championship and Ryuichi Kiyonari providing BMW their first-ever victory in the British Superbike Championship. But the 2014 BMW Motorrad Race Trophy went to Markus Reiterberger, with three race wins in the German Superbike Championship (IDM) and victory in the Superstock class in the Oschersleben eight-hour race. With a new S1000RR for 2015, BMW announced it would again contest the World Superbike Championship and expand the BMW Motorrad Race Trophy to include additional championships and a team competition.

↑ Dunlop celebrated three TT wins on the S1000RR at the Isle of Man in 2014, taking his tally to 11 victories on the legendary island circuit. *BMW Group Press*

↓ Michael Dunlop on his way to winning the Superbike race at the 2014 Isle of Man TT. His race average was 128.415 miles per hour. *BMW Group Press*

↗ The 2014 K1600GT Sport had a sportier seat and lower screen, but at more than 700 pounds, it wasn't really a sporting bike. *BMW Group Press*

2014 Facelift

K1600GT Sport, K1600GT, and K1600GTL

For 2014 the K1600GT was available as the more dynamic Sport, with black wheels, a low windshield, and sports-style seat. Light Gray was no longer available for the K1600GT, and Silver was deleted for the K1600GTL.

2014 **K1600GT SPORT, F1600GTL** *(DIFFERING FROM 2013)*	
Colors	**Orange/Black (K1600GT Sport); Beige (K1600GTL)**

S, R, F, and G Series

With replacement imminent, BMW offered a R1200R DarkWhite special model in contrasting white bodywork with black wheels and drivetrain. Also included was a sports seat and windshield. Updates to the R1200GS were primarily confined to electronic aids, notably three additional driving modes: Dynamic, Enduro, and Enduro Pro with matching ASC and ABS as an option, while the F800GS was now offered with a Dynamic package, consisting of ESA and ASC. The G650GS now came with black wheels and luggage rack. With a new S1000RR impending, the HP4 was only available in select markets this year.

2014 **R1200R DARKWHITE, S1000RR, R1200R, F800R, G650GS** *(DIFFERING FROM 2013)*	
Colors	White (R1200R DarkWhite); Gray/White, Red/White, Black (S1000RR); Black, Beige (R1200R); Orange/Black, White/Black (F800R); Black (F650GS)

→ The R1200R DarkWhite contrasted white bodywork with a gray frame and black engine and swingarm. Also included was a sports seat and small screen. *BMW Group Press*

2015

R1200R, R1200RS, S1000RR, S1000XR, F800R, K1600GTL Exclusive, K1600GTL, K1600GT, K1300S, K1300R, S1000R, R nineT, R1200RT, R1200GS, R1200GS Adventure, F800GT, F800GS, F800GS Adventure, F700GS, and G650GS

After the most successful sales year in history, it was no surprise to see five new models released for 2015. While the introduction of a new R1200R and R1200RS wasn't unexpected, that both these new models eschewed the traditional R series Telelever front suspension in favor of an upside-down telescopic fork was surprising, begging this question: Was BMW now heading back toward conservatism?

Economic conditions over the past few years had restricted the general development of Superbikes, and for 2015 BMW released an updated S1000RR, the first new Superbike platform from any manufacturer for three years. And as the company had done with the GS 35 years earlier, BMW endeavored to create a completely new adventure sport niche with the S1000R-based XR.

↑ Much sportier than before, a new R1200R appeared for 2015, an upside-down front fork replacing the Telelever. This is the sport version, with belly pan and fly screen.
BMW Group Press

R1200R

The final boxer to receive the new water-cooled engine was the R1200R, but while retaining the Paralever swingarm on the left, like on the R nineT, an upside-down front fork replaced the traditional Telelever. But while the R nineT continued with the earlier boxer engine and drivetrain, the R1200R represented a new era. The heavier crankshaft engine was shared with the R1200GS Adventure, R1200RT, and new R1200RS, while a centrally positioned radiator and new air intake snorkels allowed for the narrower front profile required for a naked roadster. The plethora of electronic aids included ABS, ASC, an onboard computer, and two riding modes, Rain and Road, with keyless ride and gearshift assistance optional.

Developed specifically for the R1200R, the tubular-steel bridge frame incorporated the engine as a stressed member, with the 45mm Sachs upside-down front fork inspired by the R nineT. This contributed to a much more modern and aggressive style, significantly more so than its rather staid predecessor. Also new were the more effective radial front brake calipers. As pioneered with the R nineT, customizing was an essential component of the new R1200R, with three models offered: standard, Sport (with belly pan and fly screen), and Exclusive (with a gold front fork and luggage rack). Although still quite heavy, but with its low-slung boxer engine providing surefooted handling, the new R1200R was extremely impressive.

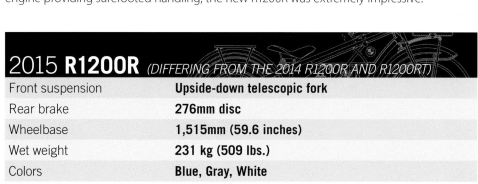

2015 R1200R *(DIFFERING FROM THE 2014 R1200R AND R1200RT)*

Front suspension	**Upside-down telescopic fork**
Rear brake	**276mm disc**
Wheelbase	**1,515mm (59.6 inches)**
Wet weight	**231 kg (509 lbs.)**
Colors	**Blue, Gray, White**

↑ Also with an upside-down front fork, the R1200RS continued the RS tradition initiated with the R100RS back in 1976. All new boxers had a left-side Paralever swingarm. *BMW Group Press*

↓ Lighter and more powerful than before, the 2015 S1000RR featured a revised frame and new styling. *BMW Group Press*

R1200RS

Although the RS was historically important, the R100RS in 1976 establishing a formula symbolizing consummate all-around sport touring, this series had been absent from BMW's range for a decade. But after this hiatus, BMW resurrected its great sports touring tradition with the R1200RS. Providing more emphasis on sport than earlier incarnations, the engine was the now familiar water-cooled boxer, tuned for more torque at lower rpm than on the R1200RT and R1200GS. As on the R1200R, the modified airbox, new air intake snorkels, and a centrally positioned radiator provided a more slender front silhouette. Endeavoring to replicate the S1000RR's dynamics, the front suspension was a 45mm upside-down fork, similar to the new R1200R, while electronic ESA (electronic suspension adjustment), with two damping settings, Road and Dynamic, provided exceptional handling and safety.

Continuing the RS practice of including a functional aerodynamic fairing, the R1200RS half-fairing fused the touring and sporting functions, while the riding position provided a slight front-wheel bias, resulting in a superb balance between steering and ergonomics. Uniting the touring qualities of the R1200RT boxer with the more sporting R1200R, the R1200RS maintained the great RS tradition.

2015 **R1200RS** (DIFFERING FROM THE R1200R)	
Wheelbase	**1,530mm (60.2 inches)**
Wet weight	**236 kg (520 lbs.)**
Colors	**Blue/Gray, Gray**

S1000RR

Six years after revolutionizing the Superbike class, BMW released a significantly updated S1000RR—effectively the successful limited-edition HP4 transformed into regular production guise. With cylinder head porting, a new intake camshaft, lighter inlet valves, shorter intakes, a larger airbox, and ride-by-wire throttle, the power increased slightly, with a smoother delivery. A lighter exhaust system contributed to a slight weight reduction, while a new frame included sharper steering geometry, a lower swingarm pivot to increase squat, and a slightly longer wheelbase. Unlike in the HP4, the Brembo front radial brake calipers were not the higher specification Monobloc but still more than adequate. Although the S1000RR came standard with three riding modes, the HP4's electronically controlled dynamic damping control (DDC) suspension was available as one of the many options.

One of the more significant updates was the restyled bodywork. The previous asymmetric headlight arrangement was retained as a characteristic distinguishing feature, but with the headlights repositioned and restyled. Another innovation was electronic speed control, allowing easier adherence to prevailing speed limits, while the new instrument panel could provide information as diverse as current and maximum banking angles and deceleration rates. A true racer with lights, the S1000RR raised the bar yet again for liter Superbikes.

2015 **S1000RR** (DIFFERING FROM 2014)	
Power	**199 horsepower at 13,500 rpm**
Fuel supply	**BMS-X**
Wheelbase	**1,425mm (56.1 inches)**
Wet weight	**204 kg (449 lbs.)**
Colors	**Red/White, Black, Motorsport**

S1000XR

Expanding the S1000RR-based platform, the adventure-sport S1000XR offered Superbike performance, adventure bike versatility, and touring motorcycle comfort. The engine was ostensibly that of the S1000R roadster, while electronic aids included standard Rain and Road riding modes and automatic stability control (ASC). The aluminum frame, suspension, and wheels were also derived from the S1000R, but with a shallower steering head angle, longer swingarm, and more suspension travel adding to the adventure capability. Carving out a crossover niche, the S1000XR provided a unique formula by combining GS, Supersport, and touring elements.

↖ Creating a new adventure sport niche, the S1000XR was an amalgam of GS, sportbike, and touring elements. *BMW Group Press*

↓ Significantly updated for 2015, the F800R now had new styling, an upside-down fork and radial front brakes. *BMW Group Press*

2015 S1000XR *(DIFFERING FROM S1000R)*

Rear brake	**265mm disc**
Wheelbase	**1,448mm (57 inches)**
Wet weight	**228 kg (503 lbs.)**
Colors	**Red, White**

F800R

With new suspension, four-piston radial front brakes, more power, lower first and second gear ratios, and more modern styling, the updated F800R provided improved sporting performance while maintaining a minimalist presence. Although the basic water-cooled parallel twin engine and aluminum perimeter frame continued much as before, front suspension was now by an upside-down fork, with braking handled by a pair of radial Brembo brake calipers. Pitched also at novice riders, the F800R had a lower seat and new conical tapered aluminum handlebars to improve rider ergonomics. Its updated styling extended to a distinctive symmetrical headlight, with new radiator shields and front fender. ASC and an onboard computer were standard, and while the weight was slightly increased, the F800R continued to provide outstanding performance in a compact package.

2015 F800R *(DIFFERING FROM 2014)*

Power	**90 horsepower at 8,000 rpm (48 horsepower at 6,750 rpm)**
Front suspension	**Upside-down fork**
Wheelbase	**1,526mm (60 inches)**
Wet weight	**202 kg (445 lbs.)**
Colors	**White, Blue**

2015 Facelift

Facelift models for 2015 included a special K1300S Motorsport and updates to the R1200GS and K1600GT and GTL. The R1200GS now featured the heavier crankshaft of the R1200GS Adventure and R1200RT, while keyless ride and shift assistant were now available as an option (also on the R1200GS Adventure and R1200RT). In an endeavor to widen the huge R1200GS Adventure's appeal to those previously deterred by the insurmountable seat height, a special 2-inch lower suspension kit and 1-inch lower seat were optional this year. The luxury touring K1600GT and GTL benefited from standard dynamic traction control (DTC), with keyless start and hill start control optional. Along with new colors, the K1300S Motorsport included a black engine spoiler and tinted windshield, HP wheels and footpegs, and an Akrapovič silencer.

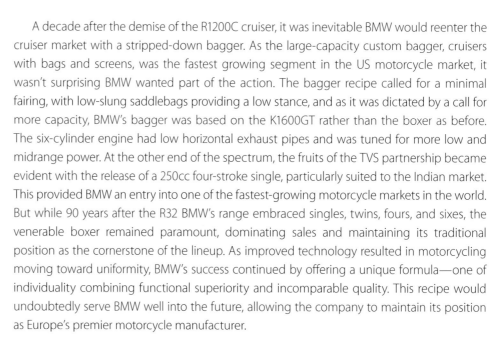

2015 **F800R** *(DIFFERING FROM 2014)*	
Power	**90 horsepower at 8,000 rpm (48 horsepower at 6,750 rpm)**
Front suspension	**Upside-down fork**
Wheelbase	**1,526mm (60 inches)**
Wet weight	**202 kg (445 lbs.)**
Colors	**White, Blue**

↑ Along with new colors and graphics, the K1300S came with HP wheels and footpegs. *BMW Group Press*

A decade after the demise of the R1200C cruiser, it was inevitable BMW would reenter the cruiser market with a stripped-down bagger. As the large-capacity custom bagger, cruisers with bags and screens, was the fastest growing segment in the US motorcycle market, it wasn't surprising BMW wanted part of the action. The bagger recipe called for a minimal fairing, with low-slung saddlebags providing a low stance, and as it was dictated by a call for more capacity, BMW's bagger was based on the K1600GT rather than the boxer as before. The six-cylinder engine had low horizontal exhaust pipes and was tuned for more low and midrange power. At the other end of the spectrum, the fruits of the TVS partnership became evident with the release of a 250cc four-stroke single, particularly suited to the Indian market. This provided BMW an entry into one of the fastest-growing motorcycle markets in the world. But while 90 years after the R32 BMW's range embraced singles, twins, fours, and sixes, the venerable boxer remained paramount, dominating sales and maintaining its traditional position as the cornerstone of the lineup. As improved technology resulted in motorcycling moving toward uniformity, BMW's success continued by offering a unique formula—one of individuality combining functional superiority and incomparable quality. This recipe would undoubtedly serve BMW well into the future, allowing the company to maintain its position as Europe's premier motorcycle manufacturer.

2015 **F700GS, F800GS, F800GS ADVENTURE, F800GT, R1200GS, R1200RT, K1600GT, K1600GTL, K1300S MOTORSPORT, K1300R** *(DIFFERING FROM 2014)*	
Colors	White, Black/Red, Blue (F700GS); Red, White/Black (F800GS); White, Kalamata (F800GS Adventure); Blue (F800GT); Dark Blue, Black (R1200GS); Blue/Gray (R1200RT); Black (K1600GT and GTL); White (K1600GT); Silver (K1600GTL); Black/White/Blue (K1300S Motorsport); Black (K1300R)

INDEX